DATE DUE

DEMCO, INC. 38-2931

Religious Fundamentalism in Developing Countries

Religious Fundamentalism in Developing Countries

Edited by
Santosh C. Saha and Thomas K. Carr

Contributions to the Study of Religion, Number 65

GREENWOOD PRESS
Westport, Connecticut • London

Library of Congress Cataloging-in-Publication Data

Religious fundamentalism in developing countries / edited by Santosh C. Saha and
Thomas K. Carr.
     p. cm.—(Contributions to the study of religion, ISSN 0196–7053 ; no. 65)
     Includes bibliographical references and index.
     ISBN 0–313–31155–2 (alk. paper)
     1. Religious fundamentalism—Developing countries. I. Saha, Santosh C. II. Carr,
Thomas K., 1962– III. Series.
     BL238.R47   2001
     291.1'7'091724—dc21   00–049084

British Library Cataloguing in Publication Data is available.

Library of Congress Catalog Card Number: 00–049084
ISBN: 0–313–31155–2
ISSN: 0196–7053

First published in 2001

Greenwood Press, 88 Post Road West, Westport, CT 06881
An imprint of Greenwood Publishing Group, Inc.
www.greenwood.com

Printed in the United States of America

The paper used in this book complies with the
Permanent Paper Standard issued by the National
Information Standards Organization (Z39.48–1984).

10 9 8 7 6 5 4 3 2 1

For my grandchildren:

Priyashi Saha

Sudip & Sumon Bagui

Contents

Religious Fundamentalism
in Developing Countries

Introduction

As a term defining a particular segment of the religious population, "fundamentalism" is a relatively new coinage. It was first used in the 1920's to label the movement, inspired by several Protestant theologians in America, that sought to make certain, divinely revealed "fundamentals" of the Christian faith (e.g., the virgin birth, the infallibility of the Bible, etc.) required for orthodoxy. From the start, the movement possessed a juridical bias. For example, in some U.S. colleges, universities, and seminaries it became fashionable to require strict adherence to the fundamentals for everything from student admission to faculty tenure and promotion. Bob Jones University (B.J.U.) in Greenville, South Carolina, founded in 1927, is one case in point. At B.J.U., students, staff, and faculty still gather together each day to recite the following list of fundamental beliefs:

I believe in the inspiration of the Bible (both the Old and the New Testaments); the creation of man by the direct act of God; the incarnation and virgin birth of our Lord and Savior, Jesus Christ; His identification as the Son of God; His vicarious atonement for the sins of mankind by the shedding of His blood on the cross; the resurrection of His body from the tomb; His power to save men from sin; the new birth through the regeneration by the Holy Spirit; and the gift of eternal life by the grace of God.[1]

The term "fundamentalism," in short, was first used to distinguish a religious movement within American Christianity; a movement which, by appeal to what were believed to be divinely sanctioned beliefs, sought both to identify and to exclude those who did not share those beliefs.

Today the term is used more broadly. Currently, "fundamentalism" is seen to define a range of movements, either religious or sociopolitical (but more often both), in all regions of the world, which aim to impose specific traditions—whether religious, national, cultural, or ethnic—on societies thought to be in danger of straying from the "fundamentals" that hold them together. What makes these movements "fundamentalist" is that their adherents seek to raise themselves and their beliefs *above* the political by appealing explicitly to some one or other supreme authority, moral code, or philosophy that cannot be questioned.[2]

Ordinarily, this appeal assumes a religious orientation. In their introduction to the first volume of the famed "Fundamentalism Project," *Fundamentalisms Observed*, editors Martin Marty and R. Scott Appleby claim that the religious aspect of fundamentalism tends to express itself in the following four ways: as a "fighting for" the worldview associated with the religion; a "fighting with" the myths, traditions and doctrines created by the religion; a "fighting against" those who do not subscribe to the religion; and finally, a "fighting under" the god or other transcendent reference thought to be the religion's ultimate source.[3]

But what is becoming increasingly clear is that, despite the term's origins, fundamentalism is no longer merely a religious phenomenon. Its supra-political emphasis notwithstanding, fundamentalists very often attach certain social and political correlates to their religious slogans. It is for this reason that some have called into question the appropriateness of using the term "fundamentalism" beyond its original, religious context. It is argued that the term only serves to obscure major differences between the disparate ideological tendencies often included under the rubric, and when used pejoratively, to exacerbate existing prejudices. Thus, there is little consensus on whether using the term without qualification is valid. Nor has any more appropriate term been found.[4] Yet there is general agreement that something is happening worldwide that deserves to be identified by a common referent and that can be understood, by means of that referent, on a global scale. Thus, despite expressed misgivings, most scholars working in the field consider "fundamentalism" the term of choice.

In the volume mentioned above, Marty and Appleby put forward three reasons for their insistence on the common use of the term "fundamentalism."[5] Against the background of acknowledged problems with the term, they state that:

1. "fundamentalism" creates a necessary distinction over against cognates like "traditionalism," "conservatism," and "orthodoxy" whose meanings overlap with "fundamentalism" but are not fully synonymous with it;
2. it is a word that is now used by journalists, public officials, scholars and others to connote a commonly understood set of references;
3. and when asked to define their proposed alternatives—alternatives like "revolutionary neotraditionalist Islamic (or Jewish, Christian, Hindu, etc.) radicalism"—it was found that authors invariably describe what others more commonly call "fundamentalism."

It is for these and similar reasons that we decided to use the term in the title of this book. In our understanding, and based on what has been said in the foregoing, "fundamentalism" refers to *any sociopolitical movement that requires of its members a strict adherence to specified "fundamentals" or doctrines; that seeks to impose those fundamentals, by persuasion or force, on any who are outside the movement; and that claims for its motivation in doing so a divine, or otherwise transcendentally grounded, mandate.* Additionally, our focus is restricted to those fundamentalist movements, so defined, which have arisen within developing nations, or among subcultures that have emigrated from developing nations.

Having now rendered this apology for our use of a common term, the reader may be surprised to find in the chapters that follow a variety of terms for identifying fundamentalist movements worldwide, such as "neo-fundamentalism," "religious radicalism," "religious Zionism," "biblical literalism," "Pentecostalism," or "Hindu revivalism." We thought it best not to impose the uniform use of the term fundamentalism on the authors, as the variety of their terms seems better to represent our editorial intent of identifying nuances within the broader spectrum of fundamentalist movements. But this is not to say that there is not common ground among those movements; nor that they cannot each be called "fundamentalist" as we have defined the term.

There is evidence to suggest that religious fundamentalism, or at least religious *conservatism*—which is differentiated from fundamentalism only by reason of its greater doctrinal flexibility (a term which is used here relatively)—is on the rise around the world. As mainstream (i.e., more "liberal") religious organizations are losing membership, the rolls of conservative and fundamentalist churches, mosques and synagogues appear to be growing. In the developed West, this observation is somewhat misleading, since religious practice on the whole, and church attendance in particular are on the decline. But in the developing nations, the story is very different. Consider as one example the growth of Pentecostal-fundamentalist Christianity in Latin America in the past two decades:[6]

- In El Salvador Pentecostal churches grew an astonishing 400 percent in the years 1980-1985.
- In 1979, there were 53,500 overseas missionaries in Central American countries; by 1990 there were three times that number.
- If present growth rates continue in Guatemala (44 percent annual increase), conservative Christians will account for the total population of the country in the year 2015.
- In 1988, Penny Lernoux reported that "every hour 400 Latin Americans convert to the Pentecostals or other fundamentalist . . . churches."[7]
- In 1991, Pablo Deiros predicted that "by the end of the 1990's . . . half of the [Latin American] population will belong to the spectrum of evangelical-Pentecostal-fundamentalist churches."

Though Deiros's prediction did not come to pass, it is clear, as the other statistics show, that the appeal of fundamentalist religion in the last two decades of the last century was very strong in the developing nations of Latin America. As evidence that the same "conservative drift," as it has been called,[8] is being felt around the world, consider the following statistics:

- 5.4 million copies of the Book of Mormon were published last year, including 1.5 million in Spanish and 600,000 in Portuguese. This accounted for over 3 percent of all religious publishing world-wide.[9]
- The Watch Tower Society (Jehovah's Witnesses) grew 2 percent worldwide in 1999, reporting over 1 billion hours of missionary work and 330,000 baptisms.[10]
- At their annual meeting last May, more than 94 percent of Exxon's worldwide shareholders rejected a measure that would have extended benefits to the domestic partners of homosexual employees. Mobil decided to drop the same plan after it merged with Exxon in December 1999.[11]
- In March 2000, conservative military police in Iran were ordered to round up women and men who flout dress codes or socialize with the opposite sex. They were also ordered to search for satellite dishes which can pick up Western programming.[12]
- For four years now in Afghanistan, strict Islamic policies called "Taliban" have denied young girls the right to an education, and women the right to a divorce.
- Egyptian women were recently granted the right to divorce without their husbands' approval. But while Egyptian men can get divorced automatically, a woman can do so only if she can prove the husband beat her, was a drug addict, was sterile, or refused to support the family. It is reported that few women are ever granted a divorce.[13]

Reasons for the observed increase in religious and political conservatism tend to center around three sources: the globalization of economic markets, which leads to the importation of foreign products and brands, and therefore foreign values, into indigenous cultures; the weakening of the autonomy and power of national, religio-political sovereignties, either through revolution and overthrow, the formation of multinational unions, or the subtler processes of secularization; and the "corruption" of ethnic and cultural symbols and modes of discourse through their mediation, via global information and communications networks, with foreign elements.[14] In summary, it has been said that fundamentalism is a reactionary gesture in a world that is moving too fast toward conformity and unity; a world that demands tolerance for the sake of the "new world order." As a countermeasure to such a world, fundamentalism offers its adherents the consolation of a stable, discrete identity—which includes certain individuating markers as lifestyle management strategies and well-interpreted mythologies — over against the din of competing versions of the same.

Establishing a genealogy of fundamentalism, however, is not the primary concern of this volume. This important topic has been treated at length elsewhere.[15] Rather, our editorial concern is to engage critically, within a variety of contexts, with the claims made by fundamentalist movements and to assess the impact such claims have had, and are having, upon the cultures and societies that play host to them.

It is the general aim of the chapters that follow to narrate the history and implications of this worldwide drift towards radical conservatism as it has expressed itself in the form of fundamentalist movements. This is to say, the methodological approach that unites this volume is part historical, part phenomenological, and part critical-evaluative. Not all of the essays treat present forms of fundamentalism, but all seek to address issues that arise in the contemporary world as the presence of fundamentalism makes itself known. Some of the authors are more sympathetic to fundamentalism than others; some are coreligionists aligned with the belief system of the fundamentalism described, but who do not share the same degree of militancy; and some respond as antagonists. But this variety of perspectives seems appropriate to a sociopolitical phenomenon as varied and as evocative as fundamentalism.

Leading off the works is Mir Zohair Husain's chapter, "The Politics of Islam in Pakistan," which sheds light on the religiously charged politics of a predominantly Muslim country, but which also has a large Hindu constituency. Husain's very detailed historical narrative provides highlights from the dramatic rise and fall of fundamentalist political movements in Pakistan— some fuelled by religious revival, others by political ideology—starting with the turn of the last century and bringing the story up to our own day. Of special interest in Husain's description is the use of religious symbolism (e.g., the sword as symbolic of the Islamic *jihad* to inspire the people to uphold specific political aims. Husain ends his historical journey with a current assessment of Pakistani politics and culture, which also foreshadows possible future directions.

Co-editor Thomas Carr then writes on "Apartheid and Hermeneutics: Biblical Interpretations, Neo-Calvinism and the Afrikaner Sense of Self (1926-86)." His essay contends that Afrikaner identity during the years of apartheid's rise and political dominance was and is a construction of both a Calvinist mythologizing of historical events and a politically charged biblical hermeneutics. Carr's historical survey demonstrates that the Dutch Reformed Church (DRC) used both forms of discourse to encourage popular support for the policies of apartheid. The author concludes his chapter by suggesting that when the DRC.disallowed the teaching of German hermeneutical philosophies from its universities and seminaries, it made room for its dual strategies of historical revisionism and biblical "proof-texting," which in turn served to legitimate the DRC's support of apartheid.

Jacob Abadi's "Religious Zionism and Israeli Politics: Gush Emunim Revisited" offers a timely analysis which traces the rise, impact and decline of this conservative Israeli political movement. Abadi concludes that the rise to power of *Gush Emunim* coincided fortuitously with the declining power of the Labour Party and the rise to power of Begin's Likud Government while its demise can be attributed, in part, to internal factionalizing within the movement and its boycott on principle of the 1990s peace talks.

In "*Swadeshi* Economics: Toward a Critical Assessment of Hindu Revivalist Economics in India," co-editor Santosh Saha tackles the intricacies of Hindu religious politics within a larger frame: namely, the question of national identity as a synthesis of religious devotion and secular statehood. Saha argues that while post-colonial Hindu revivalists, in the interest of furthering national identity, put forward a coherent political platform—based mainly on Gandhian economics—their penchant on religious grounds to view "cooperation" as economic capital and technological advancement as a threat ensured the failure of that policy in the global marketplace. Saha closes by locating India's competitive disadvantage in that marketplace, as well as its relatively underinsured status, as within the sphere of influence of this viable but, in Saha's view, "analytically deficient" political alternative.

In "The Rise of Neo-Fundamentalism in Egypt," Rudolf Zarzar seeks first to clarify what he means by Islamic "neo-fundamentalism" as it is expressed within the particularities of recent Egyptian history. Next, he orients this form of fundamentalism within the larger movement of Islam-based politics, which he views as in a present state of "crisis." The bulk of the chapter then details Zarzar's analysis of the causes of the presence and increasing influence of neo-fundamentalism in Egyptian culture. The essay concludes with a forward-looking treatment of the uneasy alliance, currently in place, between Egyptian neo-fundamentalists and the broader, and more pluralistic, Egyptian culture. Zarzar contends that the merger of devotional Islam and mainstream democracy is possible in Egypt, so long as violence is shunned, and human rights, economic growth and the electoral process are upheld as worthy values and goals.

Harriet Harris places her concern in a developed nation, Britain, but chooses to focus on a subculture there that has its roots in several developing nations. In "Mission UK: Black Pentecostals in London," Harris describes the life and struggles of immigrants from Africa, the Caribbean, and the Indian sub-continent as they seek to express their charismatic Christian faith in a culture very largely secularized. Harris states that black émigré Pentecostals in Britain find themselves confronted by two principal ironies: that of the lack of faith in the culture that once taught them faith, and that of the antagonism to their growth and vitality from indigenous churches that are no longer growing and vital. Through the use of interviews and on-site observation, Harris takes us into the churches and organizations of this subculture as it seeks to understand what it means to "be church," to be Pentecostal and missionary, in a city largely indifferent to its message and mission.

Syed Serajul Islam applies an approach to the politics of Bangladesh similar to that of the previous article. In his "The Politics of Islam in Bangladesh," Islam renders an analysis of the interaction between Islamic revivalism and post-colonial political rule in another country riven with Muslim-Hindu strife. Included in the article is a brief cultural and political history of Bangladesh prior to its 1971 War of Liberation, as well as an assessment of the causes particular to the rise of religious fervor in the country. The author concludes by saying that, while no post-colonial political regime has ignored, or indeed can ignore, the strength of Islam as a force for social and cultural cohesion, neither has any exclusively Islamic regime succeeded to political power, for reasons that the author explains at length.

Finishing off our book Vivienne SM. Angeles's chapter, "The State, Moro National Liberation Front, and Islamic Resurgence in the Philippines." Angeles narrates the thirty-year history of the MNLF, a revolutionary movement seeking, among other things, the Islamization of the Philippines. The author puts forward the provocative thesis that the Philippine government, in making certain concessions to the MNLF in the interests of peace, served to further the cause of Islamization—a development the author considers to be an infringement of the anti-establishment clause of the Philippine constitution.

The last thing that needs to be said is that the views and interpretations included here are those of the individual authors, and would not necessarily be affirmed by the publisher of this volume or, except for their own chapters, by the editors.

NOTES

1. Taken from the Bob Jones University website. URL: www.bju.edu/aboutbju/creed/.

2. C.S. Kessler, "Religious Fundamentalism: Questioning the Term, Identifying its Referents. Paper Presented to the Conference Challenging Fundamentalism: Questioning Political and Scholarly Simplifications," April 26-27, 1996, Kuala Lumpur (unpublished).

3. Cf. Martin Marty and R. Scott Appleby (eds.), *Fundamentalisms Observed* (Chicago: University of Chicago Press, 1991), pp. ix, x.

4. Cf. Kessler, "*Religious Fundamentalism.*"

5. For the following, see Marty and Appleby, *Fundamentalisms Observed*, p. viii.

6. Except as otherwise noted, the following statistics come from Pablo Deiros, "Protestant Fundamentalism in Latin America," in Marty and Appleby, *Fundamentalisms Observed*, p. 144.

7. Penny Lernoux, "The Fundamentalist Surge in Latin America," *The Christian Century*, 20 (January 1988), p. 51.

8. Frances Kissling, "The Appeal of Fundamentalism," from a website devoted to fundamentalism URL: www.mosaic.echonyc.com/~onissues/w95kissling.html.

9. Cited in *World Pulse*, 63 (April 7, 2000), p. 13.

10. Cited in *World Pulse*, 63 (April 7, 2000), p. 14.

11. Cited in *Frontline*, 14 (March/April, 2000), p. 6.

12. Cited in *World Pulse*, 63 (April 7, 2000), p. 14.

13. Caroll Turnbull (ed.), "Global Trends and Updates," April 23, 2000 URL: www.3rdworld.org/trends.html

14. Cf. Bronislaw Misztal and Anson Shupe (eds.), *Revival of Religious Fundamentalism in East and West* (Westport, Conn.: Praeger Publishers, 1992).

15. Cf. Karen Armstrong, *The Battle for God* (New York: Knopf, 2000); Martin Marty and R. Scott Appleby (eds.), *Accounting for Fundamentalisms* (Chicago: University of Chicago Press, 1994); Bassam Tibi, *The Challenge of Fundamentalism* (Berkeley: University of California Press, 1998).

Chapter 1

The Politics of Islam in Pakistan

Mir Zohair Husain

Islam is the *raison d'être* of Pakistan. Consequently, all Pakistani leaders, both civil and military, have found it necessary to identify themselves, at least nominally, with Islamic concepts so as to further legitimize their stewardship, and to unify an otherwise diverse country. However, three prominent leaders in Pakistan's history engaged in the politics of Islam more than anyone else, namely Muhammad Ali Jinnah, Zulfikar Ali Bhutto, and Muhammad Zia-ul-Haq. This chapter focuses on their use of Islam in contributing to Islamic revivals that profoundly affected their political fortunes and the destiny of Pakistan for better or worse.

MUHAMMAD ALI JINNAH

Muhammad Ali Jinnah (1875-1949), known reverentially by his fellow countrymen as *"Quaid-e-Azam"* (Great Leader), was the chief architect and founding father of Pakistan. Though Westernized and secular in his orientation, he infused the Pakistan Movement — struggling for an independent Muslim homeland —with new life and vigor when he became its leader in the late 1930s. In less than a decade, Jinnah brought about an unprecedented Islamic resurgence in twentieth-century India and created the new nation of Pakistan. His miraculous achievement—that still endures and thrives—establishes his place among the great leaders of Islamic history.

Jinnah: The Elitist and Moderate Secular Indian Nationalist

A barrister with British secular legal training and Western political values, Jinnah began his political career in 1906 when he joined the All-India National Congress Party. He was hailed as "an ambassador of Hindu-Muslim unity" in the anti-colonialist struggle. The famous Indian Hindu nationalist Gopal Krishna Gokhale (whom Jinnah greatly admired and emulated for his good character and commitment to social service) said of Jinnah: "He has the true stuff in him, and that freedom from all sectarian prejudice which will make him the best ambassador of Hindu-Muslim unity."[1]

As an Indian nationalist in the Congress Party (which had been boycotted by the Indian Muslim majority), Jinnah was critical of the Muslim League's demands for separate but equal electorates and even convinced a number of Muslims to join his political party.[2] Furthermore, after being persuaded to join the Muslim League in 1913, he did so without adversely affecting his Congress Party membership, which he held for the next seven years. In fact, in 1917 he called on Muslims to join with their "Hindu brethren": "To the Muslims my message is: join hands with your Hindu brethren. My message to the Hindu brethren is: lift you backward brothers up. In this spirit, let the foundation of Home Rule League be consecrated and there is nothing for us to fear."[3]

Generally, Muslim leaders would never refer to Hindus (who are considered polytheistic infidels in Islam) with such affinity. Moreover, in the same speech he rejected the fear in the Muslim community that Muslim identity and culture would be undermined by majority Hindu domination. He said: "Fear not . . . this is a bogey which is put before you to scare you away from the cooperation and unity which are essential to self government."[4] In 1931, Jinnah referred to himself as "an Indian first and a Muslim afterwards."[5]

As a secularist, Jinnah opposed mixing religion and politics. Consequently, he objected to Gandhi's use of Hindu rhetoric and symbolism to mobilize and unite Indian Hindus for his civil-disobedience movement against British rule. Jinnah regarded this as the Hinduization of the nationalist movement. Soon after becoming the president of the Muslim League in 1934, Jinnah gave a speech in the Indian Legislative Assembly, in which he stated that religion was "merely a matter between man and God" and should be disassociated from politics.[6]

His secularism and desire to cooperate with the Congress Party leadership in order mutually to resolve problems facing India was evident in a public speech, in which he stated: "There is no difference between the ideals of the Moslem League and of the Congress; the idea of complete freedom for India."[7]

Moreover, in his correspondence with Muhammad Iqbal,[8] Jinnah usually avoided taking religious positions Iqbal urged upon him. Instead, Jinnah concentrated on the economic, political, social, and cultural plight of the Indian Muslims.[9]

However, Jinnah was an extremely astute and visionary politician. While disagreeing with the advocates of the *Khilafat* and *Hijrat* movements launched by the conservative *ulama* (Islamic scholars) of the Indian subcontinent, he was nevertheless impressed by the *ulama's* successful mobilization of Indian Muslims using the rallying cry of Islam.[10] While abhorring Mohandas Karamchand Gandhi's strategy of using Hindu rhetoric and symbolism and engaging in the ideologization of religion to mobilize the Hindu masses, Jinnah was nevertheless profoundly impressed with the Mahatma's[11] aura of saintliness, charisma, and mammoth following among Indian Hindus.[12]

Jinnah's Transition from Secular Nationalism to Islamic Populism

Nehru's marginalization of the Muslim League leadership during and just after the 1937 provincial elections infuriated the arrogant and sensitive Jinnah who felt disillusioned and betrayed by the Congress Party leadership. At this time, Jinnah finally took heed of Muhammad Iqbal's constant encouragement to pursue greater autonomy for the Muslim minority and left the familiar realm of elitist politics (primarily limited to drawing rooms, offices and legislative assemblies) for the unfamiliar and unpredictable political landscape of mass politics. To reach, excite, and mobilize the Indian Muslim masses in the great struggle for a separate Muslim homeland, Jinnah shed his Western suits for the *sherwani* and Jinnah cap worn by many Indian Muslims, and laced his speeches with religious and colloquial terms.[13]

Jinnah's disillusionment deepened when he observed the performance of the Congress Party provincial governments. Not only did these Congress-run provincial governments exclude Muslim Leaguers from power, but were also perceived by Muslims as promoting Hindu ideas and ideals.[14] Thus, by the end of the 1930s, Jinnah, who had spent most of his political life attempting to preserve and protect the rights, interests, and culture of the Muslim community on the Indian subcontinent through peaceful dialogue with the leadership of the Congress Party, became convinced that "the Congress Party was a Hindu organization dedicated to the establishment of Hindu *raj* [rule] in India and that it had no intention of developing a non-sectarian, genuinely liberal polity, which might value the diversity of religious and cultural expression in India."[15] Moreover, by the late 1930s the slogan "Islam in Danger" had become so loud that Jinnah, as leader of the Indian Muslims, could not ignore it any longer. He, therefore, adopted the rallying cry of Islam and called for an "Islamic state." With this move, Jinnah's transition from secularist to Islamic populist was complete.

By 1938, Jinnah had come to believe that the Muslim League was not merely a political party representing Indian Muslims, but the standard-bearer of Islam in the Indian subcontinent. In the same way, Jinnah identified the Congress Party as the representative of India's Hindu majority, the standard-bearer of Hinduism, and future governors of Hindustan (land of the Hindus).

In 1940, Jinnah—who had become a convert to the ideas and ideals of Sir Sayyid Ahmad Khan,[16] Muhammad Iqbal, and the Muslim League in general—formulated the now famous "two-nation theory," a significant innovation in Islamic political theory and practice. In this theory he maintained that the Muslims and Hindus were not merely members of two different religions, but of two comprehensive and entirely different belief systems that diverged completely, whose adherents pursued two strikingly different and frequently antagonistic ways of life. They neither intermarried nor dined together. They drew inspiration from different historical episodes and heroes; in fact, often the historical or cultural hero for one was the villain for the other. The most succinct and refined version of the "two-nation theory" was forwarded by Jinnah in his letter to Mahatma Gandhi in 1944, when he wrote:

We are a nation of a hundred million and what is more we are a nation with our own distinctive culture and civilization, language and literature, art and architecture, names and nomenclature, sense of value and proportion, legal laws and moral codes, customs and calendar, history and traditions, aptitude and ambitions; in short, we have our own distinctive outlook on life and of life. By all canons of international law, we are a nation. We maintain and hold that Muslims and Hindus are two major nations by any definition or test of a nation.[17]

Although Jinnah espoused Islamic rhetoric and even called for the establishment of an "Islamic state"—albeit a very liberal, tolerant, and democratic one—he never once referred to instituting the *shariah* (Islamic Law), even partially or in a revised form, which is mandatory in such a polity.[18] Instead, most of Jinnah's speeches and statements after he had popularized the "two-nation theory" dwelt on the threat that Hindu majority rule posed to the physical, cultural, economic, political, and spiritual interests and well-being of the Muslim minority in India. In a speech at a civic reception in Chittagong on March 26, 1948, Jinnah said: "You are only voicing my sentiments and the sentiments of millions of Mussalmans when you say that Pakistan should be based on sure foundations of social justice and Islamic socialism, which emphasize equality, and brotherhood of man."[19]

In his 1945 *Eid*[20] Message, Jinnah alluded to his kind of liberal and democratic "Islamic state" in which every Muslim would be encouraged to practice his faith in his own way without being forced to follow the puritanical or traditional interpretation of the *ulama*. Jinnah declared: "our Prophet has enjoined on us that every *Mussalman* should possess a copy of the *Qur'an* and be his own priest."[21]

Jinnah's Return to Secularism

Although ecstatic at the creation of Pakistan through the use of the potent emotional message of "Islamic nationalism," Jinnah was agonized by the bloody communal massacres spawned by both the Islamic resurgence and its equally powerful response in the form of reactionary Hinduism. The communal bloodshed reached a climax in 1947, when millions of Muslim refugees crossed the border into Pakistan and millions of Hindus crossed the border into India. Witnessing this painful experience, and determined to bring the full weight of his charismatic personality against this communal carnage and to allay the fears of all minorities (both non-Muslim and Muslim) within Pakistan, Jinnah spoke to the Constituent Assembly of Pakistan in August 1947 in which his proclivity towards secularism resurfaced:

If you change your past and work together in the spirit that every one of you, no matter to what community he belongs . . . is first, second, and last a citizen of this state with equal rights, privileges and obligations, there will be no end to the progress you will make. . . . You may belong to any religion or caste or creed—that has nothing to do with the business of the state.[22]

It is, indeed, noteworthy that Jinnah's "two-nation theory," formerly the foundation of the Pakistan Movement, was not even mentioned. No longer were Hindus and Muslims considered two incompatible nations, but religious communities that could and ought to get along as citizens of one state where all were equal in the eyes of the government and law. In fact, the last sentence of the above quotation, which implies that religion has nothing to do with the state, is a rather clear espousal of secularism.

Jinnah may have believed that the two-nation theory, which was situation-specific and pertinent largely to pre-partition India, had now outlived its utility. But rather than stating this, he alluded to how Catholics and Protestants, who had fought each other for generations, lived harmoniously as equal citizens of Great Britain.[23] He went on: "Now, I think we should keep that in front of us as our ideal and you will find that in the course of time Hindus would cease to be Hindus and Muslims would cease to be Muslims, not in the religious sense, because that is the personal faith of each individual, but in the political sense as citizens of the state."[24]

This was the first and most important speech given by Pakistan's founding father to the Constituent Assembly responsible for framing the country's constitution. The ideological thrust of Jinnah's speech was entirely consistent with his general worldview well-known throughout his long political career. Having failed to establish Hindu-Muslim unity in predominantly Hindu India, Jinnah was determined to succeed in the predominantly Muslim "homeland" that he had established. Having witnessed the insecurity of the Muslim minority in predominantly Hindu India, he did not want the non-Muslim minorities to suffer the same fate in predominantly Muslim Pakistan.

While Jinnah had failed to bring Hindus and Muslims together in pre-partition India, he resolved to succeed in the little time remaining to him in the predominantly Muslim homeland of Pakistan. In a radio broadcast to the people of Australia in February 1948, Jinnah said that "The great majority of us are Muslims . . . but make no mistake: Pakistan is not a theocracy or anything like it. Islam demands from us the tolerance of other creeds."[25] Indeed, Jinnah feared that the new-born Pakistan might be exposed to new dangers if heated debate over the creation of a theocratic state led to divisions and disunity. It might then sooner or later result in Muslims of one sect or school of thought taking up arms against other Muslims, a situation which the fledgling nation could ill-afford and which Jinnah did everything to avoid.

Summing up, Jinnah greatly accelerated the conversion of the 1930s incipient Islamic revival started by the Muslim League into the Islamic resurgence of the 1940s. It was quite an achievement for Jinnah to have prevailed in establishing Pakistan despite strong opposition from the Congress Party that enjoyed overwhelming support in predominantly Hindu India; the British colonialist rulers who wanted to leave behind a united India; and even some Islamists, such as Sayyid Abul A'la Maududi and his *Jama`at-e-Islami* (henceforth simply *JI*).[26] It was also an amazing achievement since Jinnah was a Westernized and predominantly secular elitist, who spoke refined English, which was spoken by the Indian Muslim elite, but very poor Urdu, which was spoken by the Indian Muslim masses. However, despite these attributes, Jinnah managed effectively to inspire, mobilize and galvanize the majority of Indian Muslims and yet create a tolerant, moderate, and liberal "Islamic state" in the very short span of seven tumultuous years.

ZULFIKAR ALI BHUTTO

Zulfikar Ali Bhutto (1928-79), a Berkeley and Oxford educated secular Sindhi *zamindar*[27] and lawyer, occupied several ministerial positions (including the prominent position of foreign minister from 1963 to 1966) in General Muhammad Ayub Khan's secular regime that came to power in a bloodless military *coup d'état* in October 1958. After a falling out with President Ayub Khan in June 1966, Bhutto resigned from government. In November 1967, Bhutto launched his own Pakistan People's Party (PPP), which was based on secular socialism. In less than a year, Bhutto's opposition to Ayub Khan's autocratic, capitalist, and pro-American regime sparked nationwide demonstrations. In spring 1969, Ayub Khan resigned and handed over power to General Agha Muhammad Yahya Khan, who in turn held free and fair national elections in December 1970. The PPP won those elections in the country's western wing due to Bhutto's enormous political acumen, experience, and charisma; a palpable fear among West Pakistanis that the East Pakistani Awami League (People's League) and its charismatic East Bengali leader, Sheikh Mujib-ur-Rahman, would win a landslide victory and treat West Pakistan as a stepchild; the PPP's tantalizing promise to provide all Pakistanis with *roti, kapra, makan* (food, clothing, and shelter); and Bhutto's eloquent defense of his party's "socialist" ideology.

Indeed, a few concise quotations from Bhutto's speeches and statements should make the point as to how far Bhutto moved from his original ideology of "secular scientific socialism" embodied in the PPP documents of November 1967 to his emphasis on "Islam" in "Islamic socialism" at the end of the 1970 election campaign. For instance, in an address to the Mazzaffargarh Bar Association on January 17, 1968, Bhutto said, "We have to tackle basic anomalies and no basic anomaly can be tackled without the application of the principle of scientific socialism."[28] On another occasion, Bhutto wrote, "Only socialism, which creates equal opportunities for all, protects from exploitation, removes barriers of class distinction, is capable of establishing economic and social justice. Socialism is the highest expression of democracy and its logical fulfillment."[29] Again, in a public address to the Sindh Convention in Hyderabad on September 21, 1968, Bhutto said: "No power on earth can stop socialism—the symbol of justice, equality, and the supremacy of man—from being introduced in Pakistan . . . . I am a socialist . . . . Some ridicule me for being a socialist. I don't care."[30]

However, as the election campaign progressed, Bhutto came under increasing criticism from the Islamists for promoting an "un-Islamic" socialist ideology. Bhutto fought back by increasing the Islamic content in his party's ideology. For instance, in his address to the District Bar Association in Hyderabad on June 26, 1969, Bhutto said:

Islam is our religion. Pakistan came into being because we were Muslims. We will sacrifice everything for Islam. If you want to serve Islam, if you want to serve Pakistan, then serve the Muslims of Pakistan . . . . Make the people powerful, and in this way, you will be doing a service to your God, to your Prophet, to your country . . . . There is undoubtedly the principle of democracy in Islam . . . . Islam emphasized . . . equality [more] than on anything else. . . . We want to create equality, but when we talk of equality, of socialism, we are dubbed anti-Islamic.[31]

At a public speech in Liaquat Gardens, in Rawalpindi, on January 17, 1970, Bhutto said:

We are first Muslims and then Pakistanis. Unlike "Islam *Pasands*" we not only like Islam, we love Islam...our foremost principle is "Islam is our religion." We are prepared to offer any sacrifice for the glory of Islam....In Islam, socioeconomic equality or *"Musawat"* has been given highest priority. The Prophet (peace be upon him) emphasized the importance of *Musawat*. We shall, therefore, bring about *Musawat*.[32]

In the 1970 PPP Election Manifesto, Bhutto declared that his party's ultimate objective was the creation of a classless society, which would ensure the true equality of Pakistanis. Since this aim was deeply embedded in the socioeconomic and political philosophy of Islam, Bhutto felt that the PPP was merely striving to implement the noble ideals of the Islamic faith.[33] On yet another occasion, he said, "Islam was the first religion to give a message of equality for everyone. That is why we want Islamic equality to be established. Poverty and hunger cannot be stamped out without adopting the principles of equality."[34]

In a radio and television address to the nation on November 18, 1970, a couple of weeks before the December elections, Bhutto said:

There was a time in the history of Islam when the Great Umar declared that if along the banks of the Euphrates should a dog die of starvation, the *Khalifah* of Islam would be answerable before Almighty *Allah*. Here in Pakistan—in the largest Islamic State—men and women die of starvation by the thousands. Our children sleep in the streets without shelter. Our toiling masses live an appalling life . . . . The struggle in Pakistan is not between Muslim and Muslim, but between the exploiters and the exploited, between the oppressors and the oppressed. If the citizens of Pakistan are provided with employment, with food and shelter, with schools and hospitals, indeed with normal facilities, we would be acting in conformity with the injunctions of the Holy *Qur'an* and *Sunnah*.[35]

Bhutto's effective use of potent religious imagery is illustrated by his designating a sword as his party's election symbol, thereby alluding to the legendary *Zulfiquar-e-Ali* (Ali's sword). In so doing, Bhutto sought identification with Prophet Muhammad's wise and courageous cousin and son-in-law as well as Islam's fourth *khalifah* (caliph),[36] who had defeated many an enemy of Islam with his famous sword, thus contributing to Islam's expansion and glory.

Moreover, Bhutto wanted the image of the sword to inspire the masses with the ideal of a *jihad* (holy war) to be waged by the PPP regime against the evils of capitalism and feudalism in particular and against exploitation and injustice in general. In the realm of foreign affairs, he promised a *jihad* against the evils of imperialism, colonialism, and neo-colonialism. He also stirred his audiences by saying that he was prepared to lead Pakistan into a one-thousand-year-long *jihad* against India and celebrate *Shaukat-e-Islam* Day (Glory of Islam Day) in New Delhi and Srinagar.[37]

During his whirlwind tours of West Pakistan, Bhutto pointedly made very publicized visits to the religious shrines of a few famous *pirs* (spiritual guides). He performed public prayers at popular Islamic festivals like *Eid*[38] in an attempt to counteract his conservative Islamic opponents' criticism that he was a *kafir* (unbeliever).

Instead of bringing the eastern and western wings of Pakistan together, the 1970 national election contributed to the further polarization of the two regions of the country. While Bhutto's PPP won 59 percent of the votes cast in West Pakistan, Mujib-ur-Rahman's Awami League secured 74.9 percent of the votes cast in East Pakistan.[39] The military junta as well as the influential civilian politicians of West Pakistan found Mujib's landslide victory unacceptable because most West Pakistanis perceived Mujib's demand for east wing autonomy as striking at the very foundations of a united Pakistan. When the West Pakistani power elite dishonored the election results to prevent Mujib-ur-Rahman from assuming the prime ministership of Pakistan, the Awami League leadership retaliated by calling for a civil-disobedience movement in East Pakistan. This civil-disobedience movement snowballed into a nine-month-long civil war that culminated with India's military intervention in East Pakistan, a third Indo-Pakistani war, the breakup of Pakistan, and the birth of Bangladesh from the crucible of East Pakistan on December 16, 1971.

The creation of Bangladesh led not only to a transfer of power from Yahya Khan's discredited military regime to that of the PPP—which had won the mandate of the West Pakistani people in the elections held a year earlier—but also profoundly traumatized West Pakistanis and resulted in a vigorous debate about the very foundations of Pakistan's nationhood.[40] Critics of the two-nation theory—the basis on which Pakistan was established–felt vindicated. So did those who felt that the slender thread of Islam wouldn't be sufficient to hold the two distant and strikingly different wings of Pakistan together. The Islamists believed that "un-Islamic" leaders, the lack of Islamization, and God's displeasure with a nation that had failed to be truly Islamic were responsible for regionalism, class conflict, and the dismemberment of the country.

Bhutto's Manipulation of Islam in Domestic Policy

Zulfikar Ali Bhutto was acutely aware of the identity crisis, soul-searching, and powerful Islamic current generated in the aftermath of Bangladesh. He, therefore, turned to Islam to heal the nation's wounds much more aggressively than he otherwise would have. Besides conceding a constitution that was far more Islamic in letter and spirit than the previous two, Bhutto instituted a number of Islamic measures to appease, yet undercut, the powerful Islamic interest groups in the country. These measures tended to cast an Islamic overtone onto Pakistani society. Thus, between 1973 and 1976 Bhutto: "endorsed an Act of Parliament declaring the Ahmadis to be a non-Muslim minority despite the fact that they had overwhelmingly supported him in the 1970 elections";[41] changed the name of the Red Cross to Red Crescent, thereby symbolically, though superficially, Islamizing the humanitarian organization in Pakistan;[42] ordered copies of the *Qur'an* to be placed in all the rooms of first class hotels throughout Pakistan; established a Ministry of Religious Affairs for the first time in Pakistan's history;[43] encouraged the national radio and television stations to increase the number of religious programs; promoted Arabic instruction in schools and on radio and television;[44] provided increased facilities for the separate Islamic instruction of *Shi`ah* and *Sunni* children in all schools;[45] sponsored an international conference on the life and work of Prophet Muhammad; and removed quota restrictions imposed on those wanting to go to perform the *haj* (pilgrimage to Mecca), increased the pilgrim's foreign exchange allowance, and saw to it that more ships and planes were made available during the *haj* season to transport the pilgrims to and from Saudi Arabia.[46]

In his desire to win over the hearts of the Sindhi and Punjabi village folk, who revere their *pirs* and saints, Bhutto ordered ornate gilded doors from Iran to be placed at the entrance of two very popular shrines in Pakistan: one at Shahbaz Qalander in Sewan (Sind) and the other at Data Ganj Bakhsh in Lahore (Punjab). In addition, he invited the *imam* (prayer leader) of the Prophet's mosque in Medina and later the *imam* of the mosque at the *Ka`aba* to Pakistan.

Bhutto's Reorientation of Pakistan's Foreign Policy Toward the Muslim World

Given the importance of overcoming misunderstandings of Muslim countries regarding Pakistan since the mid-1950s, when it was allied to the West, and when Pakistani Prime Minster H. S. Suhrawardy angered the Muslim world by referring to it as "Zero plus zero plus zero is after all equal to zero," Bhutto embarked on what he called a "journey of renaissance" or a "journey among brothers," which took him to twenty predominantly Muslim countries in the Middle East. His journey helped rebuild Pakistan's bridges of understanding and friendship with the Muslim nations.[47]

During the Arab-Israeli War of October 1973, Bhutto supported the Arabs diplomatically, politically, and even materially.[48] He instructed Pakistan's UN delegation to assist other Muslim delegations in making common cause. His regime dispatched doctors and nurses to Egypt and Syria.[49] Pakistani pilots were sent to assist the Syrian air force, and a few army battalions were kept on alert in the event Damascus was attacked.[50]

Pakistanis saw the nomination of Pakistan as the host of the Second Islamic Summit Conference of the Organization of the Islamic Conference (OIC)[51] in Lahore as a result of Pakistan's espousal of Arab and Islamic causes since the nation's inception as well as Bhutto's astute statesmanship. In fact, because of Bhutto's careful orchestration and the propitious political climate in the Muslim world, the Lahore Summit was not only the biggest gathering of its kind in the post-World War II period, but also very successful.[52] The Lahore Summit enhanced Pakistan's stature in the world, made Bhutto one of the most popular figures in the Muslim World, facilitated Pakistan's export of manpower to and inflow of remittances from the Middle East, and dramatically increased the inflow of aid from the oil-rich Muslim countries.

In Bhutto's opinion, his "greatest achievement" lay in being the major architect of Pakistan's nuclear energy program and the father of the yet-to-be-exploded "Islamic Bomb."[53] He considered this achievement greater than stabilizing and consolidating West Pakistan, his domestic socioeconomic reforms, the July 1972 Simla Agreement with India, the 1973 Constitution, the strengthening of ties with the Muslim world, and hosting the 1974 Lahore Islamic Summit Conference.

In a book entitled *If I Am Assassinated*, published in India, Bhutto is said to have written: "We know that Israel and South Africa have full nuclear capability. The Christian, Jewish, and Hindu civilizations have the capability. The Communist powers also possess it. Only the Islamic civilization was without it, but that position was about to change."[54]

Circumstantial evidence suggests that Bhutto promised to share Pakistan's nuclear technology with his Arab benefactors once his country had built the "Islamic Bomb" with their money. Israel's past military successes and probable nuclear capability helped Bhutto convince them that the existence of an Islamic Bomb would not only deter Israel from ever using its nuclear arsenal against the

Arabs but also dissuade it from invading and occupying more Arab land. Moreover, Bhutto firmly believed and was able to convince his Arab brothers that with the "Islamic Bomb," the Islamic bloc would no longer be weak and vulnerable; rather it could proudly reassert itself as an influential power in international affairs.[55]

Bhutto's allegation that foreign agents (alluding to America's Central Intelligence Agency) and domestic opposition forces (particularly the Islamists and pro-Western rightists) were conspiring to overthrow him in order to prevent the completion of the "Islamic Bomb" was intended to make him a martyr, dying in the honorable cause of Islam,[56] thus enhancing his Islamic credentials.

Bhutto accurately perceived the mutuality of interests between Pakistan and the Muslim Middle East. Bhutto's regime, therefore, facilitated labor migration to the Middle East by easing passport and visa formalities; allowed Pakistani emigrants to hold dual nationalities; allowed "labor exchange" arrangements with several Middle Eastern countries; allowed a large number of experienced civilian technicians and armed forces personnel to go to the Middle East; signed agreements to provide training for air force personnel from these countries at academies in Pakistan; allowed migrating labor to bring back earnings in the form of consumer or capital goods; and made special arrangements with the Pakistan International Airlines (PIA) and the National Shipping Corporation to service the migrating labor force.[57] These policies resulted in the migration of an estimated 600,000 Pakistanis to the Middle East by 1977, remitting about $700 million annually to Pakistan.[58]

Using the "politics of Islam," Bhutto was able to make Pakistani export of manpower one of the country's major export items, bringing in nearly 48.9 percent of Pakistan's foreign exchange earnings by the fiscal year 1977-78, compared to only 15.1 percent in the fiscal year 1974-75.[59] In fact, by 1977, according to an International Monetary Fund (IMF) report, Pakistan topped the list of labor-exporting countries both in numbers of workers, which was estimated at over 500,000, and in volume of remittances, which was estimated at $1 billion, nearly double its 1976 figure of $590 million.[60]

Bhutto's same skillful policies generated increased Middle Eastern grants, loans, oil at concessionary prices, and investments. Statistics reveal that prior to Bhutto's assumption of power, foreign aid to Pakistan from Muslim countries was inconsequential. Starting in 1974, Pakistan became one of the prime recipients of generous aid from the oil-rich Muslim countries. By the end of 1976, foreign assistance to Pakistan, mainly from the Middle East, contributed about half of the approximately $1.7 billion Pakistani development budget.[61]

Bhutto's Use of Islam in the 1977 Elections and After

The PPP's Election Manifesto of 1977 was different in style and content from its 1970 Election Manifesto. It contained none of the socialist rhetoric that had characterized the PPP ideology when the party was founded. While socialism and even "Islamic Socialism" were underplayed both in the 1977 Election Manifesto and in the party's official pronouncements, Islam (minus socialism) was prominently highlighted. The PPP Manifesto promised to "hold high the banner of Islam . . .; ensure that Friday is observed as the weekly holiday instead of Sunday . . . making the teaching of the Holy *Qur'an* an integral part of eminence as a center of community life . . .; [and] establish a federal *Ulama* academy."[62]

As the spring 1977 election campaign in Pakistan gathered momentum, the eight opposition political parties constituting the Pakistan National Alliance (PNA) used Islam and Bhutto's authoritarianism to combat Bhutto's regime. Sensing the Islamic thrust of the PNA's successful election campaign strategy, Bhutto instructed the PPP rank and file to drop references to "Islamic socialism," and use the much more appealing term of *musawat-e-Muhammadi* (Islamic egalitarianism) instead. Moreover, Bhutto and his PPP candidates stressed the regime's service to Islam in domestic as well as foreign policy during the past six years and promised to do much more for the cause of Islam if reelected. As one perceptive editorial in a local Pakistani newspaper pointed out: "The major emphasis in the People's Party programme for the future is on Islam. This is in sharp contrast to the concept of trinity propounded in the last election—socialism, Islam and democracy."[63]

Despite Bhutto's appeal to Islam, his credentials were suspect because of his secular orientation. But Bhutto and the PPP orators confidently repeated the charges made in the successful 1970 election regarding the political inexperience, pro-Western bias, and potential sectarian clashes if their opponents came to power. The PPP also listed its accomplishments in the service of Islam with particular emphasis on Bhutto's role as chairman of the successful Islamic Summit Conference in Lahore.[64]

The PPP's overwhelming victory at the polls, despite the PNA's success in drawing mammoth crowds during the election campaign, left the PNA disillusioned and furious. Its members accused Bhutto of election fraud and launched a movement to remove him from office if he did not concede to new national elections under the direct supervision of the judiciary and the army. When Bhutto refused to hold new elections, the PNA launched a civil disobedience campaign that succeeded because Bhutto had alienated many influential groups in the country during his years in power.

Numerous mosques throughout Pakistan encouraged their congregations through religio-political sermons and even organized many of their members to engage in a *jihad* against the secular and un-Islamic Bhutto regime. The rallying cry of the PNA, influenced by the Islamic political parties, was to replace the regime of the "Whiskey party leader," under whom "Islam was in Danger," with the pristine purity of *Nizam-i-Mustafah* (Prophet Muhammad's system) or *Nizam-i-Islam* (the Islamic system).

As the PNA-led movement drew upon the enormous reservoir of genuine Islamic sentiments among the majority of Pakistani people, Bhutto reacted by announcing a series of Islamic measures in his press conference on April 17, 1977, including the immediate prohibition of alcohol in the country (i.e. all bars and wine shops were to be closed), and Pakistani embassies abroad were forbidden to offer alcoholic drinks at receptions; a ban on all forms of gambling and the closure of night-clubs; the Islamization of Pakistan's civil and criminal laws, which were to be streamlined and completed in six months instead of the four years allowed by the 1973 Constitution; and the reconstitution of the Council of Islamic Ideology responsible for the introduction of *Shariat* Law to include leaders of three Islamic political parties. Though these moves did not check the erosion of his support, they only heightened the Islamic revival sweeping Pakistan.

Having attempted to appease his opponents with little or no success, Bhutto imposed martial law on April 21, 1977; placed tighter censorship on the mass media; and jailed hundreds of people who opposed his regime.[65] However, when the use of force also failed to crush the opposition movement, Bhutto requested the Saudi Arabian Ambassador to Pakistan and the foreign ministers of the United Arab Emirates (UAE), Kuwait, and Libya to do all they could to bring the Pakistani political parties to the negotiating table to resolve their differences in the "spirit of Islamic solidarity and brotherhood." This Islamic Solidarity Committee provided a face-saving device to both the PPP-led government and the PNA-led opposition to negotiate issues. Arab mediators also promised financial assistance for new elections.[66] But even as a compromise was near, the PNA Central Council, sensing victory, rejected the deal that had been tentatively approved by the negotiators. Now that PPP-PNA negotiations had failed, an intensification of violence inevitably leading to civil war loomed on the Pakistani horizon. To prevent such an eventuality, the Pakistani army—increasingly restive about its task of controlling civilian unrest for a leadership that had lost its legitimacy—acted out its time-honored extra-constitutional role by executing a swift and bloodless *coup d'état* on July 5, 1977.[67]

In summary, the secular and liberal Bhutto—whom most people would least identify as an Islamic revivalist—brought about an Islamic revival in Pakistan through his skillful manipulation of Islamic symbolism in domestic and foreign policy. However, the politics of Islam in which Bhutto so astutely engaged in order to enhance his own power and popularity came to haunt him in the twilight months of his tenure, and ultimately resulted in his overthrow.

MUHAMMAD ZIA-UL-HAQ

The leader of the Pakistani armed forces who overthrew Bhutto's regime was General Muhammad Zia-ul-Haq, a pious, apolitical, loyal, and mediocre career army officer whom Prime Minister Bhutto had personally promoted to the position of army chief-of-staff a little over a year earlier.[68] In his first national address on radio and television, General Zia clearly stated that his dual mission was to restore law and order as well as hold free and fair elections on the basis of adult franchise within ninety days. In that same speech, Zia stated that Pakistan was "created in the name of Islam" and would "survive only if it sticks to Islam."[69]

Zia-ul-Haq's Islamization Campaign

Just five days after coming to power, General Zia imposed martial law and assumed the august position of Chief Martial Law Administrator. He then introduced a broad spectrum of punishments that are recommended in the Islamic *shariah,* such as public flogging for the commission of several crimes including murder, rape, theft, drinking of alcohol, fornication, prostitution, adultery, bearing false witness, and destroying government property in demonstrations and riots. These punishments were intended not only to deter the criminal elements in society, but also to intimidate his opposition.

When Zia released Bhutto from "protective custody" on July 28, 1977, the former prime minister started to effectively campaign for the October 1977 elections. What alarmed the military clique was that the overly confident Bhutto had begun to scathingly denounce the martial law authorities at huge campaign rallies and had even suggested retribution against them if reelected. The military rulers began to imagine a miserable future for themselves if the charismatic and vindictive Bhutto was reelected with the mandate of the people. They probably not only feared being dishonorably dismissed from the armed forces and losing their pension, but suffering a long and humiliating period of imprisonment, and possibly even capital punishment for violating the Constitution and overthrowing a democratically elected government. Therefore, on September 3, 1977, merely thirty-six days after releasing Bhutto, General Zia had the former prime minister rearrested and imprisoned for "the gross abuse of power" during his six-year-long rule. Then, less than a month later, General Zia postponed the promised October elections and instituted a period of "accountability" to look into the gross corruption, abuse of power, and the serious allegation that Bhutto had ordered the murder of a political rival, Ahmad Raza Kasuri.[70]

On September 1, 1977, General Zia called on the Islamic Ideology Council (IIC)—that General Ayub Khan had established and Bhutto had revived—to recommend feasible ways of bringing the existing laws in conformity with the *Qur'an* and *Sunnah* (Prophet Muhammad's words and deeds) and help him in establishing a *Nizam-i-Islam* (Islamic System) in the country. After nominating a number of prominent *ulama* from the ranks of the Islamic parties and interest groups to the IIC, the council got down to the task of formulating feasible measures to introduce a *shariah*-based penal code, *zakat* (2 ½ percent annual tax on wealth), *ushr* (a 10 percent tax on farmland paid by well-to-do landholders to the poor), and an interest-free banking system. Zia also revitalized the Ministry of Religious Affairs, the *Auqaf* Department for the administration of religious institutions, and other governmental institutions, which affected religious practice. Within a couple of years, the IIC became a major policy-planning body responsible for the Islamic reformation of the country.[71]

Less than three weeks later, in a speech to an audience in Lahore, President Zia criticized the Westernized and secular intellectuals in the elite for demanding the restoration of Western democracy. However, in the Islamic Republic of Pakistan, "sovereignty does not belong to the people," but "belongs to Almighty Allah and we are His servants." By this Zia was implying that Islam did not have such "alien" concepts as popular sovereignty, Western-type elections based on adult franchise, and liberal parliamentary democracy. Zia also claimed that Pakistan had not come into being merely to provide *roti, kapra aur makan* (ridiculing the PPP's popular vote-getting slogan of bread, clothing, and shelter). Therefore, he stated, that he would hold elections in November 1979, only after he was convinced that the future leaders of the country would safeguard Pakistan's national integrity and enforce *Nizam-i-Islam*.[72]

Soon after postponing elections for an additional two years, General Zia increased governmental censorship of television programs and movies, and began to introduce a broad spectrum of Islamic measures. Women were told to dress modestly, wear the *hijab* (head covering or veil), and wear little (preferably no) make-up in public. Very soon, women were wearing the *hijab* on television and to work. Zia himself rejected Western dress in favor of the dress worn by most Muslims in Pakistan and India, namely, the *kurta* or *kameez* (a cotton or linen shirt), *shalwar* (baggy cotton trousers), and an *achkan* (waist-coat) or *sherwani* (long baggy knee-length coat) for men.[73] He also made it a point to start all his press conferences and public speeches with the recitation from the *Qur'an*.[74] The government began to strictly monitor entertainment programs in all educational institutions to see that they were complying with Islamic standards of morality and ethics. In fact, the Zia regime encouraged Pakistanis to adorn the walls of educational institutions and governmental offices as well as calendars and billboards with quotations from the *Qur'an* and *hadith* (Prophet Muhammad's sayings).[75] Furthermore, President Zia officially designated Friday as the weekly holiday instead of Sunday[76] and picked up Bhutto's idea of renaming streets, parks, and public buildings (including schools, colleges, and universities) with the names of Muslim leaders, heroes, and heroines. The city of Lyallpur was renamed Faisalabad in honor of King Faisal of Saudi Arabia.[77]

In August 1978, Zia invited a number of prominent leaders and scholars from the Islamic parties and groups within the PNA to officially join his administration as advisors (a few with cabinet rank) in order to help the martial law authorities "in the prompt and effective introduction of *Nizam-i-Mustafah*."[78] Although *JI*'s founder and first *amir* (Islamic leader), Maududi, had written and spoken against an Islamic state being ruled by a military despot, his successor, Mian Tufail Muhammad, had great faith in Zia-ul-Haq's commitment to Islam and said that this was "a golden opportunity for the establishment of an Islamic system which should never be allowed to go unavailed of."[79]

While *JI* leaders joined Zia's regime as cabinet members and official advisors for the first time in Pakistan's history, they resigned eight short months later because of the government's unpopularity and their own desire to actively campaign and win the November 1979 election. However, on October 16, 1979, President Zia indefinitely postponed the November 1979 elections and outlawed all political parties (including the *JI*). In fact, President Zia, who had come to see himself as the *amir* of the Islamic state he was ushering in, justified his actions with Maududi's long-advocated ideas regarding an Islamic state.[80] Maududi's main ideas included: (1) Almighty *Allah's* (God's) sovereignty and not "popular sovereignty" (rule of the people, by the people, and for the people as in Western democracies) should be the paramount and fundamental constitutional principle of an Islamic state; (2) only a devout Muslim can rule an Islamic state, and his tenure in office should be limited only by his dedication to protecting, defending, and promoting the Islamic ideology of the state; (3) a leader called an *amir* (ruler) should be elected from among devout Muslim candidates; (4) a *Majlis-i-Shura* (Advisory Council) "composed of men with the educational qualifications to make valid applications of the fundamental law of the *Qur'an* and the *Sunnah*" should advise the *amir* of an Islamic state; (5) political parties in an Islamic state should be discouraged because they only cause conflict and divisions within the *ummah* (Muslim community); (6) non-Muslims should be allowed to reside safely in an Islamic state, but should not be permitted to hold any powerful or influential policy-making position; and (7) minorities can vote in elections, but only in separate electorates.[81]

On December 2, 1978, President Zia initiated the process of establishing a legal system based on *Nizam-i-Islam*. He established a permanent law commission to simplify the legal system and to bring all the existing laws in conformity with Islamic guidelines. The ultimate goal was to make the *shariah* the basis of all law in Pakistan. In February 1979, Zia announced the establishment of special *Shariat* Benches (courts that would decide cases on the basis of the *shariah*), and religious courts were established as a supplement to the existing judicial system to review a limited range of laws and adjudicate cases brought under the *shariah*. With the addition of a *Shariat* Bench as part of the Supreme Court, cases could be brought challenging the validity of any law. The *Shariat* Bench consisted of five judges who were to be advised by competent *ulama* in matters of Islamic law. The main function of these Islamic legal bodies was to exercise a form of Islamic judicial review, where any citizen could request the judiciary to declare a law either wholly or partially un-Islamic. This was a big step towards establishing the supremacy of Islamic law over the Anglo-Saxon secular law that Pakistan had inherited from its British colonial masters.[82]

On February 10, 1979, President Zia utilized the happy occasion of *Eid-e-Milad-un-Nabi* (Prophet Muhammad's birthday) to introduce a more comprehensive Islamic penal code. Though far from the comprehensive Islamic system that Zia wanted to introduce, his Islamic measures nevertheless constituted additional "concrete steps and solid measures" in his effort to transform the country's sociocultural, economic, and political institutions and processes in accordance with Islamic principles and incorporate Islam more fully into the nation's daily life.[83]

The elite and the regime's opponents viewed Zia's imposition of Islamic punishments for a broad spectrum of crimes as so medieval and barbaric that they began referring to Zia-ul-Haq (literally, "Light of Justice") as *Zulumul Haq* ("Haq the Oppressor"). Even the *JI,* which had initially supported Zia and his Islamic penal code, realized how unpopular the Islamic punishments were among the majority of Pakistanis, and reverted back to Maududi's view that the introduction of the Islamic penal code prior to its socioeconomic prerequisites (i.e. the establishment of Islamic economic and sociocultural system, which included the elimination of poverty and the attainment of the basic necessities of life by all citizens) was neither a good policy nor recommended in Islam.[84]

The Zia regime's Islamization campaign significantly affected Pakistan's educational system. The government established numerous cells, committees, commissions, university departments, and other agencies assigned to study, plan, or implement the Islamic transformation of Pakistani society. The government arranged many conferences on Islamic subjects, topics, and themes. It ordered the mass media to cover international, regional, national, and local conferences and seminars pertaining to Islam. It hosted national conventions of the *ulama* and *mashaikh* (spiritual leaders). It undertook a thorough revision of textbooks and course curricula in order to "prepare a new generation wedded to the ideology of Pakistan and Islam."[85] *Islamiyat* (Islamic studies) was made compulsory for all Muslims. More government money started flowing to mosque-based primary schools where children were taught Arabic, the *Qur'an,* and *hadith*. A *Shariat* faculty was established at the *Quaid-e-Azam* University in Islamabad in 1979; a year later, it became a separate educational institution, and was called the Islamic University.[86] Radio and television productions were ordered to conform to strict Islamic standards of morality and ethics as well as reinforce the national identity of the citizenry. A law was introduced severely punishing those who defiled the names of the Prophet Muhammad and the *Khulafah-i-Rashidin* (the rightly guided caliphs).[87] Furthermore, after considerable pressure from Islamic groups, the government even tried to establish separate educational facilities for males and females, but then abandoned the idea for lack of money and strong opposition from educated and vocal women's groups.[88]

In 1980, Zia's government publicized the Report of the Committee on Islamization. The report stated that the main goal of an Islamic economic system was a "just society," which could only be achieved by providing free and universal education, increasing the availability of basic consumer goods, and increasing the level of employment so that people could lead a decent life.[89] The committee also recommended an active governmental role in the just redistribution of physical assets (especially land reform) and in satisfying the basic human needs of the masses; rejected the "growth strategy" or "trickle-down strategy," in which the government primarily assisted wealthy industrialists and large landlords to accelerate economic growth, as un-Islamic because it increased the gap between the rich and the poor and thereby violated the principles of Islamic egalitarianism and justice; advised against excessive foreign borrowing to promote development in the short run because that would negatively affect the standard of living of future generations; and called on the government to produce and deliver the basic necessities of life because that matter was too important to be left to Adam Smith's "invisible hand" and the unpredictable market forces of supply and demand.[90]

Although the Committee on Islamization considered the adoption of *zakat* and *ushr* as important, but not necessary, to the introduction of an Islamic system, the Zia regime, desirous of giving the public the feeling that the regime was serious about ushering in an Islamic economic system, proceeded to collect *zakat* and *ushr* during the holy month of Ramadan with much fanfare. A Central *Zakat* Fund was established to help the poor and needy (such as those who were widowed, orphaned, handicapped, and aged) and President Zia proudly inaugurated the distribution of *zakat* on the national radio and television. Despite the fact that most of the *Zakat* Fund came from the governments of Saudi Arabia and the United Arab Emirates (and not from reluctant Pakistanis), President Zia confidently and optimistically bragged that as a result of *zakat* and *ushr*, Pakistan would be transformed into a welfare state and an egalitarian society in which "hunger and beggary would be eliminated" and "no citizen would go to bed hungry."[91]

In a 1983 press conference Zia said: "My only ambition in life is to complete the process of Islamization so that there will be no turning back. . . . The Islamization process is a lifetime job . . . . you have to put their [general society's] aims and objectives straight on the path of righteousness. And that is what I call Islamization."[92] Then, during the holy month of Ramadan, Zia's regime glorified and encouraged all able-bodied Pakistani Muslim adults to fast. In this regard, Zia's regime even forbade restaurants, motels, and hotels to serve food to Muslims from dawn to dusk, and pressured government officers to lead the mid-day prayer in governmental offices. The government publicized the annual *haj*, with high government officials photographed and shown on television sending off and welcoming home pilgrims at the docks and airports.[93] In fact, even General Zia was shown in the mass media personally seeing off shiploads and planeloads of pilgrims going to perform the *haj* or shown embracing *hajis* returning from the *haj*.[94]

Pakistan's *Shi`ah* minority, emboldened by Iran's Islamic revolution, vociferously protested the state-organized mandatory *zakat* and *ushr* because the obligatory collection of these taxes was not in keeping with their school of jurisprudence.[95] On June 20, 1980, General Zia's government realized the destabilizing effect of the *Shi`ah* anger and appointed a committee of *Shi`ah* and *Sunni ulama* to study the *Zakat* and *Ushr* Ordinance. Based on this committee's recommendations, the Zia regime defused the sectarian time-bomb by announcing that there would be no interference in people's deeply held religious beliefs; that no one dogma would be imposed on any Muslim sect; and that the *Shi`ah* community would be allowed to formulate its own procedures and establish its own institutions to collect, administer, and distribute *zakat*.[96] Indeed, in 1981, *zakat* as a compulsory requirement for *Shi`ahs* was completely withdrawn.

An attempt to deduct *zakat* from the savings accounts of all Pakistani citizens according to the Hanafi (*Sunni*) school of Islamic jurisprudence created another uproar among the *Shi`ah* minority in March and April 1983. Increased demands by *Sunni* parties and interest groups to make Hanafi jurisprudence the law of the land, and to declare all other Islamic sects as minorities, thereby giving them second class citizenship, tended to polarize *Sunnis* and *Shi`ahs* and resulted in sectarian violence.[97]

On August 14, 1984 (Pakistan's Independence Day), Zia again annoyed and frightened the *Shi`ahs* as well as liberal *Sunni* Muslims, when he announced the immediate appointment of a *nazim-i-galat* (organizer of prayers) in every village and urban precinct. These prayer organizers were to not only organize the mid-day prayers on Fridays, but also encourage Muslims to say all five prayers daily.[98] To quote Zia:

Only those persons are being appointed for this service of religion who have sound moral character and their piety is so exemplary that their words will have deep effect on the hearts of people. The procedure for this exercise *for the time being* (italics added) is based on persuasion and motivation and not on compulsion. But we are determined to succeed in establishing the system of prayer at all cost.[99]

Zia's continued implementation of policies and programs based on the Hanafi school of Islamic jurisprudence continued to provoke the *Shi`ah* minority into actively opposing those governmental measures. That, in turn, resulted in some *Sunni* zealots harassing and attacking *Shi`ahs* and their property, and going so far as to demand that Pakistan be declared a "Sunni state" which would restrict the public performance of *Shi`ah* religious rituals. The *Shi`ahs*, fearing the worst, decided to create greater solidarity in their ranks by establishing a political party in 1987 called the *Tehrik-i-Nifaz-i-Fiqh-i-Jaffariah* (TNFJ). The TNFJ actively opposed a uniform *shariah* code, requested the government to consult them when formulating Islamic laws, and supported the implementation of *Quranic* and *shariah* injunctions for each sect according to its own interpretation.[100] In late summer 1988, a few *Sunni* zealots were so incensed with the influential *Shi`ah* lobby getting its way that they assassinated a leading *Shi'ah alim* (Islamic scholar), Arif Hussain al-Hussaini, in Peshawar. The *Shi`ahs* responded by crying "Blood for Blood" and accused Zia of complicity in the crime.[101]

While Zia sometimes gave in to Pakistan's influential *Shi`ah* minority, which comprises over 15 percent of the Pakistani population, he adopted an uncompromising stand against the much smaller and weaker Ahmadi or Qadiani minority. In 1984, Zia issued presidential decrees forbidding Ahmadis from calling themselves Muslims, preaching to Muslims, calling their place of worship a *masjid* (mosque), and utilizing such Islamic religious practices as the *azan* (call to prayer).[102]

Some of the most controversial Islamic measures introduced in the Zia era were those pertaining to the role of women in the emerging Islamic state. The *Majlis-i-Shura* (Consultative Assembly or Advisory Council) angered many women when it unanimously approved the *Qanun-i-Shahadat* (Law of Evidence) ordinance on March 3, 1983. This Ordinance brought the Law of Evidence in conformity with Islamic injunctions present in the *Qur'an* and *Sunnah*. Conservative *ulama* both within and outside the *Majlis-i-Shura* adamantly argued that only in matters, which were confined to women's activities, could there be women witnesses. In all other matters, there should be two men, and if only one man was available, there should be one male and two female witnesses (i.e., the evidence of two female witnesses would be considered equivalent to that of one male witness). Though no laws were changed, many women in the elite class of Pakistani society were concerned with the direction the Zia regime was taking the country.[103]

Women's concerns were further heightened when they heard that in an Islamic system charges of rape had to be corroborated by as many as four witnesses (an almost impossible requirement) to find the alleged rapist guilty. Failure to convict the rapist made the woman guilty of fornication in the *shariah*. A large segment of the female population was furious at Zia and other high-level government officials for saying that women should stay at home and not work in public places where they would be interacting with men and vulnerable to sexual harassment, adultery, and rape. Female athletes vociferously protested against the Zia regime for forbidding them from competing in national, regional, and international competitive sports and games. Many women denounced the Zia regime for prohibiting women from participating in dramas and plays when male spectators were in the audience.[104]

General Zia, like most Islamic fundamentalists, interpreted *riba* as "interest" and not as "usury" (excessive interest charged by avaricious money lenders and "loan sharks") as Muslim Modernists do. He, therefore, attempted to prohibit *riba*. As a first step, the Zia regime decided that the House Building Finance Corporation, National Investment Trust, and Investment Corporation of Pakistan would begin interest-free lending and deposits. The House Building Finance Corporation, for instance, adopted the gimmick of making certain types of loans on the basis of sharing of rental income rather than sharing interest. Zia also asked the Islamic Ideology Council (IIC) to come up with some feasible recommendations for the transition to an interest-free economy. After about three years of deliberations, the IIC came out with a 118-page report which, except for a change of terminology (such as referring to "interest" charged and given by banks to "profit and loss" loans and deposits in banks), recommended no Islamic solutions to the country's serious economic problems. Instead, the IIC recommended the formation of more study groups and committees to do more in-depth research on establishing an interest-free economy. However, Zia's target of introducing interest-free Islamic banking in Pakistan by June 1985 was unrealistic and has still not been implemented.[105]

The Zia regime also tried to Islamize Pakistan's secular political system. In August 1979, Zia amended the 1962 Political Parties Act. The amendments incorporated allowed for the registration of only those political parties with the Election Commission that had limited their party funds to the lower levels mandated, swore allegiance to the Islamic ideology of Pakistan, propagated no opinion against the Islamic ideology of Pakistan or against the judiciary or the armed forces, and held party elections annually.[106] A month later, Zia said: "The present political system in which political parties flew at each other's throats had no relevance to the Islamic concept."[107] In late October 1979, Zia was even more emphatic about establishing an Islamic system: "The main need of this country is an Islamic, democratic, and stable government for which elections for the sake of elections have no meaning . . . . I want that our democracy should be imbued with the spirit of Islam and those people who are elected in such a democratic system should have a genuine love for Islam."[108]

In order to formulate feasible recommendations for the Islamic governmental system, Zia appointed a twelve-member committee of "scholars, jurists, *ulama*, and prominent persons from other walks of life." On the recommendations of this body, Zia decided to hold non-party elections at the appropriate time; utilizing separate electorates (Muslims and non-Muslims voting separately for their political representatives); in which the political candidates running for office would have to be practicing Muslims of established honesty, ability, and competence; and the voters would have to be practicing Muslims as well.[109]

In his address at the *Quaid-i-Azam* University on October 8, 1979, General Zia denounced the propaganda that Pakistan had been established merely to fulfill the material needs of the people. In this speech, Zia stressed that Pakistan would be an Islamic state based on Islamic ideology. He denounced the PPP's secular socialist ideology that was antithetical to Islam and Pakistan's Islamic ideology.[110] In fact, Zia's regime systematically harassed, imprisoned, whipped, and tortured many PPP activists.

At a press conference on October 16, 1979, Zia referred to "Islam" a number of times when announcing the postponement of the November 1979 elections: "I want to introduce Islam in Pakistan in the true sense. Our present political edifice is based on the secular democratic system of the West, which has no place in Islam. . . . This country was created in the name of Islam, and in Islam, there is no provision for Western-type elections."[111]

President Zia later stated his desire to introduce an electoral system based on proportional representation, which he suggested was more in keeping with the spirit of Islam. He probably got this idea from Professor Khurshid Ahmed, chairman of Pakistan's Institute of Policy Studies and a well known Islamist, who had written and popularized a fifty-page paper in which he called the proportional representation system closer to Islam than any other.[112]

In his October 1980 speech, Zia stated that: "As long as I am at the helm of affairs and there is with me the overwhelming force of Islam-loving people, we will not let the country go into the hands of anti-Islam and secular elements."[113] In the same speech, Zia announced his decision to create a *Majlis-i-Shura* (Consultative Assembly or Advisory Council), comprising 250 to 300 "true Pakistanis and *momins*" (devout Muslims) to debate public issues, within limits.[114] In late 1981, Zia established the *Majlis-i-Shura* as promised, and claimed that Pakistan was moving toward's a *Shurocracy*, or an Islamic type of democracy. But the *Majlis-i-Shura* remained merely an advisory body (with no powers) to the president.[115]

Perhaps the most blatant example of Zia's exploitation of Islam was the unprecedented nationwide referendum of December 19, 1984. In this referendum, voters were asked:

Do you support Pakistani President General Muhammad Zia-ul-Haq's programme . . . to bring Pakistani laws in line with the Islamic principles, in accordance with the injunctions of the Holy Quran and the Holy Prophet—peace be upon him—and to safeguard Pakistan's ideology; and do you support the continuance, the further strengthening of this programme and the transfer of power to the elected representatives of the people in an organized and peaceful manner?[116]

The proposal in the referendum was phrased in such a way that a negative answer would cast the respondent as an "enemy of Islam and Pakistan." On the other hand, if the majority replied in the affirmative, then Zia would, in his opinion, have the mandate of the people to continue as president for an additional five years. While opposition groups were banned from participating in the referendum and threatened with punishment for even advocating a boycott of the referendum, Zia toured the entire country campaigning for support of the proposal. Zia dismissed the "need for the parliamentary opposition to challenge the government's programme, because the programme is based on the Koran " "and the Holy Koran is my manifesto," "so what is there to oppose?"[117] There were rumors of demonstrations throughout the country in opposition to the referendum, yet on the day following it, despite considerable skepticism from critics, the government claimed a 97.7 percent approval vote, with 62 percent of the 35 million registered voters casting ballots. Sources close to the Election Commission maintain that only 20 percent of the eligible electorate actually cast their "votes." Zia interpreted the referendum results as a mandate to remain as president for an additional five years and continue the Islamic sociocultural, political, legal, and economic transformation that he had initiated.[118]

After twice postponing scheduled elections (October 1977 and November 1979) because President Zia regarded them as too divisive and "un-Islamic," "party-less," and "non-partisan," elections were held on February 25, 1985, to choose members for the newly established National Assembly and Provincial Assemblies. But these elections were only partially free because political candidates could use only a limited amount of campaign funds; public meetings and processions were tightly controlled to prevent any anti-government agitation or movement from developing; television, radio, and the written press were heavily censored to prevent major criticism of the regime; and whatever the verdict, President Zia had reserved the right to appoint the prime minister, dissolve the National Assembly, and remain commander-in-chief of the armed forces.[119]

The Movement for the Restoration of Democracy (MRD) comprised of eleven political parties told their rank and file to boycott the fraudulent elections. But many of their followers did not obey. Having the rare opportunity to cast their vote, Pakistani voters turned out in large numbers. According to reliable reports, over 50 percent of Pakistan's eligible voters cast their vote. Much to Zia's chagrin, a number of his cabinet members and allies were defeated by unknown politicians, while those identified with the PPP did well.[120]

On March 18, 1985, Zia took steps to protect himself when he promulgated new amendments to the constitution, one of which specified that "the president's orders made since the 5th of July, 1977, shall not be altered, repealed, or amended without the previous sanction of the president."[121] A couple of days later, President Zia appointed Muhammad Khan Junejo, a prominent Sindhi politician, as prime minister. Then, on December 30, 1985, the wily Martial Law Administrator succumbed to intense domestic and foreign (mainly American) pressure to lift martial law and allow political activity. However, even here there was a catch, as political parties had to register with the election commission made up of Zia's loyal civil servants and prove that they were sufficiently committed to Islamic ideology. Needless to say, this "ideological litmus test" prevented the PPP and other opponents of the Zia regime from qualifying and contesting the elections.[122]

In 1987, when enforcing *Nizam-i-Islam*, Zia once again banned political parties claiming that it was a Western innovation, that was antagonistic to the Islamic notion of governance. This was obviously intended to undermine the influence of secular groups; it also provided Zia with an excuse to nominate a *Majlis-i-Shura*, which he emphasized was an advisory board and not an elected assembly. He won over some of the most prominent *ulama*, despite their lack of electoral support, and requested them to serve in the *Majlis-i-Shura*.[123]

On May 29, 1988, President Zia dismissed Prime Minister Junejo along with the latter's cabinet, and then dissolved the National Assembly on grounds that the Junejo cabinet had failed to maintain law and order and had done little "to make the *shariah* the basis of Pakistani law."[124] Less than half a month later, Zia unilaterally enacted the *Shariat* Law—a presidential ordinance decreeing the *shariah* as the supreme law of the land. This meant that any law passed by the National Assembly or the Provincial Assemblies would thereafter be required to conform to the *shariah*; any laws that were found to be "repugnant" to Islam would have to be discarded or revised to conform to Islamic guidelines.[125]

Zia's Foreign Policy Emphasizes Pakistan's Relations with the Muslim World

When General Zia came to power, he inherited Bhutto's successful foreign policy vis-à-vis the Muslim world. Like Bhutto, Zia believed that close ties with the Muslim World constituted "a firm pillar" of Pakistan's foreign policy.[126] While Pakistani military advisors, technicians, and even soldiers had been serving in a number of Arab countries since 1965, there numbers increased during Bhutto's tenure in office and further increased during Zia's tenure in office. The export of Pakistani civilian manpower and goods to the oil-rich Arab states also substantially expanded during the late 1970s and early 1980s. In fact, by 1985, more than half a million Pakistanis were living and working in the Arab world. According to a reliable estimate, the overall total funds from official and unofficial (including remittances) sources abroad came to $4 billion per year by 1983. Pakistan was able to buy the latest military hardware from the West with funds from the oil-rich Arab countries and even got oil from these countries at bargain prices and with soft loans (low interest loans that are payable over the long term). Pakistan also benefited from investments and purchases made by wealthy Arabs in major cities like Karachi.[127]

Pakistan's military strongman was fortunate to be the leader of a geostrategically located country at a time when the West and the conservative oil-rich Arab monarchies feared the spill-over of Iran's Islamic (*Shi`ah*) revolution, American diplomats being held hostage in the U.S. Embassy in Tehran, the Iran-Iraq war, and the Soviet invasion and occupation of Afghanistan. Fears of Iran's brand of revolutionary anti-Western Islamism or Soviet Communism spreading in the oil-rich Persian Gulf permeated the global environment. In December 1980, Crown Prince Fahd ibn Abdul Aziz (king of Saudi Arabia since 1982) visited Pakistan and declared that Saudi Arabia envisioned its security interests tied to Pakistan's, and that "any interference in the internal affairs of Pakistan would be considered interference or injury to the Kingdom of Saudi Arabia."[128] Fahd's robust support for Pakistan was music to Zia's ears as it implied an increased flow of Saudi aid.

President Zia, with the generous help of the United States and the oil-rich Persian Gulf kingdoms, orchestrated the Muslim world's support for the Afghan *mujahidin* (freedom fighters). Pakistani military advisors trained the Afghan *mujahidin* on weapons supplied by the United States and organized them into an effective fighting force that prevailed in their *jihad* against the army and air force of a Communist and atheist superpower. Gulbuddin Hekmatyar's *Hezb-i-Islami* (Islamic Party)—a revolutionary Islamic group committed to an Islamic state in Afghanistan—got more assistance from the Zia regime than any of the other seven Afghan *mujahidin* groups. In fact, Pakistan's Muslim Fundamentalist president was so committed to helping the people of Afghanistan that he allowed his country to become a haven for over 3 million Afghan refugees. According to one estimate, the

Pakistani government was spending approximately $1 million a day to feed, house, clothe, educate, and provide health care for these Afghan refugees.

Despite the opposition of some Arab states, Zia was one of the Muslim leaders who called for greater understanding of both Egypt and Iran in the OIC. While maintaining good relations with Western and pro-Western Arab states, Zia also maintained good relations with Iran's Islamic theocracy, which was hostile to the West and pro-Western Arab monarchies. Zia sent Pakistan's Ithna Ashari (Twelver) *Shi`ah* foreign minister, Agha Shahi, a number of times to visit high level Iranian government officials (including, Ayatollah Ruhollah Khomeini). In fact, Pakistan earned Iran's goodwill by withdrawing from the Central Treaty Organization (CENTO) in March 1979 (after Iran did so), selling Iran wheat and rice, and maintaining genuine neutrality in the Iran-Iraq war despite heavy pressure from the West (especially the United States) and the conservative Persian Gulf monarchies to take Iraq's side in the fratricidal war.

Furthermore, Zia continued former Prime Minister Bhutto's nuclear program. Indeed, Zia's commitment to building Pakistan's "Islamic Bomb" was so strong that he even rejected U.S. President Jimmy Carter's $400 million aid package when it was conditioned on abandoning Pakistan's nuclear ambitions. In fact, Zia belittled Carter's economic and military aid to Pakistan as "peanuts." Fortunately for Zia, President Carter's successor, Ronald Reagan, was committed to an aggressive anti-Soviet crusade from the moment he moved into the White House in 1981. Reagan, therefore, overlooked Pakistan's nuclear program and gave Zia's Islamic Republic a generous six-year aid package worth $3.6 billion (approximately $600 million a year). In fact, U.S. aid kept flowing to Pakistan till 1990.[129]

The Soviet invasion of Afghanistan made neighboring Pakistan a "front-line" state and an important member of the OIC.[130] President Zia took full advantage of the opportunity and became a major spokesman for the forty-five nation Islamic bloc. In fact, in September 1980, the plenary session of the eleventh annual meeting of the Islamic Foreign Ministers Conference unanimously elected Zia to address the thirty-fifth session of the United Nations General Assembly. As spokesman for the OIC, Zia made several trips to Iran and Iraq to end their eight-year-long war, but with little success. High-level Pakistani diplomats also played a major role in the U.N.-sponsored talks in Geneva that finalized the Soviet troop withdrawal from Afghanistan. Furthermore, Zia told all Pakistani diplomats in international bodies to complain about the persecution and killing of Muslims in several parts of the world, especially in Jammu and Kashmir, Bombay, and Bhiwandi, at the hands of the Hindus.[131]

The Zia Era in Retrospect

President Zia's eleven-and-a-half year rule came to an abrupt end on August 17, 1988, when he and twenty-eight others (including nine senior generals) died in a mysterious plane crash near the Pakistani city of Bahawalpur. He was the only leader in Pakistan's political history who believed that Pakistan's founding fathers (Sayyid Ahmad Khan, Iqbal, and Jinnah) wanted to create an "Islamic state" based on the *shariah*. He pushed an Islamization campaign from above in a more concerted and sustained manner than any previous Pakistani leader.

In short, there were several major reasons for General Zia-ul-Haq's vigorous and sustained Islamization campaign. First, there was Muhammad Zia-ul-Haq's own religious upbringing, profoundly Islamic socialization, and sincere devotion to and practice of Islam.[132] Second, Bhutto had already engaged in a significant amount of Islamic symbolism and rhetoric to create an Islamic revival in the country. Zia just rode the crest of the Islamic wave sweeping Pakistan at the time. Third, Zia was profoundly impressed with the awesome power and amazing success of the *Nizam-i-Mustafah* Movement which had politically paralyzed Bhutto's secular regime. Fourth, the failure of capitalism during the Ayub era (1958-69) and socialism during the Bhutto era (1972-77), resulted in the Pakistani people (especially the mass media and politicians) talking about the "Islamic Alternative" as a way of addressing the country's socioeconomic problems (such as poverty, inequality, corruption, nepotism, and socioeconomic injustice). Fifth, Zia was acutely aware of the fact that his autocratic military regime lacked legitimacy, and so Islam, which had always been his security blanket and anchor in life, became a useful weapon with which to neutralize his political adversaries, as well as the key to consolidate, expand, and remain in power longer than any other Pakistani political leader. Sixth, this apolitical and reluctant "soldier of Islam" used the "Islamic card" to trump not only his domestic political adversaries at the political game they thought they knew better than him, but obtain generous aid from oil-rich Muslim countries. Seventh, intense lobbying by Islamic parties and interest groups persuaded Zia to establish a *Nizam-i-Islam* in the country. Eighth, the success of the first Islamic Revolution in modern times in Iran and the rapid spread of Islamic revivals all over the world, may well have reinforced the Islamic revival in Pakistan and helped the Zia regime remain in power and continue promoting its Islamic message. And ninth, the Zia regime effectively used its well-established Islamic credentials at home and abroad (especially in the help they gave to the Afghan *mujahidin* fighting the Soviets in Afghanistan and the Afghan refugees in Pakistan) to get more aid from the oil-rich Arab Persian Gulf countries and the West (especially the United States) than most other countries.

MUHAMMAD ALI JINNAH, ZULFIKAR ALI BHUTTO, AND MOHAMMAD ZIA-UL-HAQ COMPARED

Jinnah and Z. A. Bhutto had a secular formal and informal education for the most part; spent time studying, working (mainly Jinnah), and traveling in the West before assuming power in Pakistan; were heavily influenced by Western ideas and practices; were considered relatively nominal, non-practicing, and secular Muslims;

and looked to a broad spectrum of philosophies and ages for models of political and socioeconomic development. Zia, on the other hand, seems to have been profoundly influenced by his Islamic socialization at home and in the neighborhood *madrassah* (Islamic school) where his father taught Islamic classes; spent relatively little time studying, working, or traveling in the West; had a predominantly Islamic worldview in which he looked primarily to Islam's classical period (that of Prophet Muhammad and the rule of first four caliphs) for inspiration and emulation; and was a devout and austere *Sunni* Muslim.

While it is true that Zia, like Jinnah and Z. A. Bhutto, did not want a theocracy—the fusion of mosque and state and the rule by Islamic theologians—his desire to make Pakistan a genuine Islamic state, where the *shariah* was the supreme law of the land, seems to have been sincere and not merely a machiavellian political ploy to legitimize his rule and consolidate his power. Jinnah and Bhutto, on the other hand, were far more broad-minded, cosmopolitan, liberal, and pragmatic, and wanted Pakistan to be a modern, moderate, pluralistic, and tolerant "Muslim homeland." In fact, these two astute politicians had absolutely no qualms about adopting and adapting modern, Western secular ideas, programs, policies, and practices such as nationalism, socialism, democracy, and secularism. However, political expediency demanded that they pay lip service to Islam and sugarcoat their secular ideology with Islamic rhetoric and symbolism by adding prefixes, such as "Islamic" nationalism, "Islamic" socialism, and "Islamic" democracy.

Unfortunately, for Pakistan and Pakistanis, Jinnah died only fourteen months after establishing the new Muslim homeland. Had the charismatic and cosmopolitan founding father of Pakistan lived for a decade or more after achieving his independent Muslim homeland, the newborn Islamic Republic would not have experienced the leadership crisis that it did. It also may not have been as seriously polarized between the secular elite and religious forces as it is today. Likewise, Z. A. Bhutto's cynical exploitation of Islam sowed the seeds of an Islamic revival that General Zia greatly broadened and deepened with his fundamentalist brand of *Sunni* Islam over the next eleven years. As a result, Pakistan today is a profoundly schizophrenic society where there is an on going struggle between secular and religious forces as well as where sectarianism (the *Sunni-Shi`ah* conflict) simmers beneath the surface and erupts in bloody tit-for-tat killings from time to time. In fact, if Jinnah were alive today, he would be deeply disillusioned with the current political, economic, and sociocultural environment in the country that he founded.

CONCLUSION

The use of Islam by most Pakistani leaders since the country's independence has been intended to appease and undermine their political adversaries, win over a predominantly illiterate, religious, and gullible population, and get money from the oil-rich Muslim countries (especially from the early 1970s). Yet, it is indeed truly ironic and curious that although Islam has played such a prominent role in Pakistani politics for much of its existence, Islamic political parties—such as the *JI*, the *Jama`at-e-Ulama-e-Islam* (Association of Muslim Theologians), and *Jama`at-e-Ulama-e-Pakistan* (Association of the Muslim Theologians of Pakistan)—have never been elected to govern the Islamic Republic of Pakistan and its religious Muslim population. This amazing lack of electoral success on the part of Islamic parties is probably due to several major reasons.

First, Islamic political parties in Pakistan have been too dogmatic and doctrinaire in their Islamic worldview. Their insistence on ideological purity; literalist or narrow interpretation of their religious theory and practice, and zealous propagation of their conservative or puritanical brand of faith tend to not only frighten non-Muslims, but also alienate the secular-minded Muslims and the non-Hanafi Muslims who comprise the economic, bureaucratic, and political elite of the country. In fact, Zulfikar Ali Bhutto vividly painted the nightmare scenario of a fratricidal sectarian war, or even a civil war, should any of the religious political parties come to power and impose a narrow interpretation of Islam on the entire country.

Second, the Islamic political parties have still not been able to evolve a working strategy of economic, social, and political development in a modern and increasingly interdependent world. In the late 1960s, for instance, when Pakistan had a military dictatorship and serious economic problems of inflation, unemployment, underemployment, and the increasing gap between the tiny wealthy minority and the poor majority, the Islamic parties continued to rely on the age-old bogey of "Islam in Danger" instead of eloquently and persuasively articulating the most basic and pressing needs of the masses, namely, liberal parliamentary democracy and the promise of food, clothing, and shelter. On the other hand, the *JI's* revolutionary rhetoric of drastically and fundamentally altering the lord-serf relationship in the rural areas (where 60 to 70 percent of the Pakistani population resides) tends to provoke stiff opposition from the status quo *zamindars, sardars* (tribal chieftains), and *pirs*. Moreover, the *JI's* rhetoric of segregating women from men in educational institutions and places of work alienates many women.

Third, most Pakistanis have thus far regarded the *ulama* and the leaders of the Islam parties to be knowledgeable about Islam but lacking the knowledge, experience, and necessary qualifications to run a modern-day nation-state in a rapidly changing and globally interdependent world. Moreover, Pakistani voters are terribly disillusioned by the poor performance of the Islamic regimes in Iran, Sudan, and Afghanistan, and are thus even more weary of voting for Islamic parties.

Fourth, intense doctrinal disputes and serious personality clashes lead to exaggerated images of hopeless fragmentation and constant feuding among the Islamic parties. It seems that a very strong self-righteous, judgmental, and emotional tone pervades the politics of the Islamic parties and interest groups. They see everything in terms of black and white, right and wrong, and good and evil. It should, therefore, come as no surprise that coalitions and alliances of Islamic parties and interest groups do not last long enough to bring them to power.

Fifth, pragmatic, and secular-minded politicians such as Jinnah and Z. A. Bhutto used religious symbolism and rhetoric in a much more seductive and effective way than the Islamists. For instance, during the 1940s, the secular Jinnah inspired, mobilized, and galvanized many more Indian Muslims behind him and his ideology of Islamic nationalism than did Maududi with his ideology of Islamism. Maududi and his brand of Islamism fared no better in the late 1960s and in the 1970 national election in Pakistan when he and his *JI* came up against the secular Bhutto and the PPP with their ideology of Islamic socialism and *roti, kapra aur makan.*

Sixth, Islamic parties in Pakistan have been highly selective in their recruitment of party members. Such highly exclusive cadre parties are often successful as interest groups and in influencing those in positions of governmental authority, but have a difficult time capturing power and running a government. Mass parties (like the PPP and the Pakistan Muslim League) that are open to anyone and everyone are in a far better position to capture power and have done so whenever elections have been held.

Seventh, some religious groups were accused of being against the establishment of Pakistan and the leadership of the Pakistan Movement. That has always been a great embarrassment and liability for them because their opposition opportunistically exploits this controversial canard as an effective election issue. Maududi of the *JI,* for instance, expressed his strong opposition to the Pakistan Movement's efforts to create an independent Muslim homeland based on Islamic nationalism and scathingly attacked its leaders.

On a final note, it ought to be pointed out that while Islamic parties, movements, and interest groups may very well continue having a difficult time winning the mandate of the electorate and coming to power through the ballot box in free and fair national elections, their ranks continue swelling with many new Islamists every day. It is, therefore, quite probable that as the economic, social, and political environment in Pakistan continues to deteriorate, some future Pakistani generals may well follow in General Zia-ul-Haq's footsteps and try to impose an Islamic revolution from above, *à la Iran*, with the active support of some Islamic parties and interest groups.

NOTES

1. Quoted in Sarojini Naidu (ed.), *Mohamed Ali Jinnah: An Ambassador of Unity* (Madras: Ganesh, 1918), p. 1.

2. In 1906, a large number of Indian Muslims who had been active in Sir Sayyid Ahmad Khan's All-Indian Muhammadan Anglo-Oriental Educational Conference (founded in 1885), went on to establish the All-India Muslim League in order to represent the Indian

Muslims in British India. Sir Sayyid had established the Anglo-Oriental Educational Conference for the active exploration of Islamic theology, history, culture, and civilization, and to assist needy *madrassah*s and *maktab*s (Islamic elementary schools). For more about Sir Sayyid Ahmad Khan see note 16.

3. Nazir Ahmad Sheikh, *Quaid-i-Azam: Father of the Nation* (Lahore: Qaumi Kutub Khana, April 1968), p. 32.

4. Quoted in P. Moon, *Divide and Quit* (Berkeley, CA: University of California Press, 1962), p. 270.

5. Sharif al-Mujahid, *Quaid-i-Azam Jinnah: Studies in Interpretation* (Karachi: *Quaid-i-Azam* Academy, 1981), p. 18.

6. Speech delivered by Jinnah in February 1935, which is reproduced in its entirety in Jamal-ud-Din Ahmad (ed.), *Speeches and Writings of Mr. Jinnah* (Lahore: Shaikh Muhammad Ashraf Publications, 1960), pp. 1, 5.

7. Quoted in Khalid Bin Sayeed, *Pakistan: The Formative Phase* (Karachi: Pakistan Publishing House, 1960), p. 84.

8. Muhammad Iqbal (1873-1938) was a famous Indian Muslim poet, philosopher, leader of the All-Indian Muslim League from 1930, and close friend of Muhammad Ali Jinnah. Like Sir Sayyid Ahmad Khan, Iqbal feared that the Indian Muslims were in danger of losing their distinct faith, culture, and identity in a predominantly Hindu country. In 1930, Iqbal conceived of a Muslim state based on a common history, race, religion, and language in the northwestern region of India (comprising Punjab, Northwest Frontier Province, Sindh and Baluchistan) where Muslims comprised the overwhelming majority of the population. He spent the last eight years of his life encouraging the Muslim League leadership to pursue the establishment of such a Muslim homeland, inspiring millions of Indian Muslims through his powerful poetry.

9. C.M. Naim, "Afterword," in *Iqbal, Jinnah and Pakistan: The Vision and the Reality* (Utica, N.Y.: Syracuse University Press, 1979), pp. 184-89.

10. A conservative Indian Muslim *alim* (Islamic scholar) by the name of Qayyam-ud-Din Muhammad Abdul Bari was instrumental in initiating the *Khilafat* Movement in the Indian subcontinent in the immediate aftermath of World War I or around December 1918. The *Khilafat* Movement with conservative Indian Muslim clerics—especially the *Jamia`at-e-Ulama-e-Hind* (Association of the Islamic scholars of India)—in the vanguard, protested British attempts to carve up the Ottoman Empire and agitated in support of the Ottoman Caliphate.

When the *Khilafat* Movement was at its peak in the summer of 1920, a segment of the conservative *ulama* (Islamic Scholars) began the *Hijrat* Movement, in which about 50,000 devout Indian Muslims were persuaded by the *ulama* to abandon their homes and immigrate to the neighboring Muslim homeland of Afghanistan because India under the British *raj* (rule) was no longer a *dar-al-Islam* (abode of Islam or abode of peace), but a *dar al-harb* (abode of conflict). Afghanistan was under the Muslim rule of Amir Amanullah and considered safe for the Muslims of the Indian subcontinent. Initially, the ruler, government, and people of Afghanistan warmly welcomed the refugees. However, as the penniless Indian Muslim refugees became a socioeconomic burden to Afghanistan, Amanullah's armed forces sealed the Afghan border. By autumn 1920 many of the Indian Muslim pilgrims had returned to India disillusioned, alienated and angry. See M. A. Naeem Qureishi, "The Ulama of British India and the Hijrat of 1920," *Modern Asian Studies*, vol. 13, no. 1 (1979), p. 41; Leonard Binder, *Religion and Politics in Pakistan* (Berkeley: University of California Press,

1963), pp. 54-57; Martin Kramer, "Political Islam," *The Washington Papers*, vol. 8, no. 73, (Beverly Hills: Sage Publications, 1980), p. 33; Stanley Wolpert, *Roots of Confrontation in South Asia* (Oxford: Oxford University Press, 1982), pp. 94-95.

11. *Mahatma* is a Sanskrit term meaning "great soul," and is used in Hinduism for one who has attained great knowledge and wisdom. *Mahatma* was the title given to Mohandas Karamchand Gandhi because of his honorable character, praiseworthy mission, immense wisdom, and noble deeds.

12. Naim, "Afterword," pp. 184-85.

13. Stanley Wolpert, *Jinnah of Pakistan* (London: Oxford University Press, 1984), pp. 147-48 and 152.

14. For instance, encouraging the use of Hindi and discouraging the use of Urdu; compelling Muslim children in municipal and government schools to sing the Congress Party's national anthem, a hymn entitled *"Bande Mataram"* (I Hail Thee Mother India) with strong anti-Muslim undertones, hoisting the Congress flag on public buildings; and condoning the discrimination occurring against them in a broad spectrum of government and non-government jobs. Hafeez Malik, *Moslem Nationalism in India and Pakistan* (Washington, D.C.: Public Affairs Press, 1963), pp. 334-35.

15. Anwar H. Syed, "Was Pakistan to Be an Islamic State? Iqbal, Jinnah, and the Issues of Nationhood and Nationalism in Pakistan," *The Indian Review*, vol. 1, no. 1 (Autumn 1978), pp. 38-39.

16. Sir Sayyid Ahmad Khan (1817-98) was the Indian Muslim educationist, Islamic jurist, and author who encouraged the Muslims of India to learn English and get a Western education in order to enhance their economic position, social status, and political influence in British India. In 1864, he established a library and scientific society to translate Western works into Urdu and publish a newsletter in both English and Urdu to enable the British to understand and appreciate the Muslims more fully. In 1875, Ahmad Khan founded the All-India Muhammadan Anglo-Oriental College at Aligarh (later called Aligarh College) that graduated the vanguard of the Pakistan Movement and the future governing elite of modern-day Pakistan; In the immediate aftermath of Sepoy Mutiny of 1957 (in which many junior Muslim and Hindu soldiers rose up to overthrow British rule and were brutally crushed), Ahmad Khan was instrumental in reducing British-Muslim tensions. While a staunch supporter of British *raj*, he strongly discouraged Muslim cooperation with the Hindu-controlled All-India Congress Party. In fact, Sayyid Ahmad Khan advocated and supported separate electorates for Muslims in India and alluded to the "two-nation" separatist concept that posited that Hindus and Muslims were not only two different religious communities, but also two different "nations" living within India—an idea further developed and effectively utilized by Muhammad Ali Jinnah to create an independent "Islamic state" or "Muslim homeland" of Pakistan.

17. Quoted in Aziz Beg, *The Quiet Revolution: A Factual Story of Political Betrayal in Pakistan* (Karachi: Pakistan Patriotic Publications, 1959), p. 34; also see Syed Sharifuddin Pirzada (ed.), *Foundations of Pakistan: All India Muslim League Documents, Vol. II (1924-1947)* (Karachi: National Publishing House, 1969), pp. 335-37; Jamil-ud-Din Ahmad (ed.), *Speeches and Writings of Mr. Jinnah,* vol. I (Lahore: Ashraf Publications, 1960), pp. 159-63; and Sharif al-Mujahid, *Quaid-i-Azam,* pp. 491-93.

18. The *shariah* is the comprehensive, eternal, and immutable body of sacred Islamic law that governs the individual and community life of Muslims. Most Islamists consider it their Islamic duty to struggle actively and ceaselessly to implement the *shariah* because without

it they believe you cannot have a genuine "Islamic state."

19. Cited in Javid Iqbal, *The Legacy of Quaid-i-Azam* (Karachi: Ferozsons, 1967), p. 40.

20. *Eid* means "festival" in Arabic. There are two *Eids* in Islam that are celebrated annually: *Eid al-Fitr* and *Eid al-Adha. Eid al-Fitr* means "the festival breaking the fast" because it is celebrated with much fanfare one day after the ninth Islamic lunar calendar month of *Ramadan. Eid al-Fitr* is one of the happiest days in the year for Muslims because it marks the end of the auspicious month of *Ramadan* when Muslims fast from dawn to dusk each day. The month of *Ramadan* is very holy for Muslims because they believe that is when God revealed the *Qur'an* to Prophet Muhammad. *Eid al-Adha* means "festival of the sacrifice." It comes at the end of the *haj* (pilgrimage to Mecca in present-day Saudi Arabia), which goes on from the seventh to the tenth of *Dhul Hijj*—the last month in the Islamic lunar calendar. At the end of the four-day *haj*, Muslims have been enjoined by their faith to slaughter animals (sheep, goats, cows, or camels). This Islamic ritual of slaughtering animals is in memory of Abraham's willingness to sacrifice his son, Ishmael, when Abraham was commanded by God in a dream to test his faith.

21. Cited in Ikram Azam, *Pakistan and the Nationalities Notion* (Lahore: Amir Publications, 1980), pp. 207-8.

22. Quaid-i-Azam, *Mahomed Ali Jinnah: Speeches as Governor General of Pakistan 1947-1948* (Karachi: Pakistan Publications, n.d.), pp. 8-9.

23. Ibid., p. 9.

24. Ibid.; also in *Constituent Assembly of Pakistan Debates*, vol. I, no. 2 (August 1947), pp. 18-20.

25. Azam, *Pakistan and the Nationalities Notion*, p. 209.

26. Sayyid Abul A'la Maududi (1903-79) was a radical Islamic theoretician, ideologue, pamphleteer, agitator, organizer, and political activist. He struggled for most of his life to protect, defend, promote, and propagate his fundamentalist version of Islam. In 1941, Maududi established a religio-political party called *Jama`at-e-Islami* (Islamic Association) in India to influence those in positions of authority not to overlook the needs and aspirations of the Muslim community. He passionately tried to instill South Asian Muslims with Islamic fervor and spark an Islamic renaissance first in India and then in Pakistan.

Maududi considered the Pakistan Movement's espousal of Islamic nationalism to be similar to secular nationalism, which he felt would divide the *ummah* (Muslim community), breed parochialism, and create love for one's particular territory. Maududi said: "When I look at the Muslim League's resolution [demanding Pakistan] my soul laments." He also regarded the leaders of the Pakistan Movement to be Westernized secular nationalists and non-practicing Muslims. To quote Maududi: "Sad it is, that from the *Quaid-i-Azam* of the League to its lowliest followers there is not one who has an Islamic mentality and . . . looks at matters with an Islamic viewpoint." In fact, Maududi considered the term "Islamic nationalist" or "Muslim nationalist" to be an oxymoron: "'Muslim Nationalist' and 'Muslim Communist' are as contradictory terms as 'Communist Fascist,' 'Socialist Capitalist,' and 'Chaste Prostitute'!" Therefore, Jinnah's Pakistan, in Maududi's opinion, would be "pagan" and "its leaders pharaohs, nimrods, and infidel tyrants." No wonder, writing as early as 1942 (only two years after the Pakistan Resolution and with Jinnah leading the Pakistan Movement), Maududi stated that "why should we foolishly spend our time in waiting for, or in struggle for the creation of, this so-called Muslim government, which we know will be not only disadvantageous for our objective but a substantial hindrance to it?" However, once Pakistan was established, Maududi settled in the new Muslim nation and began a tireless campaign with the help of his *JI* to transform the country into an Islamic state. See my article titled "Maulana Sayyid Abul A'la Maududi: An Appraisal of His Thought and Political Influence," *South Asia: Journal of South Asian Studies*, vol. IX, no. 1 (June 1986), pp. 61-81.

27. A Sindhi *zamindar* is a wealthy and influential landlord who owns huge tracts of land in the southeastern desert region of the Sindhi province of Pakistan. Zulfikar Ali Bhutto's family was part of the landed aristocracy of Pakistan.

28. Zulfikar Ali Bhutto, *Awakening the People: A Collection of Articles, Statements, and Speeches, 1966-1969,* edited by Hamil Jalal and Khalid Hasan (Rawalpindi: Pakistan Publications, 1969), p. 45.

29. Ibid., pp. 94-95.

30. Bhutto's address to the Sindh Convention in Hyderabad on September 21, 1968. This address is quoted in ibid., p. 32.

31. Ibid., p. 240.

32. Zulfikar Ali Bhutto, *Marching Towards Democracy: A Collection of Articles, Statements and Speeches, 1970-1971*, edited by Hamil Jalal and Khalid Hasan (Rawalpindi, Pakistan: Pakistan Publications), pp. 10-11.

33. Pakistan People's Party, *The Election Manifesto* (Lahore, 1970), p. 1.

34. Bhutto's speech to a public gathering in Abbottabad on April 19, 1970, quoted in Bhutto, *Marching Towards Democracy*, p. 63.

35. Ibid., pp. 153-54.

36. A *khalifah* or caliph is the religio-political successor of Prophet Muhammad and the leader of the worldwide *ummah* (Muslim community).

37. Meenakshi Gopinath, *Pakistan in Transition* (New Delhi: Manohar Book Service, 1975), pp. 53, 57, 66, 75-76. New Delhi is the capital of India, while Srinagar is the capital of the Indian state of Jammu and Kashmir. Pakistanis claim that, based on the British Partition Plan of the Indian subcontinent in mid-1947, India's predominantly Muslim region of Kashmir should have been given to Pakistan. India and Pakistan have fought two wars over Kashmir (1947 and 1965).

38. See note 20 for a discussion of *Eid* festivals in Islam.

39. Craig Baxter, "Pakistan Votes, 1970," *Asian Survey,* vol. XI (March 1971), pp. 197-218.

40. See Waheed-uz-Zaman, "Editor's Note," in *The Quest for Identity*, Proceedings of the First Congress on the History and Culture of Pakistan held at the University of Islamabad, (April 1973) (Islamabad: University of Islamabad Press, 1974), p. i; Sarfraz Hussain Khawaja, *The Quest for Identity*, p. 112; Lawrence Ziring, "Introduction," in Lawrence Ziring, Ralph Braibanti, and W. Howard Wriggins (eds.), *Pakistan: The Long View* (Durham, N.C.: Duke University Press, 1977), p. 6.

41. The Ahmadis are an off-shoot of *Sunni* Islam. The sect was founded by Mirza Ghulam Ahmad (1837-1908). Ahmad was born in a village in the Indian Punjab called Qadian. Thus, Ahmadis are also called Qadianis. Ahmad wrote the *Barahin-i-Ahmadiya* (Arguments of the Ahmadiya) in the 1880s. Subsequently, he claimed to have received a series of revelations from God and proclaimed himself to be the Mahdi, the second Christian messiah, an incarnation of the Hindu god Krishna, and the *buruz* (reappearance) of Prophet Muhammad. In 1901, he founded the *Jamaat-i-Ahmadiya* (Ahmadiya Society), and had it listed as a separate Islamic sect in the official census of the Indian government. He died in 1908, leaving behind a body of theology that differs fundamentally from that of mainstream

Muslims.

Mirza Ghulam Ahmad was succeeded by *Khalifah* Maulvi Nur-ud-Din. The latter died in 1914. The founder's son, Mirza Bashir al-Din Mahmud Ahmad was then chosen as the second *khalifah* (caliph). This group, calling itself the "True Ahmadis" or "Qadianis," believes in Mirza Ghulam Ahmad's claim to prophethood (unlike Muslims, who regard Muhammad as Allah's last prophet). Another group, led by Khwaja Kamal-ud-Din and Maulvi Muhammad Ali, seceded, forming the Lahori Party. This group renamed itself *Ahmadiya Anjuman-i-Isha`at-i-Islam* (Ahmadi Society for the Propagation of Islam), insisting that Mirza Ghulam Ahmad had never claimed to be the promised messiah, but that he was a great *mujaddid* (renewer of the Islamic faith) instead. *The Encyclopedia of Islam* (rev. ed.) (Leiden, Netherlands: E. J. Brill, 1960); H.A.R. Gibb and J. H. Kramers, *Shorter Encyclopedia of Islam* (Leiden, Netherlands: E. J. Brill, 1974); *The New Encyclopedia Britannica* (15th ed.) (Chicago: Encyclopedia Britannica, Inc., 1984).

The anti-Ahmadi demonstrations in May-June 1974, resulting in widespread rioting, destruction of Ahmadi property, and the loss of innocent lives, were responsible for Bhutto's decision. But despite the same sort of happenings in 1953, Khwaja Nazimuddin, known to be one of the most devout Muslim leaders Pakistan has had (save Zia-ul-Haq), refused to concede to any of the demands made by the Islamic groups.

42. Zulfikar Ali Bhutto, *My Execution* (London: Musawat Weekly International, January 1980), p. 1.

43. A.H. Syed, *Pakistan: Islam, Politics and National Solidarity* (New York: Praeger Publishers, 1982), p. 126.

44. Within a very short space of time numerous privately owned Arabic tutorial centers sprang up throughout the country. Arabic also began to be taught in the Open University that came on public radio and television once a week.

45. *Shi`ah* is an Arabic word that literally means "partisan" or "follower." Members of this minority sect of Islam (15 to 20 percent of the Pakistani population) are partisans or followers of Ali ibn Abu Talib (literally, Ali, son of Abu Talib). *Shi`ahs* believe that Ali ibn Abu Talib, who was Prophet Muhammad's cousin, and son-in-law, was Allah's, and therefore Prophet Muhammad's, choice to become Islam's first *khalifah* (caliph). In fact, Ali actually ended up becoming the fourth caliph in Islamic history. All *Shi`ahs* also regard Ali as their first *imam* (religio-political leader).

Sunni is an Arabic word that means "those who follow the *sunnah*" (Prophet Muhammad's words and deeds). *Sunnis* (mostly belonging to the Hanafi sect of *Sunni* Islam) make up 80 to 85 percent of the Pakistani population.

46. Syed, *Pakistan,* p. 126. *Haj* is an Arabic word that means pilgrimage. Adult Muslims of sound mind and body have been enjoined by their faith to undertake the *haj*, the spiritual journey to Mecca, once in their lifetime, if they can afford it. *Haj* is the fifth pillar of Islam and it is formally undertaken between the seventh and tenth of *Dhul-Hijj*, the last month in the Islamic calendar. Muslims who successfully complete the *haj* during the annual *haj* season assume the honorific title of *haji* and are respected in the Muslim community.

47. See Z. A. Bhutto, *A Journey of Renaissance* (Ministry of Information, Government of Pakistan, November 1972), p. 7.

48. See Bhutto's press statement made in Karachi on October 20, 1973, and quoted in *Prime Minister Zulfikar Ali Bhutto: Speeches and Statements, August 14, 1973-December 31, 1973* (Karachi: Department of Films and Publications, Government of Pakistan, 1973), pp. 126-27.

49. *The Pakistan Times* (Rawalpindi, October 13, 1973), p. 1.

50. M. G. Weinbaum and Gautam Sen, "Pakistan Enters the Middle East," *Orbis*, vol. 22, no.3 (Fall 1970), p. 600.

51. The Organization of the Islamic Conference (OIC) was established in 1969 to promote Islamic solidarity and to foster political, economic, social, and cultural cooperation among member Muslim states. This organization is comprised of fifty four Muslim member states today. See Mir Zohair Husain, *Global Islamic Politics* (New York: HarperCollins Publishers, 1995), p. 20.

52. Rafiq Akhtar (ed.), *Pakistan Year Book, 1976* (Karachi: East-West Publishing Company, 1976), pp. 122-25. This was because Bhutto made a particular effort to ensure attendance of the distinguished guests by sending special Pakistani envoys to persuade leaders to attend the conference. In light of the disputes that arose over the agenda at the First Islamic Summit Conference, Bhutto noted that the agenda for the Lahore Summit was carefully prepared so that it won unanimous approval. The biggest reason for the success was the fact that the Muslin world was ecstatic over its perceived victory in the 1973 Arab-Israeli War and the Muslim-dominated OPEC's oil-price increases.

53. Akhtar, *Pakistan Year Book, 1976*, p. 299. It should be pointed out, however, that Pakistan conducted five underground atomic tests in late May 1998 after India conducted four underground atomic tests two weeks earlier.

54. Zulfikar Ali Bhutto, *If I Am Assassinated* (New Delhi: Vikas Publishing House, 1979), p. 137.

55. Steve Weissman and Herbert Krosney, *The Islamic Bomb: The Nuclear Threat to Israel and the Middle East* (New York: Times Books, 1981), pp. 53, 62-64.

56. On April 28, 1977, Bhutto made a dramatic and impassioned speech to Pakistan's National Assembly, in which he disclosed the fact that when U.S. Secretary of State Henry Kissinger visited Pakistan on August 8, 1976, he personally threatened him (Bhutto) to drop Pakistan's plans to build the atomic bomb, or else "Carter, if he comes to power, will make a horrible example of your country." *Dawn* (April 29, 1977), p. 1; Salamat Ali, "The Options Finally Run Out," *The Far Eastern Economic Review* (July 1, 1977), p. 8.

57. Shahid Javed Burki, "Employment Strategies for Economic Stability in Pakistan," paper presented at the *Quaid-i-Azam* Conference on Pakistan at Columbia University, March 9-11, 1978, p. 12.

58. Ibid.

59. Jamil Rashid, "The Political Economy of Manpower Export," in Hassan Gardezi & Jamil Rashid (ed.), *Pakistan, The Roots of Dictatorship: The Political Economy of a Praetorian State* (London: Zed Press, 1983), p. 222.

60. *Dawn Overseas Weekly* (January 6, 1979), p. 3.

61. Weinbaum and Sen, "Pakistan Enters the Middle East," p. 603.

62. "PPP Manifesto: Text of Third Chapter," *Dawn* (Karachi) (January 26, 1977), p. 4.

63. "A Great Manifesto," editorial, *Baluchistan Times* (January 26, 1977); also quoted in Richter, "The Political Dynamics of Islamic Resurgence in Pakistan," *Asian Survey*, vol. 19, no. 6 (June 1979), p. 551.

64. See *Dawn Overseas* from January 23, 1977 (when Bhutto started his election campaign by giving a speech at a mass meeting in Rawalpindi) to March 6, 1977 (one day before election day).

65. William Border, "Bhutto in Crackdown on Critics Orders Martial Law for Three Cities," *The New York Times* (April 22, 1977), p. 1.

66. Surendranath Kaushik, "Aftermath of the March 1977 General Elections in Pakistan," *South Asian Studies*, vol. 13, no. 1 (January-July 1978), p. 75.

67. *Dawn* (Karachi) (July 6, 1977), p. 1; *The New York Times* (July 6, 1977), p. 1; *Time* (July 18, 1977), p. 29.

68. Always suspicious and afraid of politically ambitious generals in the army overthrowing him, Bhutto engaged in periodic purges of the army's top brass and pursued selective promotions aimed at placing absolutely loyal and obedient generals in the senior-most positions of the armed forces. Zia, whom Bhutto regarded as an apolitical, professional, and loyal soldier, moved up to the top of the army ladder this way. Zia was also fortunate to be the presiding judge at a heavily covered court martial in 1972-73 of two dozen junior army officers, in a conspiracy to overthrow the Bhutto regime and eliminate some of the senior military officers responsible for the Bangladesh fiasco. Zia gave conspirators lengthy prison terms on grounds that they were guilty of treason in attempting to subvert and overthrow a popularly elected constitutional government. Zia was also one of the generals who loyally and faithfully carried out Prime Minister Bhutto's order to quell the Baluchi uprising for greater autonomy in 1973. Bhutto promoted Zia on March 1, 1976, to the rank of a full four-star generals, and elevated him to the senior-most position of army chief-of-staff, intentionally superseding eight more senior and competent three-star general, who were much more entitled to promotion. Asif Hussain, *Elite Politics in an Ideological State* (Folkestone, England: Dawson, 1979), pp. 142-43; Ian Mather, "The Soldier Who Hanged Bhutto," *The Observer* (April 8, 1979), p. 8.

69. *The Pakistan Times* (July 7, 1977), p. 1.

70. Ahmad Raza Kasuri had been elected on a PPP ticket to the Pakistan's National Assembly in 1970. It is alleged that when Kasuri began to criticize Bhutto, the latter ordered his assassination. But Bhutto's hit team murdered Ahmad Raza Kasuri's elderly father by mistake instead. Bhutto spent nineteen months in jail for the allegation of being a co-conspirator in the elderly Kasuri's murder. On March 18, 1978, Bhutto was sentenced to death by the Lahore High Court after being convicted of conspiracy in the murder charge. On March 25, 1978, Bhutto appealed the death sentence to the Supreme Court of Pakistan. After a year's deliberation, the Supreme Court upheld the Lahore High Court's conviction in a close four-to- three verdict and called for hanging as the punishment for Bhutto's complicity in the murder. President Zia, who had the power to pardon Bhutto, refused to do so despite enormous pressure from Bhutto loyalists in Pakistan and even bigger pressure from leaders, organizations, and individuals abroad. On April 4, 1979, Bhutto was secretly hanged and only his immediate family was allowed to bury him. Shahid Javed Burki, "Zia's Eleven Years: A Chronology of Important Events," in Shahid Javed Burki and Craig Baxter, *Pakistan Under the Military: Eleven Years of Zia-ul-Haq* (Boulder, CO: Westview Press, 1991); Craig Baxter, "Introduction," in Craig Baxter (ed.), *Zia's Pakistan: Politics and Stability in a Frontline State* (Boulder, CO: Westview Press, 1985), pp. 1-2, 156-58; Baxter, "Restructuring the Pakistan Political System," in Burki and Baxter, *Pakistan Under the Military*, pp. 31-32; William L. Richter, "Pakistan," in Mohammed Ayoob (ed.), *The Politics of Islamic Reassertion* (New York: St. Martin's Press, 1981), p. 144.

71. Mumtaz Ahmad, "Islamic Revival in Pakistan," in Cyriac K. Pullapilly (ed.), *Islam in the Contemporary World* (Notre Dame, IN: Cross Roads Books, 1981), p. 266. Also see Shahid Javed Burki, "Economic Management within an Islamic Context," in Anita M. Weiss (ed.), *Islamic Reassertion in Pakistan: The Application of Islamic Laws in a Modern State* (Utica, N.Y.: Syracuse University Press, 1986), pp. 49-57; Grace Clark, "Pakistan's Zakat

and Ushr as a Welfare System," in Weiss, *Islamic Reassertion in Pakistan*, p. 80; Hakim Mohammad Said, "Enforcement of Islamic Laws in Pakistan," *Hamdard Islamicus*, vol. II, no. 2 (Summer 1979), pp. 80-83.

Sunnah, which means custom or tradition, encompasses both the words and deeds of Prophet Muhammad and therefore complements the *Qur'an* as the major source of Islamic faith and practice. *Zakat* is the fourth pillar of Islam in which Muslims are enjoined by their faith to annually donate 2 ½ percent of their wealth in alms to the poor and/or to charitable institutions. *Ushr* is a 10 percent voluntary tax that is expected from farmers owning irrigated farmland. Landholders can pay levy in money or kind to the poor or to charitable institutions. *Auqaf* are charitable organizations operated by the government and/or private organizations that help mosques, Islamic educational institutions (including mosque schools for children), orphanages, and the poor and needy.

72. Nisar Osmani, "Polls only when Enforcement of Islamic System Assured," *Dawn* (September 24, 1979), p. 1.

73. Kemal A. Faruki, "Islamic Government and Society," in John Esposito (ed.), *Islam in Asia: Religion, Politics, and Society* (New York: Oxford University Press, 1987), p. 59. In fact, according to Faruki, when Zia's personal example failed to have much effect on male members of the elite (who continued wearing Western dress), a *quomi* (national) dress code—involving a *pyjama* or *shalwar* (baggy pants) worn with *kamiz* or *kurta* (baggy shirts) and with or without a *sherwani* or *achkan* (types of long coats)—was made obligatory for government employees and popularized in the mass media from 1981 onwards (Faruki, "Islamic Government and Society," p. 59).

74. Urdu is the national language of Pakistan. It is a hybrid of Arabic, Persian, and Sanskrit. It is written from right to left like Arabic and Persian. Spoken Urdu is similar to Hindi (the national language of India that is written from left to right in the Devnagri script). Urdu started in the army barracks during the Muslim-dominated Mughul Rule that lasted from 1525-1857. Ironically, most of Pakistan's governor generals, presidents, and prime ministers were fluent in English, but not in Urdu, and that is why most of their public speeches and press conferences were in English.

75. Faruki, *"Islamic Government and Society,"* p. 59.

76. It was initially Bhutto who made Friday instead of Sunday a holiday because Muslims are enjoined by Prophet Muhammad to go to the mosque for congregational prayers on Friday afternoons. President Zia just made the Friday holiday and Sunday workday official.

77. Richter, "Pakistan," p. 150.

78. Quoted in Ahmad, "Islamic Revival in Pakistan," p. 265. Prominent Islamists (*ulama* and Islamic party leaders) were unofficially advising General Zia from the time he took over the reins of government.

79. Quoted in Barbara D. Metcalf, "Islamic Argument in Contemporary Pakistan," in William R. Roff (ed.), *Islam and the Political Economy of Meaning: Comparative Studies of Muslim Discourse* (Berkeley: University of California Press, 1987).

80. Ibid., p. 136.

81. Richter, "Pakistan," p. 151. Also see Charles J. Adams, "The Ideology of Mawlana Mawdudi," in Donald Eugene Smith (ed.), *South Asian Politics and Religion* (Princeton: Princeton University Press), pp. 371-97; "Maulana Sayyid Abul A'la Maududi: Founder of the Fundamentalist Jammat-e-Islami," *Journal of South Asian Studies,* vol. IX, no. 1 (June 1986), pp. 61-82.

82. Baxter, "Restructuring the Pakistan Political System," p. 36; Ahmad, "Islamic Revival in Pakistan," p. 266; Richter, "Pakistan," p. 146. Also see Jan Mohammed, "Introducing Islamic Laws in Pakistan—I," *Dawn* (July 15, 1983), p. 15, and Said, "Enforcement of Islamic Laws in Pakistan," pp. 71-80.

83. Richter, "Pakistan," pp. 143-144.

84. Ahmad, "Islamic Revival in Pakistan," p. 268.

85. Ibid., pp. 155 and 150.

86. Anita M. Weiss (ed.), "The Historical Debate on Islam and the State in South Asia," in *Islamic Reassertion in Pakistan: The Application of Islamic Laws in a Modern State* (Utica, N.Y.: Syracuse University Press), p. 15; Lucy Carrol, "Nizam-i-Islam: Process and Conflicts in Pakistan's Programme of Islamisation, with Special Reference to the Position of Women," *Journal of Commonwealth and Comparative Politics,* no. 20 (1982): 74; also see President General Mohammad Zia-ul-Haq, "The President on Pakistan's Ideological Basis," address at the inauguration of the *Shariat* Faculty of the *Quaid-i-Azam* University, Islamabad, October 8, 1979, Ministry of Broadcasting, Government of Pakistan.

87. *Khulafah-e-Rashidin* or *Khulafah-e-Rashidun* means the "rightly-guided caliphs" in Arabic. In Islamic history, it often refers to the religio-political rule of the first four righteous caliphs—Abu Bakr, Umar, Usman, and Ali—who followed Prophet Muhammad in ruling the Islamic empire.

88. Richter, "Pakistan," p. 150.

89. Burki, "Economic Management," pp. 50-51. Also see Shahid Hamid, "Pakistan: Towards a Just Islamic Economic System," *Arabia* (January 1986), pp. 64-65.

90. Burki, in "Economic Management," pp. 51-52.

91. Ahmad, "Islamic Revival in Pakistan," p. 267. Also see Said, "Enforcement of Islamic Laws in Pakistan," pp. 80-83. But the amount distributed among the needy was so little ($4.00 per individual and $8.00 per family) that the entire program was a fiasco, especially if considered on the basis of Zia's inflated expectations at the time of its inauguration.

92. Reeves, "Journey to Pakistan," *The New Yorker,* vol. LX, no. 33 (October 1, 1984), pp. 97-98.

93. Faruki, "Islamic Government and Society," p. 59.

94. Richter, "Pakistan," pp. 150-51. Also see the discussion on *haj* in note 46.

95. The Isthna Ashari or literally "Twelver" school of *Shi`ah* jurisprudence, also known as *Fiqh-e-Jafariyyah*, was compiled and codified by their sixth *Imam*, Jafar-i-Sadiq (d. 765). The Twelver *Shi`ahs*, comprising the mainstream and majority of the *Shi`ah* sect, believe that Prophet Muhammad had appointed Ali, who was Abu Talib's son, to be Islam's first caliph. Twelver *Shi`ahs* are called as such because they follow "twelve" infallible *imams* (religio-political leaders) beginning with Ali and concluding with Muhammad Mahdi. Twelver *Shi`ahs* follow Prophet Muhammad's *sunnah* (sayings and deeds) as well the *hadith* (sayings) of their twelve *imams*.

96. *Dawn* (July 7, 1980), p. 1; *Pakistan Affairs*, vol. XXXIII, no. 14 (July 16, 1980).

97. *Crescent International* (March 16-31, 1983); William Claiborne, "Rival Moslem Groups Quarreling in Pakistan," *Washington Post* (March 25, 1983), p. 28A; Safa Haeri, "Proxy War in Karachi," *South* (April 1983), p. 28; Trevor Fishlock, "Zia Stirs Up Shia and Sunni Enmities," *The Times* (London) (April 6, 1983), p. 7; Tyler Marshall, "Islamization Drive in Pakistan Spurs Violence, Unrest," *The Philadelphia Inquirer* (May 1, 1983), p. 5D.

98. Faruki, "Islamic Government and Society," p. 61.

99. Ibid.; *Dawn* (August 16, 1984), p. 1.

100. Mahnaz Ispahani, *Pakistan: Dimensions of Insecurity* (N.J.: Brassey's for the International Institute for Strategic Studies, Winter 1989/1990), p. 20.

101. Ibid., p. 21.

102. Richter, "The Political Meaning of Islamization in Pakistan," in Weiss (ed.), *Islamic Reassertion in Pakistan*, p. 134.

103. "Majlis-i-Shoora Approves Law of Evidence Draft," *Dawn*, vol. VII, no. 11 (March 10-16, 1983), p. 3; Barbara Metcalf, "Islamic Arguments in Contemporary Pakistan," in William R. Roff, *Islam and the Political Economy of Meaning* (Berkeley: University of California Press, 1987), pp. 132-33.

104. Baxter, "Restructuring the Pakistan Political System," p. 37; Michael Hamlyn, "Pakistan's Prisoners of Purdah," *Times* (London) (September 8, 1983), p. 4; Qutubuddin, "Back to the Burkha?" *India Today* (June 15, 1982), p. 57; "An Orthodox Directive," *Link*, vol. 22, no. 42, pp. 30-31; Romey Fullerton, "Problems Beneath the Veil," *Far Eastern Economic Review*, vol. 120, no. 26 (June 30, 1983), p. 35.

105. Baxter, "Restructuring the Pakistan Political System," pp. 37-38; Ahmad, "Islamic Revival in Pakistan," p. 269.

106. Richter, "Pakistan," p. 147.

107. Zia-ul-Haq, quoted in the *Edmonton Journal* (September 29, 1979); also quoted in Saleem Qureshi, "Islam and Development: The Zia Regime in Pakistan," in Kenneth P. Jameson and Charles K. Wilber, *Religious Values and Development* (New York: Pergamon Press, 1980), p. 568

108. President Zia's speech quoted in *Pakistan Affairs* (November 1, 1979), p. 1.

109. Richter, "Pakistan," p. 148. The idea of separate electorates was to exclude religious minorities from voting for leaders in the emerging Islamic State. The fear was that non-Muslims would vote for secular rather than religious leaders and thereby undermine the Islamic State.

110. President Zia-ul-Haq, "The President on Pakistan's Ideological Basis," address at the inauguration of the *Shariat* Faculty of the *Quaid-i-Azam* University, Islamabad, October 8, 1979, Ministry of Information and Broadcasting, Government of Pakistan, p. 1.

111. Quoted in D. H. Butani, *The Future of Pakistan* (New Delhi: Promilla & Co., 1984), p. 36.

112. Richter, "Pakistan," p. 147.

113. *Dawn* (October 26, 1980), p. 12.

114. Ibid.

115. Craig Baxter et al. (eds.), *Government and Politics in South Asia* (2nd ed.) (Boulder, CO: Westview Press, 1991), p. 207.

116. Richter, "The Political Meaning of Islamization in Pakistan: Prognosis, Implications, and Questions," p. 132.

117. Ibid; *The Economist* (January 19, 1985), p. 33.

118. Richter, "The Political Meaning of Islamization," p. 132.

119. Anita Weiss, "Islam and the State in South Asia," in Weiss (ed.), *Islamic Reassertion in Pakistan*, pp. 16-17; William L. Richter, "Pakistan: Out of the Praetorian Labyrinth," *Current History*, vol. 85, no. 509 (March 1986), p. 114.

120. Ibid.; Burki, "Zia's Eleven Years," p. 172.

121. Ibid., pp. 172-173; Richter, "Pakistan: Out of the Preatorian Labyrinth," p. 114.

122. Weiss, "Islam and the State in South Asia," pp. 16-17.

123. Rafiq Zakaria , *Muhammad and the Quran* (New York: Penguin Books, 1991), pp. 235-236.

124. Baxter, "Restructuring the Pakistan Political System," p. 38.

125. While the Pakistani constitution does give the president the right to legislate a presidential ordinance when parliament is not in session, it is widely understood that such ordinances are only to be issued during emergencies or periods of utmost urgency. This was clearly not the case with the *Shariat* Law. Ordinances must also be confirmed by the parliament within four months and, further, are not to be renewed. The ordinance expired before the 1988 election, but a modified version was promulgated by the acting president, Ghulam Ishaq Khan, when the four months expired, violating the spirit if not the letter of the constitution. The Benazir Bhutto parliament permitted the ordinance to expire. However, Nawaz Sharif's government, which succeeded Benazir's government, had influential members of Islamic parties, and therefore half-heartedly continued to pursue Zia's goal of establishing a *shariah*-based state. Baxter, "Restructuring the Pakistan Political System," pp. 38-39.

126. Quoted in Shirin Tahir-Kheli, "In Search of an Identity: Islam and Pakistan's Foreign Policy," in Adeed Dawisha (ed.), *Islam in Foreign Policy* (New York: Cambridge University Press, 1983), pp. 75-76.

127. Craig Baxter, "Pakistan Becomes Prominent in the International Arena," in Burki, *Pakistan Under the Military,* pp. 142-45.

128. *New York Times* (December 11, 1980).

129. Baxter, "Pakistan Becomes Prominent in the International Arena," pp. 145-46.

130. See note 51.

131. *The* Economist (September 1, 1984), p. 28.

132. Zia-ul-Haq's father—who was a senior clerk in the Indian civil service (dealing with military audits)—was a devout Muslim, an Islamic studies instructor at the local mosque, and a strict disciplinarian. He personally taught his children the *Qur'an*, saw to it that they said their prayers every day, and indoctrinated them never to question God's words in the *Qur'an* Mary Anne Weaver, "Pakistan's General Zia: From Soldier to Politician," *Christian Science Monitor* (May 16, 1983), p. 7.

Chapter 2

Apartheid and Hermeneutics: Biblical Interpretations, Neo-Calvinism, and the Afrikaner Sense of Self (1926–86)

Thomas K. Carr

It has been said that the Afrikaner sense of self rests upon three pillars—"kerk, volk en taal"—or, more specifically, membership in the Dutch Reformed Church (DRC), the National Party, and the use of the Afrikans language.[1] But with the inevitable secularization of Afrikaner culture, the teaching of liberation theology in the universities and seminaries, and the growing influence in the Republic of South Africa of independent, charismatic churches, the first pillar has come to be seen by many to be in a state of weakness. The second pillar, the National Party, in the wake of its dismissal from dominance by the African National Congress, and burdened since then by the task of assimilating the very varied ideologies of its leaders, is also threatened by a growing impotence. In addition, with English steadily replacing Afrikans as the language of commerce and diplomacy, the strength of the third pillar seems also to be in jeopardy. In short, it appears increasingly likely that a post-apartheid South Africa will soon have little place for the sort of Afrikaner nationalism that fueled the politics of apartheid; and that that loss may alter irrevocably the Afrikaner sense of self.

This chapter explores the role DRC theologians played in the construction of Afrikaner nationalism. It is my contention that the Afrikaner sense of self, as it came to be expressed in the rhetoric of apartheid, was undergirded by both a Calvinist mythologizing of history and a politically charged biblical hermeneutics, and that it was, therefore, a theological construct ripe for the sort of critical dismantling it has suffered.

TRANSFORMING HISTORY INTO MYTH

At the turn of the twentieth century, Afrikaners found themselves forging a sense of ethnic identity over and against two primary fronts. On the one hand, there was what was perceived to be a very virulent form of "capitalist imperialism" established by the British as their primary political agenda following the Boer Wars. In 1895, led by the ambitious entrepreneur Cecil

Rhodes, the British entered the Transvaal, long an Afrikaner stronghold, in search of gold. Encouraged by the success of the British in the first Boer War (1881), Rhodes managed to overthrow Afrikaner rule in the district of Johannesburg the following year. This coup initiated the second Boer War (1896-99), during which, before the eventual surrender of the Boers at Vereniging, over twenty-six thousand women and children were brutally tortured and killed in concentration camps.[2] As war-weary Afrikaner men returned to empty homes and devastated farmlands, they vowed revenge, not only on the British, but also on the form of capitalism the British were seen to represent.[3] "We have not yet forgotten," wrote one observer in 1917, "how these [British] imperialist capitalist forces attacked the South African Republic with an armed band in order to assist the Capitalist revolution of Johannesburg in overthrowing the Boer government."[4] Memories of these defeats were to play no small role in shaping the subsequent political policy of the National Party when it came to power in 1948.

During the first two decades of the twentieth century, South African society was becoming increasingly urbanized, as was Europe. In search of a more stable income, many blacks moved out of their tribal communities and into the cities. Consequently, Afrikaners found themselves competing for the first time alongside native Africans for a limited number of jobs. This led to a series of strikes in what had formerly been white-dominated industries, culminating in the economically devastating miners' strikes of 1922. In response, General Johannes Hertzog, a decorated Boer Wars hero, along with other National Party candidates, ran for election under such slogans as "the poor-White problem," and more notoriously, "the Black Danger."[5] In 1924, and subsequent to a series of pacifying treaties with a British populace weakened by losses in World War I, a coalition government was formed, with Hertzog leading several other National Party representatives into power.

Once the National Party was granted political recognition and legitimacy— for the first time in the Republic's history—and with the threat of "British imperialism" diminished,[6] there was need to formulate a coherent political plan. Hertzog therefore took immediate steps to buttress economic policy with legislation that favored white labor over that of the blacks. The stated ideal was to order the national economy so as to put in place "a protective barrier against the competition of men in a lower social and economic position, and against their encroachment upon spheres of employment and standards of living dedicated to white labour."[7] In a December 1925 speech, General Hertzog declared,

[Afrikaners] must keep to a standard of living which shall meet the demands of white civilization. Civilization and standards of living always go hand in hand. Thus a white cannot exist on a native wage scale, because this means that he has to give up his own standard of living and take on the standard of living of the native. In short, the white man becomes a white nigger [sic].[8]

With this new form of socioeconomic policy taking shape under the National Party's leadership, the DRC responded in kind by holding symposia to discuss whether Christian theology could support such a mandate of segregation. Initially, it was decided that policies of segregation, once their moral and spiritual values had been assessed, ought not to be based on "physical descent, race or colour," but rather on the demonstration of "cultural superiority."[9] At a 1929 DRC-sponsored missionary conference, it was claimed that "the native is a human being of similar nature to us and that his soul is of equal worth to any other human being in the eyes of God." But it was quickly added that, "These equal rites and equal opportunities have to be exercised by [natives] in their own community."[10]

There were a few voices of dissent among the DRC leadership, among them the influential revivalist preacher Andrew Murray. Murray and his supporters argued for a strict separation of church and state, and that the former be a model for the latter of the sort of inter-racial unity promised by the Christian gospel.[11] For the most part, however, the revivalists were shut out of DRC policy-making. It increasingly became the DRC's view that what was already seen as a "divinely ordained" segregation at the ecclesial level, with blacks worshiping in predominantly black churches and whites in white churches, was to be seen as God's plan for the nation's political infrastructure as well.

Two events in the 1930s forced the above observation to come to expression as formal DRC policy. The first, as the inevitable consequence of two decades of social urbanization, was the rising incidence of inter-racial marriages, which in turn gave rise to a new ethnic identity in the Republic, that of the "Coloureds." At a 1935 meeting of the Council of Churches, under the leadership of the DRC, the infamous "Missionary Policy" was drafted in order to address this concern. It states:

The traditional Afrikaner fear of equality between Black and White originates in his aversion to the idea of racial intermarriage. The church frankly declares itself to be against this kind of mixture and against anything, which could promote it . . . . Where the church is thus against social equality in the sense of a disregard for the racial and social differences between Black and White in daily intercourse, it wants to promote and encourage social differentiation and spiritual and cultural segregation, to the benefit of both sections. The policy of guardianship as it is presently practiced must gradually develop into a policy of independence and self-determination for the Coloured and native in his own society, school, and church.[12]

A. J. Botha notes that the Missionary Policy was the first instance of an official DRC statement using "motifs of nationalism" to further its theological ideals.[13] J. Kinghorn observes that the theological jargon used in the DRC's Missionary Policy mimics, *mutatis mutandis*, the economically motivated rhetoric of the National Party's call for racial segregation.[14] As the above citation illustrates, the Missionary Policy is a clear example of a major ideological shift in the DRC's concept of itself as a religious institution. In moving away from the Reformed ideal of church unity, so central to nineteenth-century literature proclaiming its uniqueness as "God's church in South Africa," the DRC was now seen to be heralding the ideal of "unity-in-diversity."

The second event, and the one which most transformed the intent and tone of DRC policy, came in 1938 with the centennial celebration of the "Great Trek." In the years leading up the Great Trek, the Boers had been suffering under a policy of anglicization at the decree of Lord Charles Somerset, governor of the Cape Province from 1814 to 1826. Scottish ministers were brought in to preside over DRC churches, and English teachers were put in place of Boers in the schools. In 1825, it was decreed that all official documents were to be written in English, all legal proceedings carried out in English (without translation), and all government posts reserved for the English-speaking. In 1832, with the emancipation of slaves in both England and the Republic, the British refused the Boers full compensation for their loss of labor. After the Kaffir War of 1834, in which the Boers helped the British drive the Xhosa tribe back behind the frontier, Boer cattle, which had been stolen from the Xhosa, were then sold back to the Xhosa in order to defray the costs of the war.

In response to these "twenty years of British oppression," as the Great Trek legends state, the Boers collectively decided to abandon the Cape Colony in search of "shelter in the unknown wilderness of the North."[15] But as they journeyed toward the Transvaal, they were beset upon by native warriors, who, according to the Great Trek legends, proceeded to kill their women and children and take away their cattle. Both immobilized and lacking an adequate food supply, the survivors held an all-night prayer vigil, and subsequently sent off a regiment of men in pursuit. Though greatly outnumbered, they managed "to punish the enemy and redeem their past losses."[16]

The trekkers then turned eastward in search of more fertile land as well as an outlet to the sea. They sent a commission under Piet Retief to purchase from the Zulus the coastal region later to be known as Natalia. As soon as Retief paid for the land, however, he and his band of men were ambushed by the Zulus and murdered. The Zulu chief, Dingaan, then sent out an army to attack the remaining women and children who were spread out in camps in the foothills of the Drakensbergs along the Bushman's River. "The earth swarmed with thousands of enemies," wrote one eyewitness, "and no human help was possible. Even tiny children cried to the Lord and the voice of the people came up to God."[17] What ensued was a bloody slaughter:

The wagons were smashed and burned, the earth white with feathers from the bedding. Infants nursing at their mother's breast were pierced with tens of *assegaais* so that both bodies were fixed together. Children were seized by the legs and their heads smashed against wagon wheels. Women's breasts were severed, their bodies mutilated and ravished. . . . Among the dead and the still-smoldering ashes wild animals prowled around—presently to gorge themselves on human flesh.[18]

There was a small group of survivors, however, who managed to send word to their compatriots living in the Cape. Mobilized under the leadership of

Andries Pretorius, an army of insurgents, so the stories narrate, responded to the pleas for help. There followed the Battle of Blood River on December 16, 1838, during which the Boers swore a solemn oath to celebrate that day each year if God would grant them victory. Victory was achieved, at great cost to both sides, and the Afrikaners proceeded into Natal to settle the land.

Peace in the Boer's new homeland was not long-lived, however. Within one year, the British decided to annex and occupy Natal. In protest, the Boers abandoned the area, led, according to legend, by "barefoot women carrying children." They marched five hundred miles over the Drakensbergs into the southern region of the Transvaal where they founded the Republic of the Orange Free State. There, it was hoped, "they could be free from British domination and deal with the black Africans as they saw fit."[19]

For forty years, the Boers remained in the Orange Free State, building communities and cultivating the land. But in 1877, the British again invaded in the hope of annexing the now-habitable southern provinces of the Transvaal. For three years, the Boers lived under a strict British policy of what was, in effect, martial law. But on December 16, at the annual celebration of the Great Trek, and united under the charismatic leadership of Paul Kruger, the Boers made another vow to God, and took up arms in revolt. Though outnumbered once again, the Boers managed to push the British out of the area, thereby regaining their right to self-rule.

The story of the Great Trek was destined to become the central historical motif of the Afrikaner biography, and it remains so to this day.[20] Despite attempts by historians to show how far "the religious intensity" accompanying the legends "threatens to obscure the historical reality,"[21] the Great Trek myth has furnished Afrikanerdom with an elevated sense of destiny, historicizing the Afrikaner's self-identity as crucial to God's intentions for the Republic. As such, it served to construct an effective hermeneutic within which the theological rhetoric of post-1938 DRC policy could be more fully expressed. Following the centennial, for example, stories of the Trek became interlaced with biblical imagery. In Sunday sermons and in DRC-sponsored periodicals, church leaders likened the Trek to the biblical exodus of the Hebrews out of Egypt, with Lord Somerset playing the part of the Pharaoh, and Pretorius the part of Moses, leading his people into the "promised land."[22] Celebrations of the centennial ushered in an unprecedented swell of patriotic nationalism, which the DRC was quick to assume as a mandate for its own support of "unity-in-diversity." In a September 1938 issue of the church periodical *Die Kerkbode*, the comment was made that, "Our people have in their own hands the possibility of reunification. . . . One thing the Trek has taught us is that, if we look deep enough into the matter, we find that the Afrikaner people is one at heart and that the fire of patriotism and national pride burns in every Afrikaner heart."[23]

Ten years later, at the ouster of British rule and the election to full power of the National Party, Daniel Malan, an ordained DRC pastor as well as National Party prime minister, declared in a rousing speech: "This history of the Afrikaner reveals a determination and definiteness of purpose which makes one feel that Afrikanerdom is not the work of man but a creation of God. We have a divine right to be Afrikaners."[24] Standing on the banks of the Blood River, Malan went on to identify the cause of Afrikaner unity and power with a kind of divine destiny:

Here was made the great decision about the future of South Africa, about Christian civilization in our land, and about the continued existence and responsible power of the white race. . . . Behind you, you rest your eyes upon the year 1838, as upon a high, outstanding mountaintop, dominating everything in the blue distance. Before you, upon the yet untrodden path of South Africa, lies the year 2038, equally far off and hazy. . . . The trekkers heard the voice of South Africa. They received their task from God's hand. They gave their answer. . . . There is still a white race. There is a new People. There is a unique language. There is an imperishable drive to freedom. There is an irrefutable ethnic destiny.[25]

At this apex of the transformation of the Afrikaner sense of self—from oppressed believer to vindicated servant of God—it becomes clear how closely allied are the pastoral concerns of the DRC with the political ambitions of the National Party. It seems that the rise to power of Afrikaner rule served to create the sociopolitical ethos necessary to implement, twenty-four years in gestation, the nationalistic, racially biased theology of the DRC. In addition, with the 'cultural revolution'[26] initiated by the 1948 elections, the DRC assumed the mandate to legitimize theologically the political construction of apartheid. It is imperative, therefore, to examine more closely how the DRC came to play such an important role in the rise of apartheid.

BIBLICAL HERMENEUTICS AND THE RISE OF APARTHEID

J. A. Loubser, in his 1987 study, *The Rise of the Apartheid Bible*, notes a certain "hermeneutical vacuum" at work in the DRC-sponsored seminaries in the Republic. While Dutch pastors on the Continent were being exposed between the Boer Wars to the nascent biblical theology of Bultmann and Barth, which itself was informed by the hermeneutics of Husserl and Heidegger, DRC candidates for ordination in the Republic—mostly at Stellenbosch University in the Cape—were rigorously denied such access. The DRC had 'closed its ranks'[27] to the new school of biblical demythologization and its emphasis upon the historical *Sitz em Leben* of sacred texts. Lacking the "effective-historical consciousness"—as German philosopher Hans-Georg Gadamer termed it[28]— afforded by a more hermeneutically sensitive reading of the Bible, DRC pastors were free to use biblical periscope as proof texts in support of the ideals of "unity-in-diversity" and racial segregation.

The first conscious attempt in this direction came from S. J. du Toit, a professor of theology at Stellenbosch.[29] Du Toit argued for the uniqueness of the Afrikans language by referring to the story of the Tower of Babel in Genesis 11, claiming that the diversity of tongues, and therefore of peoples, was sanctioned by the will of God. He further referred to Acts 2:5-12, Revelation 5:9, 7:9 and

14:6 to forward his view that God intentionally maintains the diversity of nations and languages "before His throne in heaven." Likewise, the fifth commandment, "Honor thy father and mother," was used to suggest that he who honors his father also honors his fatherland; and he who honors his mother honors his mother tongue. According to du Toit, therefore, and presaging the Calvinism that was to play so seminal a role in later DRC theology, each nation has a special "calling" to which it has been "elected" by God. This ideal, du Toit concluded, legitimized the Afrikaner struggle for liberation; for to fulfill it's calling, a people must be free to maintain its unique, and separate, identity.[30]

In 1942, the first biblical proofs were supplied in support of political apartheid by W. J. van der Merwe, professor of theology at the University of Capetown. Van der Merwe stated that the policy of apartheid ought to be adopted "because of our past experiences as a people." He offered for support the following passages from scripture: Joshua 23:12-13, where Israel is prohibited from "mixing" with other nations; Acts 2, in which it is claimed that at Pentecost those present heard the gospel each in his or her own language; Acts 17:26, where the command is decreed that new Christian converts need not assume Jewish practices; and Revelation 7:9, which states, "And they shall bring the glory and honor of the nations into the heavenly Jerusalem."[31]

In van der Merwe's view, there was yet no indication of a theological system in support of apartheid, but his list of biblical proof texts was to supply a ready apparatus for those who sought just that. Shortly after van der Merwe's paper was published, the DRC-sponsored Commission for Native Affairs of the Council of Churches sponsored a call for legislation, which, among other things, would establish racially segregated schools and residential areas, as well as the outlawing of mixed marriages. During the same year, and influenced as well by Van der Merwe's biblical prooftexting, the Federal Missionary and Welfare Councils of the DRC submitted a memorandum to the National Party's cabinet, outlining the main tenets of its "native policy." The memorandum came out in support of the "principle of racial apartheid and of racial purity," citing favorably the research of a biologist, H. B. Fantham. Fantham had hypothesized that, for "the sake of self-preservation," miscegenation ought to be outlawed, for it tends to result in a people who display "physical disharmonies . . . violent outbursts of temper, vanity and sexual instability."[32]

The National Party heeded the call, writing into its constitution what were to become known as the "apartheid laws"—namely, laws establishing separate "townships" for blacks, coloureds and Indians, with separate schools and community facilities, and a law making mixed marriage a crime against the Republic. W. de Klerk, in his 1975 study, *The Puritans in Africa*, marks this period of the mid-1940s as "the theologising of Afrikaner politics." "The National Party," wrote de Klerk, "was itself becoming, if not a church, then a party imbued with religion . . . at its very roots."[33] In a 1980 paper read before the South African Council of Churches, D. P. Botha spoke as well of "the overwhelming role of the Church in preparing the community to accept and vote for a sociopolitical programme that would revolutionise South African life."[34]

The marriage of the DRC's politically charged biblical hermeneutics with the National Party's apartheid policies was not uniformly welcomed, however. Taking up a more liberal position were Afrikaners who understood the collaboration to be merely a pragmatic necessity, a "temporary emergency measure,"[35] which, it was hoped, would generate a populist base for legislation designed to jumpstart an economy weakened by British imperialism and the urban emigration of native Africans. It was the Afrikaners' contention that, once revitalized by apartheid, the economy could, at some future date, support a return to racial integration. But this more moderate position failed to win much sympathy among hardliners who heralded apartheid as a divine mandate, an absolute, universal ideology justified by scripture, and therefore in need of guidance by the churches.

Eventually, the supporters of ideological apartheid won the day; and evidence suggests their victory was largely due to certain underground efforts of the DRC.[36] In congresses and seminars across the country, DRC spokesmen forwarded the ideals of racial theology, often in a manner described as "autocratic" and "bewildering" by pragmatists in the government surprised at the popularity of their opposition. In the late 1940's, public debate on the future of apartheid became increasingly one-sided; and, as J.A. Loubser writes, "it has generally been recognised that the representatives of the churches played a major role in the discussion."[37] By 1950, the debate was resolved very much in favor of the National Party's right wing, whose position was later recorded in the historic document, "Human Relations and the South African Scene in the Light of Scripture," perhaps the single most significant statement of the DRC on the political ideology of apartheid.

NEO-CALVINISM AND APARTHEID

Much of the debate leading into the "Human Relations" document was structured vis-à-vis the theological work of the nineteenth-century Dutch Calvinist scholar Abraham Kuyper. As one writer put it, Kuyper served to "lay the Calvinist blueprint for a new South Africa" under apartheid.

Kuyper (1837-1920) was, by all accounts, a brilliant, and certainly prolific, professor of philosophy at the Free University of Amsterdam who, at the turn of the century, was elected prime minister of the Netherlands. For our purposes, his most important publication was a collection of lectures that first appeared in 1898, and was widely read by theologians and philosophers of universities in the Republic of South Africa (RSA). From this text, we may distill four principles that made their way into the pre-apartheid discourse of both National Party candidates and DRC theologians:

a. *The universality of Calvinism as a coherent worldview.*[39] Kuyper maintained that every atom of material reality lay subsumed under the lordship of Christ and Christ's church; and consequently, that Calvinism as an "independent system of principles" that is rightly to guide that church at every level of its jurisdiction is a "quite unique, all-encompassing world view" which ought to be the ruling system for all manner of human dealings. Not only is Calvinism to provide the appropriate ethos for church polity and personal piety, it is also to animate the political structures, educational policies, and economic agendas of every nation.

b. *The sovereignty of ethnic groups is to be exercised exclusively within their own unique spheres of influence.*[40] Kuyper identified different levels of existence—state, society, church, family—which are interrelated, as each is only allowed to remain in being by the divine will, while at the same time possessing unique, discreet forms of authority ("sovereignty in its own sphere"). Each ethnic group is thus seen, on the one hand, as part of an organic whole under God, but on the other hand, as an independent "organ" with its own, unique form of discourse, history, values and "sense of sin."

c. *God maintains and rules each sphere of sovereignty by means of "creation ordinances."*[41] These "creation ordinances," foreordained in the mind of God from eternity and uniquely referenced to each communal sphere, lend individual nations, societies, churches, and so on their characteristic sets of values, morals, definitions of the good, and worldviews. "[F]or a Calvinist faith," writes Kuyper, "no life exists in nature unless there are ordinances, which are nowadays called laws of nature . . . or rather, not laws of nature, but laws for nature."[42] Overarching every unique ordinance is the all-encompassing mandate of God, which unifies creation within a kind of *Weltseel*. But the "oversoul of the world" was not to be understood in a Kantian sense, argues Kuyper, not as a categorical *du sollst* which reigns from on high universally, but rather as something which wells up existentially from within communal spheres, and is therefore expressed uniquely in unique circumstances.[43]

d. *Prior to the second coming of Christ, human society, including the church, will exhibit diversity, not unity.*[44] In an 1869 lecture,[45] Kuyper had argued that unity is a "Christian-historical" ideal, to be pursued with vigor by people of faith. But Kuyper is careful to distinguish between "unity" and "uniformity"—the latter of which he calls "the curse of life." According to Kuyper, "uniformity" is of Satanic origin, and therefore lures well-meaning Christians from their appointed task: to build unity within their own ordained sphere of sovereignty as an "example" of what the future world will look like. In his 1898 lectures, Kuyper illustrates his point with a Darwinian metaphor:

The lower the level of development of a nation, the less diversity in thought-patterns occurs: in almost all nations one observes that they commence with unity of religion. But as individual life-forms gain strength with further development, it is just as natural that the unity breaks up and that pluriformity makes its influence felt as the indisputable demand of a richer development of life.[46]

According to Kuyperian Calvinism, the unity of the church and the individual's freedom of conscience and expression are mutually exclusive. The former is a spiritual reality, to be realized only in the age to come, while the latter is the pragmatic rule of law governing human existence until the future age arrives. "By recognising freedom of conscience," Kuyper claims, "Calvinism in principle relinquished the unity of the visible church."[47] "The existence of difference is the motive of consciousness, the motive of all that exists and grows and develops, in short the basic motive for all life and all thought."[48]

In 1944, a national congress was held at Bloemfontein, organized by the Federation of Afrikans Cultural Organisations (FACO). Among those invited to read papers was a charismatic poet and Kuyperian scholar named Totius (J. D. du Toit), son of S. J. du Toit. Totius began his paper by stating that his views on apartheid were not based on isolated texts taken from scripture. Rather, "I do not have a text, but I have the Bible, the whole Bible."[49] Totius went on to present a series of arguments, supported by Kuyperian themes, for racial diversity and segregation. He suggested, for example, that the Boer Trek was a kind of "creation ordinance," "a force inspired by God, which dominates the whole future of Africa and to some extent the history of the world." Totius contrasted the idea of "trekking" to the tower builders of Babel, "Their [the tower builders'] watchword was not 'trek,' but 'stay together.' And as it has to be conceded retrospectively that the Cape Boers would have resisted God's order if they had not trekked, so the ancient generation in the plains of Sinear obstructed the will of the Lord by resisting dispersion."[50]

In the Great Trek, Totius implies, the trekkers were under divine mandate to carve out for themselves a unique sphere of sovereignty, to resist the evil temptation to uniformity under British rule, and to assume instead their own unique, separate destiny. Totius expanded the argument by saying that the "liberalists" in parliament were trying to "force unity and equality" by transforming what Kuyper had termed a spiritual reality—namely, "union in Christ"—into a sociopolitical fact; for in the providence of God, "every nation receives a calling,"

and that calling will last till the end of the world. . . . People thus have to preserve themselves over against a Babylonian spirit of unification. And now, thus, after the dark ages God is going to bring about something wonderful in history. The Boer nation, a new type. . . . [W]e may not join together that which God has separated. In pluriformity the council of God is realised. The higher unity based in Christ is of a spiritual nature. Therefore no equality and no miscegenation.[51]

Following Totius's address, the congress resolved that the principle of apartheid was not only grounded in scripture, it was also, in light of Totius' re-presentation of Kuyperian Calvinism, the political expression of a foreordained divine mandate, applicable not only to their unique character as a people, but to all spheres of their communal life as well. Moreover, it was determined that what was true of the Afrikaner must also be true, by Kuyperian extension, of the other South African races. R. T. Lombard, in a 1981 study, remarked that at the FACO congress, "a plea was made for the application of 'apartheid' in the social, religious, educational and economic areas, with regard, not only to Afrikaners, but also to the Bantu, Coloureds and Asiatics."[52] From this congress came the rhetoric, commonly expressed in apartheid legislation that each racial group in South Africa was to be granted the opportunity to develop "according to its own nature, in its own area."[53]

In 1947, an influential article appeared, authored by New Testament Professor J. H. Kritzinger of Stellenbosch University. Kritzinger cites both "direct" and "indirect" scriptural evidence for the policy of apartheid:

[God himself] gives us a practical example of the meaning and value of racial apartheid—something that is also fully in line with the teaching of the rest of Scripture, namely, that God willed the existence of separate races. Thus an interpretation of history in the light of God's wise rule is completely scriptural because thus Moses and the prophets, Christ and Paul had read the history of God's people. And to fulfill this divine task as well as possible they soon learnt from experience that it could not be brought about by disregarding racial dividing lines but by the acknowledgement and preservation of racial separation as God had ordained and as he had also commanded Israel under similar circumstances.[54]

In identifying the plight of the Afrikaner with ancient Israel by means of a retrogressive hermeneutics of history (i.e. just as the era of Christ fulfills Hebrew prophecy, so apartheid fulfills the promise of the Boers) Kritzinger aligned himself with the Kuyperian argument that depicted the "diversity of races" as the "divine ordinance" of God. Following Kuyper, Kritzinger claimed that scripture teaches clearly the "brotherhood of all peoples" under the common authority of the divine rule, which comes to its "highest revelation in Jesus Christ." But Kritzinger was quick to point out that, as a "spiritual ideal," such an event could only be expected to materialize "in the hereafter."

Some mediating effort was made at the FOCA congress by DRC theologians hoping to draw explicit attention to the future promise of racial unity, arguing that it was both a future goal and, at least partially, could be a present reality. Professors G.B.A. Gerdener and A. H. Murray, for example, published articles critical of Kritzinger's rather one-sided presentation of the Kuyperian dichotomy of unity and diversity, calling for more theological debate around how both "ideals" could be valued equally in the political arena. But their voices were dim in comparison with the rush of support for more permanent means of segregation.

At the 1948 meeting of the South African Council of Churches, a report legitimizing biblical and theological proofs for apartheid was accepted. At the forefront of this effort was a Kuyperian scholar of international reputation, E. P. Groenewald. In his speech to the council, Groenewald argued for apartheid by frequent reference to "creation ordinances," the Calvinist principle of preordained diversity, which was to be maintained at the threat of divine punishment, and the religious value of unique nation-states as separate spheres of authority, each with their own natures and characters.[55] Following the council, Groenewald's report was expanded, published, and widely disseminated among DRC leaders and pastors. This more detailed version highlighted several principles intended to illustrate "that the division of the human species into races, peoples and tongues was a conscious deed of God."[56] Groenewald claimed that this idea can be supported not only by a series of biblical injunctions—he listed Genesis 10-11 and 15:8, Deuteronomy 32:8, Amos 9:7, and Acts 2:8ff—but also by several statements of Calvin from the Institutes. "Just as in a company of soldiers," Groenewald cited Calvin, "each company and division has its own place, so also has the people been placed on earth that every nation is enclosed within its own boundaries."[57]

CONCLUDING REMARKS

With the report of Professor Groenewald, the rising tide of support for apartheid, consisting both of DRC-validated interpretations of scripture and Calvinist theological principles, served to sweep the National Party into power. On May 26, 1948, the National Party won handily the General Election under the promise that a "cultural revolution" was underway, a revolution that would bring into legislation a juridical system of total racial segregation. The DRC's racial rhetoric of the previous decade was now to be written into law. For the Afrikaner church, the decades of the 1950s and 1960s were to see the realization of the ideals it had been hammering out in debates and national congresses during the preceding twenty-five years.[58]

By the early 1980s, when the RSA as a whole began to feel the economic and sociopolitical pressure of international censures for its apartheid laws, the DRC found itself in the uncomfortable position of having to rethink, if not recant, its most basic convictions regarding the cohabitation of races. But its willingness to do so was slow in coming. DRC leaders had so categorically believed racial segregation to be a divine mandate, rooted in scripture and therefore enforceable under penalty of divine judgment, that to renege on its segregationist agenda seemed to them to be tantamount to blasphemy. Despite such international censures as bans on trade and on competition in the 1980 and 84 Olympics, and the revocation of emigration and travel visas, this belief remained staunchly in place. Voices of dissent among the DRC ranks, from scholars like P. V. Pistorius, professor of Greek at the University of Pretoria, and Professor B. B. Keet, a biblical scholar at Stellenbosch, were quickly discounted as the "ravings of rationalism," and an affront to the sense of self innate to Afrikanerdom.[59] Rather, it became a matter of faith to support apartheid, even as, one by one, the laws of apartheid began to be dismantled, initially in 1985 with the repeal of the Mixed Marriages and Immorality Acts—the latter of which outlawed sexual intercourse between races—and then totally under the leadership of F. W. de Klerk, who came to power in 1988. Even as National Party representatives saw the expediency of change, the DRC, for quite some time longer, continued to argue for the *status quo*.

This leads one to ask: how could the DRC, a purportedly Christian institution bound by its creed to the principles of divine justice and the equality of all peoples before God, for so long have been so shortsighted in its support of a political ideology that was clearly hostile to such principles? As Anglican Bishop Desmond Tutu declared in his influential 1983 essay, "Christianity and

Apartheid," "Apartheid is intrinsically and irredeemably evil. [I]ts most vicious, indeed its most blasphemous aspect, is not the great suffering it causes its victims, but that it can make a child of God doubt that he is a child of God."[60]

How Afrikaner Christians could have so readily embraced apartheid, and Afrikaner theologians given it scriptural warrant, are questions that have vexed theologians in South Africa for the last two decades, and to which many, sometimes competing, responses have been made.[61] It is not the aim of this chapter to assess those responses, nor to add one more to the debate. But a brief observation relevant to the manner in which the DRC proceeded in its early deliberations of apartheid is, I suggest, worthy of consideration.

I am of the opinion, and it is shared by several,[62] that the aforementioned "hermeneutical vacuum," a phrase referring to the prohibition of German theology in South African seminaries, may well have been a decisive or contributing fact to the rise of apartheid. When hermeneutical consciousness is lacking in those seeking to use a historical text like the Bible as a means for understanding the present, the tendency, as Willem Vorster notes, is "to use the bible selectively as a kind of proof text."[63] This form of biblical interpretation was common in the early and medieval church, when scholars like Sts. Augustine and Aquinas taught that the bible had several layers of meaning—the historical, the typological, the allegorical—but that these stood inferior to the *sensus plenior*, that is; the "full, spiritual sense" of the text. This last and most important sense could only be understood through faith, and once reached, was to be applied to all times and places— as per Augustine in his teachings on "original sin" and the necessity of infant baptism, and Aquinas in his defense for the punishment of "heretics." When such biblical stories as the Tower of Babel and the day of Pentecost are understood as mandating a political regime like apartheid, it would seem that, once again, the church has harnessed the undeniable, but all too often exploitative, power of the biblical *sensus plenior*.

Hermeneutical consciousness, on the contrary, stresses a reading of individual passages within a text only by reference to the text as a whole; and the text as a whole by reference to the surrounding historical-cultural milieu from which it arose; and finally, that milieu and the texts it preserved by reference to the tradition which has sought to represent those historical meanings and values in each new era. Without attention to this "part-whole" exegetical analysis, itself ever evolving as frames of reference become larger with time, the present reading of an ancient text like the bible—and considering the very various nature of its tradition, we might add: especially the bible—can too easily become burdened by biases arising from one's present situation.

The study of hermeneutics, and the consciousness that study makes possible, takes its cues from a variety of sources. The most influential of these include the Marxist critique of political discourse as a product of class struggle; Nietzsche's critique of metaphysical discourse—like the sort that informed apartheid—as an all too frequent mask for sociopolitical ideology; Husserl's emphasis on the existential life-world that inextricably embraces all forms of language; and Heidegger's insistence that historical traditions are misunderstood where they are not seen as products of their own temporal-regional placement "in the world." When such German theologians as Barth, Bultmann, and Tillich took up these themes, in part from their need to find a relevant response to the atrocities of two world wars, they made the claim that the constituents of Christian faith— its sacred texts, rituals, and social praxis—are, at least in part, products of the traditions that bear them. This is to say, a text like the bible came to be seen, not as a "book of normative significance,"[64] not as a meta-historical source of fundamental data about present concerns, but as a resource, certainly profound at many points, for insight into past forms of human self-understanding. What hermeneutical consciousness brings to a text like the Bible is a kind of prudent hesitation—or as Gadamer termed it, "a radical modesty"[65]—before the task of application. Were the DRC to have allowed its future leaders to study these important developments, the ecclesial debate surrounding the birth of apartheid might well have been better informed as to the difficult, and often inconclusive, nature of biblical interpretation, and therefore less inclined toward the sort of biblical literalism that facilitated apartheid's popular support.

There remains, of course, the difficult task of what to make of the Great Trek, and the preceding Boer Wars, which together so forcefully infuse the Afrikaner sense of self with a claim to power and, for the Afrikaner people as a whole, legitimize, at least emotionally, the expediency of apartheid. It may be possible to shed light on this problem by borrowing an idea from Nietzschean hermeneutics, for then we would find support for claiming that the Afrikaner's history of suffering and oppression, itself an inescapable fact of history, may have proven a potent catalyst for a rather virulent form of *ressentiment*. According to Nietzsche, *ressentiment* is the curse of Christian morality, an irascible passion that makes slaves of those who once were one's masters. Unable to conquer their own moral failings, says Nietzsche, Christians learned to consider themselves masters of the "virtues" of shame and guilt, and consigned to a slavish hell those "*Übermenschen*" able to rise above them. Might it not be, perhaps, that something similar took place among the Afrikaners—that in shrouding their plight in mythology and spiritually interpreted biblical imagery, Afrikanerdom sought to elevate its own defeated status to power, and in so doing felt forced to deny power to its oppressors?

There is naturally no guarantee that a greater hermeneutical consciousness of the ways in which *ressentiment* and the "will to power" tend to corrupt historical interpretation would have stemmed the rise of apartheid. But one cannot help but wonder where the state of Afrikanerdom might be today, and indeed the whole of the Republic, had there been allowed in the universities some apparatus of self-appraisal, some means of furthering an ideological critique of Afrikanerdom's sense of self.

NOTES

1. This is the motto of the Afrikaner Christian League of Women, formed in the 1970s to bolster Afrikaner solidarity. See R. J. Neuhaus, *Dispensations: The Future of*

South Africa as South Africans See It (Grand Rapids: Eerdmans Publishing Company, 1986), p. 14.

2. For the history of the Boer Wars, see L. M. Thompson, "Great Britain and the Afrikaner Republics, 1870-1899," in Monica Wilson and Leonard Thompson, *The Oxford History of South Africa* (Oxford: Clarendon Press, 1971), pp. 287-324.

3. A historian of the time, J. A. Smith, writes, "Women and children who were found on the farms were driven to the so-called concentration camps. . . . [Others who were] fearful of falling into the hands of the British fled barefoot and lacerated through the veld . . . only to end up at the murderous women's camps. Thousands of dwellings were burned down and everything on the farms was destroyed. Cattle were driven away or slaughtered in heaps. . . . Those were days of lamentation and bitterness. The suffering was indescribably great. . . . It was as though the people had been forsaken by God." J. A. Smith, *The British Among the Boers, 1814-1915* (Cape Town: National Press, 1917), pp. 133-34.

4. Cited in Thompson, "Great Britain and the Afrikaner Republics," p. 291.

5. T. D. Moody, *The Rise of Afrikanerdom* (Berkeley: University of California Press, 1975), p. 24.

6. At an imperial conference in 1926, and largely at the demand of General Hertzog, the British signed the Balfour Declaration, which allowed Afrikaner self-rule within the Republic, which was still then considered a member of the Commonwealth.

7. Cited in C. W. de Kiewiet, *The Imperial Factor in South Africa* (Oxford: Oxford University Press, 1937), p. 276. Hertzog's government took action against "poor whiteism," to cite one example, by reserving coveted positions on the government-owned South African Railways for white men only, and by paying them "white wages."

8. Cited in Moody, *The Rise of Afrikanerdom*, pp. 96-97. Emphasis added.

9. This was the decision rendered by the Cape Synod, held in 1926 following the passage of Hertzog's infamous "Colour Bar" law. See J. A. Loubser, *The Apartheid Bible: A Critical Review of Racial Theology in South Africa* (Cape Town: Maskew, Miller and Longman, 1987), p. 29.

10. Cited in ibid., p. 31.

11. Moody, *The Rise of Afrikanerdom*, pp. 58-65.

12. *1935 Acts of the Council of Churches*, pp. 94-95.

13. A. J. Botha, "Evolution of a National Theology," unpublished D. Theol. thesis, Capetown University, 1984, p. 201.

14. J. Kinghorn, *The DRC and Apartheid* (Johannesburg: Macmillan, 1986), pp. 90ff.

15. Moody, *The Rise of Afrikanerdom*, p. 5.

16. J. S. Du Plessis, *President Kruger and the Word* (Bloemfontein: Sacum, 1947), p. 94.

17. Ibid., p. 104.

18. G. Preller, *Piet Retief* (Pretoria: van Schaik, 1906), pp. 152-53.

19. Moody, *The Rise of Afrikanerdom*, p. 7.

20. "The Speech of the Afrikaner," writes R. J. Neuhaus, "is permeated with talk about the trek, talk that is similar to scriptural references to pilgrimage. Educated Afrikaners, without any apparent self-consciousness, speak of setting out on a 'new trek' . . . or 'leaving the laager.'" Neuhaus, *Dispensations*, p. 23.

21. B. Villet, *Blood River* (London: Everest, 1982).

22. During my 1988 visit to the Republic, at a DRC service in commemoration of the Battle of Blood River, I heard this very description used in the sermon.

23. *Die Kerkbode* (September 20, 1938), cited in Loubser, *The Apartheid Bible*, p. 51.

24. Cited in Villet, *Blood River*, p. 96.

25. Ibid., p. 97.

26. Loubser, *The Apartheid Bible,* p. 70.

27. Ibid., p. 28.

28. Hans-Georg Gadamer, *Truth and Method* (London: Continuum, 1960).

29. Loubser, *The Apartheid Bible,* p. 24.

30. Botha, "Evolution of a National Theology," p. 273.

31. Hexam, *The Irony of Apartheid: The Struggle for National Independence of Afrikaner Calvinism against British Imperialism* (New York: Edwin Mellon Press, 1981), pp. 156-58.

32. Cited in Kinghorn, *The DRC and Apartheid,* p. 58.

33. W. de Klerk, *The Puritans of Africa: A Story of Afrikanerdom* (London: Rex Collins, 1975), p. 199.

34. Cited in Loubser, *The Apartheid Bible,* p. 52.

35. Ibid.

36. Hexam, *The Irony of Apartheid,* pp. 95-116.

37. Loubser, *The Apartheid Bible,* p. 56.

38. Ibid., p. 38.

39. A. Kuyper, *Der Stone-lezungen* (Amsterdam: Wormeker, 1989), pp. 14-36.

40. Ibid., pp. 39-59. This idea was promulgated in South Africa by the Calvinist philosopher H. G. Stoker.

41. Ibid., pp. 61-92.

42. Ibid., p. 61.

43. Clearly there are strains of Hegelian romanticism and historicism in this statement.

44. Ibid., pp. 95-112.

45. Kuyper, "Uniformity, the Curse of Life," cited in Loubser, *The Apartheid Bible,* p. 41.

46. Kuyper, *Der Stone-lezungen,* pp. 96-97.

47. Ibid., p. 94.

48. Ibid., pp. 193-94.

49. J. D. du Toit, "Die godsdienstige grondslag van ons rassebeleid," translated in *Inspan* (December 1944), pp. 198-207.

50. Ibid., p. 201.

51. Ibid., p. 203.

52. Lombard, *The Dutch Reformed Church and the Politics of Race, with Special Emphasis on the Years 1948-1961* (Pretoria: N. G. Kerkboekhandel, 1981), p. 39.

53. K. R. Johannson, *Race and Rhetoric in South Africa* (London: Kegan and Paul, 1972), p. xxiii.

54. Cited in Lombard, *The Dutch Reformed Church and the Politics of Race, with Special Emphasis on the Years 1948-1961,* pp. 130-36.

55. Cited in Hexam, *The Irony of Apartheid,* pp. 99-102.

56. E. P. Groenewald, *Racial Apartheid* (Stellenbosch: CSV, 1947), p. 40.

57. Ibid., pp. 45-47.

58. In most cases, of course—the Mixed Marriages Act, for example—it was merely a question of elaborating, and legislating against the consequences of, ideas which had already been endorsed by previous governments.

59. Lombard, *The Dutch Reformed Church and the Politics of Race,* pp. 290-97; and Loubser, *The Apartheid Bible,* pp. 72-76.

60. D. Tutu, "Apartheid and Christianity," in J. W. deGruchy and C. Villa-Vicencio (eds.), *Apartheid Is a Heresy* (Cape Town: Eerdmans, 1983), p. 46.

61. For insightful discussion of possible theological responses to apartheid by South African theologians, see deGruchy and Villa-Vicencio, *Apartheid Is a Heresy*; Wallis and J. Hollyday (eds.), *Crucible of Fire: The Church Confronts Apartheid* (Maryknoll: Orbis Press, 1989).

62. Loubser, *The Apartheid Bible*, chapter 12; Willem Vorster, "The Bible and Apartheid," in deGruchy and Villa-Vicencio, *Apartheid Is a Heresy*, pp. 94-111; and Hexam, *The Irony of Apartheid*, chapter VII.

63. Vorster, "The Bible and Apartheid," p. 97.

64. Ibid., pp. 106-9.

65. Gadamer, *Truth and Method*, p. 246.

Chapter 3

Religious Zionism and Israeli Politics: Gush Emunim Revisited

Jacob Abadi

The Israeli religious group named Gush Emunim (Block of the Faithful), whose members became known for their religious radicalism and determination to settle in Arab land occupied by Israel after the Six-Day War of 1967, had been a topic of intense controversy since its establishment in 1974. Throughout the 1980s, Gush Emunim turned into a major issue, triggering comments by many observers. Currently, however, Gush Emunim no longer occupies a prominent place in Israeli politics. The purpose of this chapter is to trace the origins of the movement, assess its impact on Israeli polity, and explore the reasons for its success in an environment that was largely hostile to its goals. Commentators who examined the overwhelming power that Gush Emunim exerted during the 1980s often tended to emphasize the role of the right wing Likud Government, which came to power in 1977, in encouraging and supporting the movement. Despite the abundance of literature on the topic, little attention was given to the fact that during its formative years, under the domination of the Labor Party, Gush Emunim turned into an uncompromising and recalcitrant group, averse to compromise and negotiations.

This chapter argues: (i) that the success of Gush Emunim was a byproduct of political, social, and ideological changes, which occurred in the Israeli society during the second decade of the state's existence; (ii) that it was the Labor Government which was largely responsible for the enormous power that Gush Emunim later wielded in Israeli politics; and (iii) that it was largely the disagreement among the leaders of the Labor coalition that enabled the movement to achieve its goals. Gush Emunim had already acquired enormous power when the Likud Party came to power. As a disciple of Vladimir Jabotinsky, the ideologue, and mentor of the Revisionist movement that had long been criticized by its opponents for its failure to encourage practical work in the process of nation building, Menachem Begin identified with Gush Emunim's objectives. However, the enormous power and popularity that the group acquired limited his ability to curb its ambitious settlement program, to determine the location of the settlements, or to set his own timetable for their establishment. There is little doubt that had the ambitions of Gush Emunim been curbed by the Labor Government, the movement would have never achieved the enormous power it later acquired, and the Likud Government would have had greater freedom in formulating its Arab policy. Despite the identity of interests between Gush Emunim and the Likud's agenda, this movement constituted far more than just a nuisance for Begin.

Gush Emunim emerged as a powerful force, not only due to its close association with the National Religious Party (NRP), which constituted an essential part of the Labor coalition, but also due to differences among members of the Labor Party. Emboldened by the disunity within the ranks of the Labor Party and the indecisiveness of its politicians, Gush Emunim increased its power even further under successive governments. However, by the end of the 1980s, a process of decline in Gush Emunim had set in. This process was not only a consequence of disagreement among the members of the movement regarding the means and the methods by which it sought to achieve its goals, but also due to the fact that the group's main goal—the establishment of settlements in Judea and Samaria—had been achieved. Gush Emunim's failure lies in the fact that its leaders did not change its character from a protest movement to a political group with a well-defined ideology and purpose.[1] The decision of Gush Emunim's leaders to keep their group outside the political system allowed the movement to wield much power during the 1980s, but proved to be a liability during the 1990s.

THE ORIGINS AND THE IDEOLOGY OF GUSH EMUNIM

A thorough analysis reveals that one of the main reasons for the rise of Gush Emunim was the weakening power of the ideologies promoted by the legal political parties in Israel. The fact that the legal parties had turned less ideological and more prone to compromise their political agenda led to the emergence of extra-parliamentary movements such as Gush Emunim, with a distinct comprehensive ideological platform.[2] After the Labor movement lost its ideological appeal, many saw Gush Emunim as the sole authentic pioneering-settler movement.[3]

Kevin Avruch attributes the emergence of Gush Emunim to changes that occurred among the religious (predominantly European-born or Ashkenazi) youth groups in Israel a decade before the outbreak of the Six-Day War of 1967. According to his argument, the Israeli educational system provided for three educational tracks in which Jewish youth could obtain their education. Two of them, the "state secular" and the "state religious," were controlled directly by the state and placed under ministerial direction. The third was independent but received financial assistance from the state and was under the patronage of the religious Agudat Yisrael Party. It consisted of traditional religious academies (*yeshivas*), which provided religious education to non-Zionist Orthodox and anti-Zionist ultra-Orthodox youth of European background. Dissatisfaction with the state-religious Mizrahi system led to the creation of an additional track in which new secondary schools were established within that system. These were boarding schools, which emphasized the study of the Talmud and encouraged the students to serve in the Nahal, a branch of the military, which combined military training with land settlement. It was from these new *yeshivas* that the Ashkenazi "knitted skullcap" generation emerged. They became the Young Guard faction within the NRP following the Six-Day War and began supporting Gush Emunim. Unlike the Labor youth, which according to Yonathan Shapiro accepted the authority of their elders and never formulated a worldview of their own, these religious young men were very daring. They rejected the passivity of the old generation, seeking to expand the role of Judaism in both domestic and foreign policy-related issues. They became so active that they established Gush Emunim in 1974, its West Bank settlement arm, Amana, in the late 1970s, and the terrorist Underground in the 1980s.[4]

Gush Emunim has been characterized as a messianic as well as a fundamentalist movement.[5] It derived its inspiration and ideology from the teachings of Rabbi Avraham Yitzhak Hacohen Kook and even more so from his son, Rabbi Zvi Yehuda Kook. Basing their arguments on the Hebrew sacred scriptures, the mentors of the movement taught that redemption was within reach in this age. According to Rabbi A.Y.H. Kook, the rise of Zionism and the subsequent events related to the growth of the Jewish national home in Palestine were proof that the era of redemption was underway.

Israel's swift victory in the Six-Day War transformed the status of Kook's theology into an operative ideology. Members of Gush Emunim were inspired by the victory, believing that it would bring about radical changes in both the physical and the metaphysical status of the Jewish State. Israel's stunning victory over the surrounding Arab states in only six days was regarded as a miracle by many Israelis, and the capture of Jerusalem only intensified the eschatological meaning of that event.[6] Many were convinced that Israel's victory was a divine miracle and that, therefore, it ushered in the age of redemption. For the religious among Gush Emunim, it was God himself who fought for the people of Israel and granted them the land for which they had been praying for centuries. Particularly inspired by that event was a small group of religious youth, which gathered at the *Merkaz haRav* academy in Jerusalem. It was there that they absorbed Rabbi Zvi Yehuda Kook's conviction that *Eretz Yisrael* (The Land of Israel) is holy, and that if one gives up territory, one necessarily empowers the forces of evil.

Unlike the ultra-orthodox *Haredi* Jews (who repudiated the validity of the State of Israel, believing that only the coming of the Messiah could redeem the Jewish people), Kook's disciples regarded the secular establishment as instrumental in accelerating the redemption process. Not only did they speak in praise of the secular establishment, but also glorified the holy attributes of the Israeli Defense Force (IDF).[7] Rabbi Z. Y. Kook carried this trend even further, saying that all the people of Israel were part of the divine process of redemption. Thus, the students at *Merkaz haRav* were captivated by the religious theology of their mentor, and closely adhered to the notion that it was permissible and imperative to liberate *Eretz Yisrael* by means of conquest and not only settlement.[8] On Independence Day 1967, Rabbi Z. Y. Kook lamented the partition of *Eretz Yisrael*, and less than a month afterwards, the IDF managed to defeat Egypt, Syria, and Jordan. This event prompted the group members to regard themselves compelled by the *Halakha* (Divine Law) to strive toward the integrity of *Eretz Yisrael* as part of the expression of the trinity—the People of Israel, the Torah of Israel, and the Land of Israel. By adhering to such an idea, the future members of Gush Emunim positioned themselves outside the rules of Israeli democracy, which determined that the secular political institutions should set Israel's boundaries.[9] The founders and mentors of the group, like Rabbi Shlomo Avineri, aspired to turn Gush Emunim, not into a marginal group of outlaws, which it turned out to be, but into a revolutionary movement capable of transforming the nation's thinking about its redemption and the future of *Eretz Yisrael*.[10]

Gush Emunim was established in 1974 in the West Bank kibbutz, Gush Etzion. Initially, Gush Emunim was a faction within the NRP, which took part in Prime Minister Yitzhak Rabin's Labor coalition. It was only after its disillusionment with and distrust of the NRP that Gush Emunim became a powerful and effective extra-parliamentary movement. According to Gershon Shafat, one of the founders of the movement, the NRP failed to exert pressure on the Labor coalition government, of which it was a member, to make the necessary concessions sought by Gush Emunim. He said that Gush Emunim's decision to secede from the NRP was because "we could not afford the luxury of inaction."[11] The group became convinced that Israel must hold on to what it regarded as the "liberated" territories that were once given to the People of Israel, and that all efforts were to be directed toward preventing the government from embarking on territorial compromises. Israel's previous experience of having to withdraw from the Sinai following the Suez Affair of 1956 was vivid in the mind of Gush Emunim members, and they were determined to force the government not to yield to foreign pressure to withdraw from these territories. Rabbi Moshe Levinger, the future leader of Gush Emunim, warned that making territorial concessions to the Palestinians would lead to a violent war among Jews.[12] Leaders of Gush Emunim promoted the settlement of *Eretz Yisrael* as an appropriate measure designed to guarantee Israel's control over the liberated territories. However, the secular regime was more pragmatic and therefore tended to be more hesitant and cautious about laying a claim to these territories. Nevertheless, the group was not discouraged, particularly in view of the fact that the leaders of the Labor coalition were not unanimous regarding the future of the territories.

Gush Emunim's conflict with the secular establishment began when the government began considering withdrawal from the occupied territories in an attempt to obtain lasting peace with the Arab states. However, Rabbi Z. Y. Kook insisted that redemption could not take place in a truncated Israel, and that by giving up territories the government forfeited redemption. Following Golda

Meir's resignation in the aftermath of the Yom Kippur War of October 1973, Rabin became the new Prime Minister. Like his predecessor, he did not respond to the group's demand to accelerate the process of settling Judea and Samaria. In response, Rabbi Z. Y. Kook condemned the government as worthless and a farce.[13]

Such thinking led the leaders of Gush Emunim to conclude that the Palestinian Arabs were not a nation and that they had no right to any part of *Eretz Yisrael*. According to the Gush Emunim's theology, which was anchored in the Torah, the Palestinians were no more than resident aliens and therefore could hope for nothing more than full individual rights within a sovereign Jewish state. Gush Emunim's mentors argued that as long as the Palestinians did not recognize Jewish hegemony over the entire area of *Eretz Yisrael*, they should be evicted from the land, as the Canaanites were in ancient Israel. According to Gush Emunim, Zionism takes precedence over democracy, which can exist only as long as the Israeli government fulfills its duty to settle the land and make no concessions to the Arabs.

Gush Emunim was far from being a passive protest movement. Shortly after Begin rose to power in 1977, its members established a covenant, a council, and a publication, *Nekuda,* in which to express their views. Oddly enough, however, the movement did not produce much written material about either the teachings of its ideological mentors or its objectives. Members of Gush Emunim were suspicious of most politicians who did not approve of their methods. Even Prime Minister Menachem Begin and Agriculture Minister Ariel Sharon, who were known for their sympathy for Gush Emunim's objectives, were often criticized for the slow pace of settling the land. Begin gave in to their demands, increased their budget, and authorized them to build more settlements in Judea and Samaria. According to one estimate, $200 million to $250 million was invested in the West Bank annually under the Likud regime.[14]

THE EROSION OF LABOR ZIONIST IDEOLOGY AND THE RESPONSIBILITY OF THE LABOR PARTY

Gush Emunim emerged against the background of changing values caused by the waning of Labor Zionist ideology. The erosion of the Labor Zionist ideology was discernible already by the early 1960s. In September 1964, Shlomo Avineri noted, "The traditional pattern of Jewish society, middle classness, are reasserting themselves. . . . Israel is approaching not only the normal bourgeois democracies of the West, but also the traditional Jewish society in the West against whose 'inverted social pyramid' early Zionism rebelled."[15]

The socialist ideology promoted by Israel's first Prime Minister David Ben Gurion and his successors lost its vigor after the first decade of the Jewish State's existence. Consequently, there was a yearning among the public for an authentic pioneering movement. Attempts made by the ruling Mapai Party to reinforce the Labor Zionist ideology through education and indoctrination achieved meager results. This ideological bankruptcy had greatly benefited Gush

Emunim, whose leaders appeared not only as the opponents of the government's policy of territorial compromise, but also as vigorous settlers, willing to assume the burden of settling in a distant and inhospitable environment, while abandoning the comfort of middle class urban life.

Gush Emunim rose to prominence not only because of the support it had in the right wing Likud Party, but also because it had sympathy within the Labor Party, which encouraged it either by disregarding its illegal actions or by openly championing its cause. Gershon Shafat, one of the founders of the movement recalled the paternalistic and indecisive attitude of Prime Minister Levi Eshkol, who by his lack of determination unknowingly gave the settlers a *carte blanche* to settle Gush Etzion. Shafat recalled that in a meeting with the members of the movement, Eshkol reacted "with a paternalistic disapproval of their presumptuousness." For example, when asked by one of Gush Emunim's activists, Hanan Porat, whether they would be able to go there, Eshkol paused and later said that the group could go and pray there during the Rosh Hashanah holiday. But when Porat told him that the group's aim was to establish a settlement there, Eshkol responded angrily and said that they should avoid "big words" and just go to pray there.[16]

Mark Segal has rightly observed that, "the ascendancy of Gush Emunim ran parallel to the declining fortunes of the Rabin government, and coincided with the break in the 'historical partnership' between the Labor Zionists and the religious Mizrahi, as the NRP switched emphasis from religion to nationalism."[17] In his study, which explores the reasons for the rise of leftist political groups such as *Mazpen* within the Israeli system, Shaul Kantzler argues that the weakening of the Labor Party's leadership after fifteen years of powerful control, allowed such fringe groups to emerge.[18] The same argument can be applied, and probably with greater force, to the rise of opposition right wing and religious groups such as Gush Emunim, whose members were convinced that they had stronger reasons to protest the government's policy, because unlike the leftist groups, they were not only fulfilling a Biblical mission by settling in the "liberated" territories, but also providing greater security for the state by building such settlements.

Gush Emunim managed to thrive on the disunity within the Labor Party after Prime Minister Golda Meir's resignation in April 1974. Recalling the difficulties the Labor Party encountered at that juncture, Abba Eban writes:

The trouble was that since Mrs. Meir's resignation, the leading personalities had split into individual domains of thought and action. There was no authority sufficient to convert them into a team driving the nation toward visible goals. The result was that less than two years after the election of a new leader, the leadership question was still open. The Prime Minister was unable to secure the implementation of his own decision . . . such as the removal of a settlement established provocatively at Kaddum in the populated area of the West Bank by a group of political zealots belonging to an organization called Gush Emunim.[19]

In his critical study *The Zionist Dream Revisited*, Amnon Rubinstein notes that Gush Emunim had skillfully managed to benefit from the disunity within the Labor Party. He mentioned the fact that the key figures in the Labor coalition, Prime Minister Yitzhak Rabin, Defense Minister Shimon Peres, and Foreign Minister Yigal Allon, were all influenced by members of Gush Emunim, who occupied positions of power in the government.[20] Faced with the need to pacify the NRP, whose members were sympathetic to Gush Emunim, and to benefit from the experience, both military and administrative, of other right wing politicians who sympathized with the movement, the Labor Government found itself unable to resist the demands of Gush Emunim. Peres recalled in his memoirs how this issue tarnished his relations with Rabin. Peres argued that Rabin's appointment of Sharon, a well-known Gush sympathizer, as his personal defense advisor threatened his position. He felt that his long experience in the Ministry of Defense could be of great value to Rabin. In turn, Rabin blamed Peres for appointing Professor Yuval Neeman, another known Gush sympathizer, as his scientific advisor in the Ministry of Defense. Peres claimed that Neeman, who was a physicist of international repute, functioned mainly in his professional capacity, while Sharon operated outside the boundaries of accepted norms by supporting Gush Emunim.

Gush Emunim benefited from the process of radicalization, which had taken place, not only in government circles, but also among the public. Indeed, the leaders of the Labor Government had shown clear signs of annexationist tendencies after the Six-Day War. This trend became obvious under Prime Minister Golda Meir, who had stated already in 1969 that there was never a Palestinian entity or a nation, and that "Since 1948 no one ever heard about a Palestinian entity."[21] Israel's former Defense Minister Moshe Dayan's statements were even more encouraging for the leaders of Gush Emunim. In a ceremony on the peak of Massada, Dayan said that his vision of a new Israel was "with broad frontiers, strong and solid, with authority of the Israel Government extending from the Jordan to the Suez Canal." Moreover, he said in an interview on BBC on May 14, 1973, that "Israel should remain for eternity and until the end of time in the West Bank." He added that if the Palestinians did not like the idea, they could "go and establish themselves in an Arab country—Jordan, Syria or Iraq." And on July 30, 1973, he said to *Time* magazine "There is no Palestine. Finished."[22] Dayan stated in his memoirs that "The West Bank—Judea and Samaria—was in my view part of our homeland that there is a need to settle in it and not to abandon it."[23]

Such an attitude on the part of a charismatic leader of the Israeli Labor cabinet was sufficient to provide Gush Emunim the confidence it needed. The first actual step taken by the group was to settle in *Elon Moreh* in Samaria. The group then began settling in Kiryat Arba near Hebron. Following the Yom Kippur War, the group became a bitter opponent of territorial compromise. Dayan's support of the group manifested itself in his tendency to allow the settlers of Tekoa and Ofra to remain there despite the government's objection.[24]

Moreover, he was openly in favor of the establishment of Eilon Moreh settlement by Gush Emunim on privately owned Arab land near Nablus.[25]

Rabin's attitude toward Gush Emunim was far more critical than other members of his cabinet. When Gush Emunim demanded a wide-ranging debate on settlement policy in June 1976, he insisted that the government's settlement policy was not open to negotiation.[26] In his memoirs he vented his anger against Gush Emunim for the less than cordial reception they gave the American Jewish Secretary of State Henry Kissinger, who was on his shuttle diplomacy tour following the Yom Kippur War. Rabin criticized those opportunist members of his party "who maintained love affairs with Gush Emunim, the breakers of the law and order."[27] He added:

In Gush Emunim I saw a very grave phenomenon—a cancer in the body of the Israeli democracy. [I was] against their basic view, which contradicts the foundation of the Israeli democracy. There was a need to embark on an ideological struggle, which uncovers the meaning of the "Gush" positions and its methods. Such a struggle cannot be waged only by the IDF's bayonets and cannot succeed while the Labor Party is divided over its attitude toward the "Gush" men and the defense minister defines them as "true idealists" and supports them both overtly and covertly.[28]

Similarly, Foreign Minister Yigal Allon attacked Gush Emunim describing it as "a political movement of false messiahs and nationalist demagogues."[29] In a meeting of delegates of the World Labor Zionist Movement, Allon said that Gush Emunim was dictating Israel's foreign policy. He explained to his listeners that Gush Emunim was powerful due to its enormous influence in the NRP, which held the balance in the ruling coalition.[30]

Defense Minister Peres described Gush Emunim as a group of "short-term demonstrative settlers flitting from rooftop to rooftop and hill to hill in the manner of torch relay."[31] Yet, despite his commitment to the peace process, Peres was captivated by Gush Emunim. He recalled in his memoirs that he had sympathy for some of the soldier-students of Gush Emunim who performed their military duties while studying the Torah in the religious academies. He went on to say how impressed he was with the students of kibbutz Ramat Magshimin, who on the night of November 20, 1975, responded swiftly and effectively to infiltration by Arab guerrillas from Syria, as a result of which three students were killed. Despite his criticism of Gush Emunim Peres was impressed by the ability of its members to combine intensive study of the Torah with combat duties. He went on, saying:

It was then that I came to appreciate the strength of the Emunim movement, and I have never since disparaged the depth of their commitment or the vibrancy of their pioneering spirit. But I have always feared that they elevated the Holy Land to a level that supersedes the holiness of man. And in so doing, in my view, they have perverted the true scale of values of authentic Judaism.[32]

Abba Eban's view of Gush Emunim was no less critical than his colleagues in the Labor Party. He referred to Gush Emunim as a group which combined theological fundamentalism and territorial ambition and "which held their right to settle in the occupied territories as superior to the state to which they were theoretically subject." He criticized Gush Emunim for challenging the Israeli legal system and for engaging in terrorism, with the awareness that their deeds would go unpunished.[33]

When Gush Emunim settled in Eilon Moreh, the Labor Government was divided over whether or not to force the settlers to evacuate the settlement. Dovish ministers led by Yigal Allon insisted on immediate evacuation of the settlers, by force if necessary, arguing that allowing the group to settle illegally tarnished Israel's image as a state of law and order. Both Rabin and Peres argued for restraint. The entire affair proved that the government was not strong enough to resist the pressure exerted by the group.

THE RADICALIZATION OF GUSH EMUNIM

As leader of a movement, whose agenda never promoted the idea of settling *Eretz Yisrael*, Begin found it necessary to appeal to populist sentiments. According to Yonathan Shapiro such sentiments were anchored in the nationalist-religious worldview that the right wing Herut Party members acquired as a generational unit in Eastern Europe, prior to World War 11.[34] Begin portrayed himself as a leader representing the national interest. This was the source of his legitimacy and his position as leader of Herut. In the political system established by the Likud Party, which included Herut and the Liberal Party, there was no room for ideological innovations.[35]

That Gush Emunim found support among Likud members was due largely to the fact that it promoted the settlement of *Eretz Yisrael*. Such a component was missing in the Israeli right wing parties. Gush Emunim provided Begin, the disciple of Jabotinsky, the opportunity to escape the historical blame cast upon the Revisionists whose agenda, unlike the Labor movement, remained barren, full of useless rhetoric. Indeed, Jabotinsky never encouraged practical work in the process of nation building. He argued that the Zionist dream would not materialize by a gradual building of settlements, but only by obtaining a majority in the country.[36] Moreover, Gush Emunim's religious ideology reinforced the Likud's territorial claims to *Eretz Yisrael*. This was the reason why Begin was lenient toward its members. Shortly after his rise to power he responded to an appeal by Chief Rabbi Shlomo Goren to release 113 Gush members, who were arrested for demonstrating against Kissinger.[37]

In contrast to the ultra-Orthodox *Haredi* community, which remained isolated and inactive, Gush Emunim promoted activism designed to lead the Jewish nation toward redemption. Not only did the group fight against any territorial concessions to the Arabs, it also promoted settlements in the occupied territories. The group's influence went beyond the religious camp assuming even greater dimensions under the Likud. By the early 1980s, the group had many advocates and sympathizers in the NRP.[38] Moreover, influential Likud figures, such as former general Ariel Sharon and former Chief of Staff Rafael Eitan, were openly sympathetic to them. Gush Emunim had also a poet laureate Naomi Shemer, who once stated that if the choice must be between peace and *Eretz Yisrael*, she would prefer the latter.[39] Begin's reference to the occupied territories as the "liberated" homeland of the Jewish people, his promise that there will be "many Eilon Moreh's," and his habit of wearing a knitted skullcap while addressing Gush Emunim[40] were all encouraging signs to its members. Under the Likud, the Gush intensified its aggressive campaign aimed at promoting the idea of the integrity of *Eretz Yisrael*. Its members demonstrated against territorial compromises and began establishing settlements in Samaria, on the ground that this was a biblical land, promised to the people of Israel since the time of Abraham. The group succeeded in challenging Allon's peace plan and so their settlements began to dot the West Bank landscape.

Under Levinger, Gush Emunim became far more active and harder to control. Its level of enthusiasm did not subside when the more moderate Hanan Porat took control of the movement. Gush Emunim rose to prominence when Rabin's government was losing popularity and when the religious parties became less inclined to support the Labor party. It was then that the NRP became more interested in issues affecting national security and, therefore, intensified its support for Gush Emunim. It was this state of affairs which allowed Gush Emunim to insist that Begin fulfill his promise to establish "many more Elon Moreh's."[41] Yet despite their sympathy toward Gush Emunim, both Begin and Sharon made it clear that there was a limit to their support. They insisted that only the Ministerial Committee on Settlement was authorized to decide on the location and the timetable of settlements building.[42]

It was ironic that Begin and Sharon, who identified more closely with Gush Emunim's ideology than their opponents within the Labor Party, took no less strong measures to curb the movement. However, Begin's success was limited. In October 1977, he was reported to have pleaded with Porat to let him address members of two settlements. But Porat insisted that Begin meet only with the secretariat. Sharon was aware of the fact that it was largely due to Gush Emunim's pressure that he remained in the government and was given an unofficial role in defense, despite his official position as a Minister of Agriculture.[43] Sharon opposed Gush Emunim's determination to settle close to Nablus, yet while he was the "settlement czar" as the Minister of Agriculture in Begin's first government, he responded to their pressure by building nearly seventy settlements in the territories, many of which were flimsy in nature.[44] Sharon's support for Gush Emunim exposed him to intense pressure from left-of-center politicians such as Yosef Sarid, who once passed an urgent motion for a plenary discussion on the issue of granting the Gush the status of an official settlement movement. In response, Sharon implied that the government was in favor of granting the group such status.[45]

Gush Emunim had never stated that its aim was violent and never openly advocated mass transfer of Palestinians to surrounding Arab countries. Its leaders boasted that they had all along advocated coexistence with the Arabs. However, such coexistence was contingent upon acceptance by the Arabs of a minority status in a sovereign Jewish State. And when their demands were not met with favorable response from the government, some Gush Emunim members began resorting to violence. By the early 1980s, the extremists within the group were said to have planned terrorist activities against Arabs in the occupied territories. Among the terrorist activities of the group were the unsuccessful attempt to assassinate the mayors of three Arab cities in the West Bank in 1980, the attack on the Islamic College in Hebron in 1983, and the plot to blow up five Arab buses, which was discovered in 1984. The group even had an elaborate plan to blow up the Dome of the Rock.

Begin's promise to Gush Emunim that "We will have many more Eilon Moreh's" had greatly encouraged the group. Despite its aggressiveness, Begin never regarded Gush Emunim as a deviant group. Other Likud members had the same regard. Defense Minister Ezer Weizman was reported to have agreed to seizure of privately owned Arab land in the West Bank in compliance with the Gush demand for more settlements. He accepted the argument made by Gush leaders that Jewish settlements were needed in order to prevent the establishment of a Palestinian state. On November 1977, the Treasury decided to appropriate IL81 million for settlements in the West Bank.[46] The government caved in to pressure by Gush Emunim, and although it ordered its members to evacuate Eilon Moreh, no deadline had been set. Moreover, when the settlers withdrew, they obtained the right to establish a settlement on another site, in addition to the sum of IL50 million in compensation.[47] Nevertheless, Begin's differences with the Gush continued. During a stormy Knesset meeting, at the end of December 1978, he reaffirmed his commitment to build more settlements in the West Bank, but insisted that the government determine the timetable. He argued that the demonstrations of the Gush and its supporters were superfluous and condemned the way in which they had criticized him as "undignified and unmannerly."[48]

Gush Emunim was in great despair following the Camp David peace accord with Egypt. The Camp David accord allowed for autonomy for the Palestinians. This grim reality brought the Gush members into an alliance with other dissatisfied individuals. Together they formed the group called *Bnai Brit Ne'emanei Eretz Yisrael* (The Covenant of *Eretz Yisrael* Faithful). This group championed the cause of Greater Israel and later formed the radical right wing Tehiya Party, whose main aim was to oppose the Camp David accords. Gush Emunim's mentor Rabbi Z. Y. Kook joined his disciples in condemning the peace accord with Egypt as a "betrayal," a "stab in the back," and "treason."[49] When two right wing Knesset members, Moshe Shamir and Geula Cohen, broke away from the Likud and established their own faction, Hanan Porat and Gershon Shafat of Gush Emunim joined that faction. The group's aim was to demand a revision of the Sinai accord with Egypt.[50]

In April 1982, the group became among the most active opponents of the government's decision to evacuate the settlers of the Rafiah Salient. They participated in the violent demonstrations against the evacuation of the city of Yamit, which had been established by the settlers. Convinced that the Muslim presence on Temple Mount kept them out of favor with God, the group began planning the demolition of the Dome of the Rock. The purpose of the action was twofold: to eliminate the contaminating Muslim presence from the "holy of the holies," and to sabotage the peace treaty with Egypt. However, since the group did not obtain the rabbinical approval for their plan and failed to convince all the members to collaborate, it was not carried out. Dismayed by the assassination of settlers in Kiryat Arab and Hebron, and by what it saw as the indecisiveness of the government, the Underground group of settlers committed several retaliatory acts until they were caught in 1984. Although very few Gush members participated in the Underground, there was a clear connection between the two. Members of the Underground were, in fact, Gush members who were swept up by the group's ideology and sought to carry out terrorist activities in order to prove their point.

In his analysis of Gush Emunim, Professor Ehud Sprinzak of the Hebrew University of Jerusalem argues that the group's activities fall into the category of "permanent illegalism." Unlike many protest movements such as the Black Panthers, which emerge suddenly and stop after a short while, the activities of Gush Emunim persisted and had a negative impact on the entire political system in Israel. Not only did Gush Emunim establish a precedent for disobedience, it also exposed the government to criticism by many critics who saw the group's territorial demands as an obstacle to peace. Unlike the ephemeral movements, which protested against unfair distribution of wealth and benefits by the government, Gush Emunim had a clear ideology and determination to break the law. The only other extra-parliamentary group that violated the law on a continual basis was the *Neturei Karta* ultra-religious group, whose members never recognized the State of Israel. But this group remained isolated and had little impact on the political system. By contrast, Gush Emunim developed an ideology and an illegal course of action. Members of the Gush argued that a government that did not allow them to settle *Eretz Yisrael* was immoral and illegal.

What made Gush Emunim such a formidable power was the support it had within a Labor movement known as the *Ein Vered* circle, whose members were inspired by the Labor Party's *Achdut Ha'avoda* (Union of Labor). According to Sprinzak, Gush Emunim represented the greatest effort of religious Zionism to fight for hegemony in Zionism. Whereas the Orthodox Zionists of parties such as Mizrahi and HaPoel Hamizrahi had accepted the secular leadership's methods of settlement and state-building, Gush Emunim challenged the government's secular authority, seeking to sanctify the Land of Israel by settlement and to establish a Jewish religious system independent of foreign influence.

Gush Emunim had wide support within both the coalition and the opposition. However, Begin who enthusiastically supported the group, found it to be a political hindrance after his rise to power. The group opposed compromises on the settlement issue and sought to stop the peace process. Yet Begin's government did not oppose the group when its members joined the settlers of Yamit who resisted evacuation as part of the peace accord with Egypt. Gush Emunim obtained financial support from both government funds and the Tehiya Party. In addition, Knesset members such as Geula Cohen, Hanan Porat, and Rabbi Chaim Druckman gave the group greater legitimacy when they went to settle in Yamit. The dissolution of Yamit did not reduce the power of Gush Emunim. On the contrary, Gush Emunim emerged as a victim of the government's alleged evil intentions and none of its members were arrested after the event. Moreover, despite the fact that Gush Emunim challenged the government, and gave birth to a radical terrorist group that sought to destroy the Dome of the Rock, Gush Emunim remained a grassroots pioneering movement with respect to the state and its institutions. Unlike Rabbi Meir Kahane's Kach movement, whose members were known for their disregard of the law and who capitalized on the economic and social distress of many Israelis in order to promote their cause,[51] Gush Emunim managed to establish very prestigious support for its illegal actions. It managed to gain popularity among the public by promoting religious ideas and establishing settlements in areas, which many regarded as part of the Jewish biblical homeland.[52] In less than a decade Gush Emunim became a powerful organization with support from many parties.[53]

SUPPORTERS AND DETRACTORS OF GUSH EMUNIM

Gush Emunim received attention disproportionate to its size. Its supporters came not only from the religious camp but also from advocates of a Greater Israel within the government. In addition, Gush Emunim had a strong base of support among the public, both religious and secular. Many regarded the group as the only authentic organization to remain loyal to *Eretz Yisrael,* and praised its members for their patriotism and willingness to assume the arduous task of establishing settlements in a hostile land and difficult terrain. Some regarded Gush Emunim as the main defender of the Jewish tradition.

Its defenders argued that it was not concerned with more than just religion, and that the main essence of Zionism was based on the settlement of *Eretz Yisrael.*[54] Harold Fisch argued that the right of the Jews to *Eretz Yisrael* lies at the heart of Kook's philosophy, and that Gush Emunim did not stray from their mentor's teaching.[55] He writes: "If I am not mistaken, the chief representatives of an uncompromising Zionist Covenant faith at this time are the activists of the so called *Gush Emunim* . . . a powerful group mainly, but not entirely, from the religious youth of the country." Commenting on their sense of realism, Fisch mentioned that in August 1975, the members of this group staged a mass demonstration against the peace agreement with Egypt. He praised them for protesting against Israel's withdrawal from the strategic passes of Gidi and Mitla and the oil fields of the Sinai. Fisch argued that, in the end, Gush Emunim's sense of realism would be appreciated by future generations. He writes:

Gush Emunim is commonly accused of mysticism and lack of political realism. No doubt the "Zionists of Zion" in 1903 were also thus accused, but history proved them right in the end. If *Emunim* were less practical and more mystical, they might argue that oil wells are not important and that all we have to do when the time comes is to pray for oil to descend from heaven to supply Israel's needs. Instead of which they argue, as believing Jews have always argued, that salvation has to be worked for as well as prayed for.[56]

Similar ideas were expressed by Welfare Minister Zevulun Hamer, who praised the movement for their idealism saying, "Gush Emunim—whose idealism is undeniable—is one group in the country today devoted to keeping alive the idea of Eretz Yisrael-knowledge of the land, love of the land."[57] Yet, despite the success of Gush Emunim, numerous critics rejected its methods and even accused it of adopting false messianism. Charles Hoffman argues that the leaders and ideologues of Gush Emunim rejected both the European humanism practiced by the pioneers of religious Zionism and the humanist trend of the religious Zionist kibbutz movement. Instead, it preferred to adopt a militant ideology, promoting Jewish rights and denying the rights of others.[58] Gush Emunim had opponents even within the religious camp. Shortly after the establishment of Gush Emunim, a religious group of moderate intellectuals called "The Circle for Religious Zionism" was formed by NRP members Abraham Melamed and Moshe Unna and several professors from the Hebrew University of Jerusalem and Bar Ilan University. This group was established in reaction to what its members believed was Gush Emunim's dangerous deviation from the authentic tenets of religious Zionism. Zvi Yaron, an expert on the writing of Rabbi Z. Y. Kook and one of the founders of the new movement, argued that Gush Emunim had perverted the meaning of Kook's thought. He accused Gush Emunim of "undermining the moral foundations of Israeli society" and said that while Kook was sensitive to the Arabs of *Eretz Yisrael*, Gush Emunim ignored them.[59] Describing the essence of Gush Emunim, Yaron said that the group could only be described as a political movement with a maximalist agenda. He criticized Gush Emunim's opposition to withdrawal from the territories, saying that it ran counter to the teachings of religious leaders such as Rabbi Joseph Soloveitchik, who argued that there is no *mitzva* and no sanction in the *halakha,* which emphasized the need or the duty to shed blood for the sanctity of the land. He argued that the pronouncements made by Kook had nothing to do with what the group preached.

It was precisely because Yaron's criticism symbolized the disapproval of many religious people in Israel that Gush Emunim found it difficult to dismiss his remarks. Yaron emphasized the fact that his criticism represented the disenchantment of many religious people with the actions of Gush Emunim. He writes:

But those of us who oppose Gush Emunim do so precisely because we are religious Zionists and because we are convinced that Gush Emunim constitutes an utter falsification of religious Zionism. . . . There is nothing in his teaching to suggest that at a time of *atchalata digeoola* (beginning of redemption) the Jewish state should be guided by "messianic policy."

He went on to say that the leaders of Gush Emunim adopted a messianic policy while ignoring the reality of Israel's unique political and military situation.[60] Similarly, the leader of the National Religious Youth Organization Bnai Akiva, Yair Cherlow, accused Hanan Porat of inciting the youth of his movement, saying, "You fire up the youth for two or three days, and leave us with the gray work of undoing the education confusion that you create."[61] The Oz Veshalom movement, a group of national religious intellectuals from cities and kibbutzim, opposed Gush Emunim's theoretical and practical interpretations of Kook's teaching. Spokesmen of Oz Veshalom argued that despite the sanctity of the land, gaining it by force involved paying a moral price, and that the ethical and spiritual quality of Israeli life was far more important than the geographical size of the state. Leaders of Oz Veshalom insisted that militarism and chauvinism should not be part of Jewish and Zionist principles.[62] Rabbi Richard Hirsch, executive director of the World Union for Progressive Judaism, criticized Gush Emunim for opposing withdrawal and for being insensitive to the claims and rights of the Arab residents.[63] In addition, although the leaders of the new dovish religious movement Netivot Shalom praised the Gush for creating "an integrated system of Zionist fulfillment," they called upon the Gush to observe the moral values of the Torah.[64]

Naturally, criticism from non-religious groups was extremely fierce. Thus, for example, members of the Labor Party's Young Guard argued that Gush Emunim was a danger to democracy. One of their members was reported to have said, "Democracies die at the hand of groups which believe they represent the true national interest and are therefore justified in imposing their view on the majority." Avraham Hasson of the Independent Liberals warned against yielding to the group's demands saying, "A government which compromises with mobs, will not last long."[65]

Independent observers and university professors joined the chorus of Gush Emunim's critics. According to Yigal Elam, Gush Emunim distorted the authentic Zionist thought of the founding fathers, whose primary concern was to search for a solution to the problem of Jewish distress in the modern period. Unlike them, Gush Emunim gave priority to obtaining the Holy Land for the Jewish people.[66] Amnon Rubinstein argued that Gush Emunim defied authentic Zionism and deviated from Herzl's teaching by preaching false messianism.[67] Itzhak Galnoor wrote in a similar vein, saying that Gush Emunim did not grasp the essential part of Kook's ideology and instead promoted the nonessential. According to Galnoor, Kook believed in the amalgamation of national, spiritual, and material elements: "The people of Israel, the Torah of Israel and the land of Israel." Gush Emunim had turned one component, the land of Israel, into the sole expression of Jewish faith. Tinged with political, chauvinistic, and racist overtones, this element guided the group's actions and rhetoric throughout its existence. According to Galnoor, there was nothing to Gush Emunim besides the settlements, and its rhetoric about spiritual revival was nothing but deception. In the end, Gush Emunim did not contribute to the spiritual revival of the Jewish people.[68] According to Danny Rubinstein, Gush Emunim did not concern itself with the traditional social challenges of Zionism, such as absorption of Jewish immigrants, or turning the national home into a melting pot of Jews from diverse backgrounds. Liberalism, tolerance, and humanism occupied a marginal place in the worldview of Gush Emunim's members.[69]

Commenting on what he regarded as the nefarious methods of Gush Emunim and the negative impact which they had on the government's settlement policy one observer writes:

The more settlements are put up all over the West Bank, no matter where, and at what cost, the lesser the likelihood will their dismantling be if the Land is ever ceded to another rule. Therefore no part of the land will ever be ceded. This is even if it is denied, the true rationale of the government's settlement policy, and it is taken directly from the ideological arsenal of Gush Emunim. It applies in equal measure to Jabal Kabir and to, say Eilon Moreh.[70]

Another critic of Gush Emunim, Uriel Sharon said to the *Jerusalem Post*:

The charm of the irrational, or rather anti-rational, should never be underestimated. . . . The attraction of the revolutionary romanticism and messianic fervour of Gush Emunim and its offshoots to broad circles of the community, especially religious youth should not be dismissed. Because they know that the Almighty is on their side and that the End of Days is near, they feel that they can pursue their divinely inspired mission to protect the inviolability of the land of Israel. . . . The words compromise and tolerance have been expunged from their vocabulary.[71]

THE SECRETS OF GUSH EMUNIM'S SUCCESS

In their comparative study of Gush Emunim and the Peace Now Movement, David Newman and Tamar Hermann argue that successful movements manage to find a common language with policy makers while maintaining their radical or idealistic image in the public eye. According to this argument, the ability of Gush Emunim to maintain a sense of pragmatism while pushing its fundamentalist agenda is what accounts for the success of the movement. The reasons for the success of Gush Emunim become obvious when one considers the points raised by Newman and Hermann. According to the authors, the erosion of the image of the Israeli establishment during the 1970s led to the rise of movements such as Gush Emunim and Peace Now and increased their ability to influence the government's decision-making. But while Peace Now remained weak due to its distance from the political elite and the prevalent security ethos, Gush Emunim benefited by combining occasional protest with prolonged cooperation with the government of the day. Its leaders managed to work within the system while maintaining popular support. Consequently, Gush Emunim was far more successful in promoting its cause. While Peace Now promoted universalistic ideas, which seemed unrealistic and naïve in the eyes of the general public, Gush Emunim promoted particularistic and ethnocentric values, which were more relevant to Jewish experience. Another important reason for the success of Gush Emunim was that, unlike Peace Now, the decision-making process in Gush Emunim was centralized. The existence of a powerful inner secretariat which constituted the decision-making body gave the group more cohesiveness. Peace Now was never engaged in settlement activity, but it did promote acts of demonstration and protest. Moreover, its membership underwent constant change. By contrast, members of Gush Emunim could always rely on the settlers as their active supporters.

Gush Emunim had much stronger connections with the establishment and greater congruence of interest with the Likud Party than Peace Now had with the Labor Party. Moreover, Gush Emunim enjoyed support among nearly all politicians to the right of center in the Knesset, while Peace Now did not have a majority of sympathizers even in the Labor Party. The fact that leading Gush Emunim personalities were represented in the NRP and the right wing Tchiya Party in the Knesset added to its power. Also, the fact that some Knesset members of the Likud, the NRP, and Tehiya were settlers themselves enabled Gush Emunim to lobby Knesset members with considerable success. Gush Emunim activists maintained unofficial contacts with government officials and managed to obtain funds due to their membership in local councils in the territories.[72]

Gush Emunim remained popular during the incumbency of Begin's successor, Prime Minister Yitzhak Shamir, despite the fact that its leaders challenged his policy regarding the settlements. They blamed him for what they described as the "Jordanization and Palestinization" of the West Bank territories when he failed to establish new settlements, to develop the Arab sector at the expense of Jewish settlements, and to express willingness to make territorial compromises. Levinger was quoted as saying that "Shamir should either fight for the ideas of the Herut Party or admit that he cannot take responsibility for building Judea and Samaria and resign."[73]

THE CONTESTED LEGACY AND THE DECLINE OF GUSH EMUNIM

Some observers who explored Rabin's assassination by the extremist Yigal Amir on November 4, 1995, concluded that the mentality promoted and reinforced by Gush Emunim was responsible for the act. In his study of Rabin's assassination, Samuel Peleg argued that "a direct line extends from Gush Emunim of the 1970s to the Jewish Underground of the 1980s and to the violent challengers of the peace process. They are all soldiers in the religious warfare that they have initiated against the state." He went on to say that despite the fact that Gush Emunim was no longer influential at the time of the assassination, "its spirit of illegalism, ferocious idealism, and unfettered messianism coupled with new fears and abhorrence of the unfolding reality inducted a new generation of believers." He concluded by saying that Rabin's assassin, Yigal Amir, was "a direct offspring of Gush Emunim and the Jewish underground."[74] Obviously, Rabbi A. I. Kook's conviction that what the secular Zionists started in Palestine was a beginning of messianic redemption stood in sharp contrast to such an act and he would have certainly condemned it.[75]

Writing in 1987, Eliezer Don-Yehiya argued that Gush Emunim no longer played a significant role in Israel. He explained that this was due to the growing tendency of the movement's leaders to conduct their activities outside the organized framework of Gush Emunim. Many of Gush Emunim's members joined the Tehiya Party in 1981, leaving the Gush with second-rate leaders. Other leaders joined the NRP, and in 1983 some joined the newly established Morasha religious nationalist party. A similar development occurred in the settlement activities of the Gush, when specific bodies such as Amana or Yesha—the council of settlements in Judea and Samaria—took control of these activities. In addition, Gush Emunim began suffering from internal conflicts and controversies regarding strategy and tactics. Gush Emunim was divided over such issues as the participation of some of its members in Tehiya, which included non-religious Israelis. Moreover, there was no consensus among the members of the movement regarding the reaction to crucial issues like the withdrawal from the Sinai, the activities of the Underground, the behavior of the government institutions, and the attitude toward Arabs.[76]

Gush Emunim was successful as a protest movement during Labor rule, which prohibited settlement, but when the Likud gave it unqualified support, it lost its uniqueness. According to Sprinzak, clear signs of trouble in the ranks of Gush Emunim became apparent by the beginning of the 1990s. The fact that three of the movement's senior rabbis issued an unprecedented *Halachic* ruling, which allowed soldiers to disobey the government's orders to evacuate the settlements, was a radical departure from the Gush's unwavering support of the Zionist government of Israel and the IDF. The disillusionment that the members of the Gush experienced, from the 1992 election of Rabin to the Oslo agreement between Israel and the Palestinians, demoralized the movement and accelerated its decline. Until then, the practice of blessing the State of Israel during the Sabbath prayer was not only maintained by Gush Emunim, but also encouraged by it. Therefore, when several prominent Gush members who were disillusioned by the Israeli-Palestinian peace talks decided to eliminate the blessing, it became clear that a radical change within the movement had taken place. Moreover, some Gush members began adopting the attitude of the ultra-orthodox *Haredi* movement, which had long opposed the Zionist enterprise, preferring instead to live in Israel under ghetto-like conditions until the coming of the Messiah.[77] Realizing that Gush Emunim had lost much of its vitality as a result of the challenges posed by the peace process, its leaders began considering other alternatives. Porat announced his intention to resign from the Knesset and told reporters that he intended to establish a new version of Gush Emunim.[78]

CONCLUSION

This chapter discusses the origins of Gush Emunim and the circumstances that enabled it to become a powerful force in Israeli politics. Its main argument is that the responsibility for its rise lies predominantly on the shoulders of the Labor Party, whose politicians failed to agree on a concerted action aimed at curbing the movement's rise.

The fact that the rise of the Likud Party in 1977 accelerated the pace of settlement—building cannot be denied.[79] Yet, despite Begin's sympathy to Gush Emunim, his Likud Government was faced with a *fait accompli*, which constrained its freedom of action. There is little doubt that Begin would have been in a better position to decide the number and the location of Gush Emunim settlements had the Labor Government been able to resist the pressure of Gush Emunim in the early days of its existence. Moreover, the failure of the Labor Party to prevent the erosion of the Zionist pioneering ideology, which the founding fathers had labored so hard to promote, worked to Gush Emunim's advantage, and its leaders managed to exploit it to the fullest.

By the mid-1980s, there were signs that Gush Emunim was undergoing a process of radicalization, which constituted a threat to the Israeli democracy. This danger manifested itself in the willingness of the movement's leaders not only to accept the activities of the Underground, but also to provide funds for the defense of the perpetrators. Three factors contributed to this drastic change: the heavy sentences inflicted on the defendants; the increasing cases of terrorism against Jews during 1984 and early 1985, and the failed attempts to convince the government to take a firmer stand against Palestinian protesters. All these convinced the leaders of the movement to support the Underground.[80] At that juncture, Gush Emunim turned into a target of criticism by many Israelis, secular as well as religious. Ironically, the fact that Gush Emunim managed to expand the settlements in the West Bank worked to its disadvantage. While it succeeded in pressuring the government to yield to its demand to settle *Eretz Yisrael*, it did not seem capable of fashioning the agenda of an ordinary political party. The fact that its leaders preferred to operate as an extra-parliamentary group and to achieve its goals through other parties left it outside the parliamentary game.

Gush Emunim's decline was due to several factors. After the implementation of its settlement agenda it lost its appeal among its supporters. Moreover, dissension within its ranks intensified when its leaders could not agree on the means and the strategies on how to achieve the movement's goals. Moreover, they no longer operated under a common umbrella, and some of them joined other parties. And probably the most serious failure of Gush Emunim was that its leaders did not develop a coherent strategy toward the peace process, which gathered momentum during the 1990s. Realizing that Gush Emunim was no longer the force that it once had been, some of its leaders declared their intention to establish a new group with similar objectives.

It is difficult to predict what the future of Gush Emunim will be. However, the rise of a Labor-dominated government under Prime Minister Ehud Barak in the summer of 1999 was a clear sign that the group no longer maintained its erstwhile ascendancy. And if the peace process moves as quickly as Barak hopes, the prospects for the reemergence of Gush Emunim as a powerful force in Israeli politics are slim at best. Based on the negative impact, which Gush Emunim has had on the Middle East peace process, its transformation from a powerful pressure group into a marginal force in the Israeli society should be regarded as a positive development.

NOTES

1. Whether or not Gush Emunim could have succeeded in establishing a party with a well-defined ideology and objectives is open to speculation. There was one example in the history of the Jewish State where an extra-parliamentary group had attempted to take part in the legal system. This was the Fighters Party, which consisted of the previous Stern Group whose members were engaged in fighting the British authorities in Palestine until 1948. The Fighters Party promoted an odd platform, which combined both Marxist and nationalist elements. One of the reasons for the party's failure was that, as Joseph Heller put it, "the historical reality had quickly adjusted itself to the ideological and political needs of the Fighters Party." Joseph Heller, *Lehi, Ideology and Politics: 1940-1949* [Hebrew], vol. 11 (Jerusalem: Keter, 1989), p. 508. A very similar process occurred in Gush Emunim. After its success in settling *Eretz Yisrael* there was little that the movement could preach.

2. Dan Horowitz and Moshe Lissak, *Trouble in Utopia: The Overburdened Polity of Israel* [Hebrew] (Tel Aviv: Am Oved, 1990), p. 225.

3. Michael Bar Zohar, *Facing a Cruel Mirror* [Hebrew] (Tel Aviv: Yediot Aharonot, 1990), p. 80.

4. Kevin Avruch, "Gush Emunim: The 'Iceberg Model' of Extremism Reconsidered," *Middle East Review*, vol. XXI, no. 1 (Fall 1988), pp. 30-31.

5. Gush Emunim had most of the characteristics that Hava Lazarus Yafeh identified as common to fundamentalist movements. Among these are the tendency to cling to authentic tradition; the desire to establish a state in which the religious law will prevail; the willingness to accept and use modern arms and technology to further the movement's cause; the strong belief in the infallibility of the holy scriptures; the conviction of its members that they can understand the plans and deeds of God; the importance they attach to miracles as proofs of the religious truth; the expectation of radical changes in the near future; the tendency to adopt violent and revolutionary means to accelerate the redemption process; and the rejection of more moderate attitudes held by others. See Hava Lazarus-Yafeh, "Contemporary Fundamentalism—Judaism, Christianity, Islam," *The Jerusalem Quarterly*, no. 47 (Summer 1988), pp. 27-39. Gush Emunim subordinated the democratic system to the general Zionist goal. Democracy was accepted, but only if it existed within the Zionist system, and if there was collision between the two, Zionism took precedence. Ehud Sprinzak, "Gush Emunim: The Tip of the Iceberg," *The Jerusalem Quarterly*, no. 21 (Fall 1981), p. 39.

6. Horowitz and Lissak, *Trouble in Utopia*, p. 148.

7. See remarks by Moshe Levinger in the Jewish settlers' magazine *Nekuda* [Hebrew], no. 89 (1985), p. 7.

8. Aviezer Ravitzky, *Freedom Inscribed: Diverse Voices of the Jewish Religious Thought* [Hebrew] (Tel Aviv: Am Oved, 1999), p. 145.

9. Horowitz and Lissak, *Trouble in Utopia*, p. 288.

10. Dov Schwartz, *Religious Zionism between Logic and Messianism* [Hebrew] (Tel Aviv: Am Oved, 1999), p. 34 ff.

11. Gershon Shafat, *Gush Emunim: The Story Behind the Scenes* [Hebrew] (Jerusalem: Beit El, 1994), p. 20.

12. "Levinger: There Will Be Bloodshed in Struggle for Judea and Samaria," *Jerusalem Post* (December 12, 1985).

13. Ronald C. Kiener, "Gushist and Qutbian Approaches to Government: A Comparative Analysis of Religious Assassination," *Numen*, vol. XLIV, no. 3 (September 1997), p. 235.

14. Ehud Sprinzak, "The Genesis of Zionist Fundamentalism: The Case of Gush Emunim," *Orim*, vol. III (Autumn 1987), p. 22.

15. Shlomo Avineri, "Israel: Image and Reality," *The New Republic*, vol. 151 (September 26, 1964), p. 9.

16. Gershon Shafat, *Gush Emunim: The Story Behind the Scenes* [Hebrew] (Jerusalem: Beit El, 1994), p. 27.

17. Mark Segal, "Golem and Gush Emunim," *Jerusalem Post* (October 13, 1977).

18. Shaul Kantzler, *Leftism in Israel: Intelligentsia in a Tangle of Alienation* [Hebrew] (Tel Aviv: Ma'ariv, 1984), pp. 103-4.

19. Abba Eban, *An Autobiography* (New York: Random House, 1977), p. 587.

20. Amnon Rubinstein, *The Zionist Dream Revisited: From Herzl to Gush Emunim and Back* (New York: Schocken, 1984), p. 107.

21. Meron Medzini, *The Proud Jewess: Golda Meir and the Vision of Israel: A Political Biography* [Hebrew] (Jerusalem: Edanim, 1990), p. 403.

22. Cited in Eban, *An Autobiography*, p. 487.

23. Moshe Dayan, *Story of My Life* [Hebrew] (Jerusalem: Edanim, 1976), p. 491.

24. "Weizman Ready to Seize Land to Satisfy Gush Emunim Demand," *Jerusalem Post* (October 5, 1979).

25. "The Price of Blunders," *Jerusalem Post* (October 23, 1979).

26. "Rabin: Won't argue with Gush Emunim," *Jerusalem Post* (June 28, 1976).

27. Yitzhak Rabin with Dov Goldstein, *Service Diary* [Hebrew] (Tel Aviv: Ma'ariv, 1979), p. 486.

28. Ibid., p. 551.

29. "Allon: Gush Emunim Demagogues Harm Whole Jewish Settlement Effort," *Jerusalem Post* (June 13, 1976).

30. "Allon: Gush Dictates Foreign Policy," *Jerusalem Post* (June 6, 1979).

31. "Peres slams Gush," *Jerusalem Post* (August 31, 1976).

32. Shimon Peres, *Battling for Peace: A Memoir* (New York: Random House, 1995), pp. 148-49.

33. Abba Eban, *Personal Witness: Israel Through My Eyes* (New York: G. P. Putnam's Sons, 1992), pp. 462, 604.

34. Yonathan Shapiro, *An Elite Without Successors: Generations of Political Leaders in Israel* [Hebrew] (Tel Aviv: Sifriat Poalim, 1984), p. 153.

35. Yonathan Shapiro, *Chosen to Command: The Road to Power of the Herut Party— A Socio-Political Interpretation* [Hebrew] (Tel Aviv: Am Oved, 1989), p. 134.

36. Yochanan Bader, *The Knesset and I* [Hebrew] (Jerusalem: Edanim, 1979), p. 16.

37. "Begin Orders Gush Members Release," *Jerusalem Post* (March 14, 1979).

38. See M. Friedman, "Change in the National Religious Party—The Background to its Electoral Decline," *Medina, Mimshal VeYchasim Benleumiyim* [Hebrew], no. 19-20 (Spring 1982), pp. 115-20.

39. Bernard Avishai, *The Tragedy of Zionism: Revolution and Democracy in the Land of Israel* (New York: Farrar Strauss Giroux, 1985), p. 306.

40. Eric Silver, *Begin: The Haunted Prophet* (New York: Random House, 1984), pp. 160, 164, 245.

41. "Challenge for Mr. Begin," *Jerusalem Post* (September 25, 1977).

42. Joshua Brilliant, "Begin Warns Gush Emunim Against Settlement Bid," *Jerusalem Post* (September 26, 1977).

43. Sarah Honig, "Sharon to Remain in Government if Assured of Some Defense Role," *Jerusalem Post* (May 29, 1980).

44. Yosef Goell, "Gush Emunim Golem," *Jerusalem Post* (March 5, 1982).

45. "Sharon Wants to Help Gush Emunim," *Jerusalem Post* (November 10, 1977).

46. "Treasury Would Give Gush Emunim IL81m," *Jerusalem Post* (November 10, 1977).

47. "Placating Gush Emunim," *Jerusalem Post* (November 19, 1979).

48. "Begin Pledges More Settlements, but Says Gov't Will Set Timetable," *Jerusalem Post* (January 1, 1979).

49. Mark Segal, "Begin Musters Majority for Peace Accord," *Jerusalem Post* (September 24, 1978).

50. Aher Wallfish, "New Shamir-Cohen Party Will Fight Peace Policies,"*Jerusalem Post* (July 18, 1979).

51. Gabby Scheffer, "Kahane, Kahanism and Race," *Gesher* [Hebrew], vol. 114, no. 32 (Summer 1986), p. 68.

52. Ehud Sprinzak, *Every Man Whatsoever Is Right in His Own Eyes: Illegalism in Israeli Society* [Hebrew] (Tel Aviv: Sifriat Poalim, 1986), pp. 121-45.

53. Daniel Gavron, "In from the Cold," *Jerusalem Post* (March 25, 1983).

54. Moshe Kohn, "The Secular 'Gush' Speaks Its Mind," *Jerusalem Post* (August 1, 1976).

55. Harold Fisch, "Gush Emunim Claims What's Wrong with Emotionalism," *Jerusalem Post* (September 19, 1975).

56. Harold Fisch, *The Zionist Revolution: A New Perspective* (New York: St. Martin's Press, 1978), pp. 167-68.

57. "Putting Social Work into Local Hands," *Jerusalem Post* (March 11, 1976).

58. Charles Hoffman, "The Golem of the Gush," *Jerusalem Post* (May 4, 1984).

59. "Religious Group to Urge Political Moderation," *Jerusalem Post* (October 20, 1975).

60. Zvi Yaron, "Gush Emunim Undermining Religious Morality," *Jerusalem Post* (September 14, 1975).

61. Moshe Kohn, "Orthodox Opponents of Gush Emunim," *Jerusalem Post* (August 3, 1976).

62. Moshe Kohn, "Ideological Gangsterism," *Jerusalem Post* (November 9, 1976); "A small soft voice," *Jerusalem Post* (November 18, 1977).

63. Judy Siegel, "Reform Leader Says Gush Emunim Has 'Abused Jewish Tradition,'" *Jerusalem Post* (November 8, 1976).

64. Daniel Gavron, "The Path-Finders," *Jerusalem Post* (December 31, 1982).

65. "Gush Emunim Is Dangerous," *Jerusalem Post* (May 25, 1976).

66. Yagal Elam, "Gush Emunim: A False Messianism," *The Jewish Quarterly*, no. 1 (Fall 1976), pp. 60-61.

67. Rubinstein, *The Zionist Dream Revisited*, pp. 104-5.

68. Itzhak Galnoor, "The Failure of Religious Zionism," *The Jerusalem Quarterly*, no. 41 (1986), p. 70.

69. Danny Rubinstein, *On the Lord Side: Gush Emunim* [Hebrew] (Tel Aviv: Hakibbutz Hameuchad, 1982), p. 178.

70. "Gush Emunim Run Cabinet," *Jerusalem Post* (January 16, 1980).

71. Mark Segal, "Appeal to the Irrational," *Jerusalem Post* (March 12, 1982).

72. David Newman and Tamar Hermann, "A Comparative Study of Gush Emunim and Peace Now," *Middle Eastern Studies*, vol. 28, no. 3 (July 1992), pp. 509-30.

73. Joel Greenberg, "Gush Says Shamir Is Jordanizing," *Jerusalem Post* (January 22, 1987).

74. Samuel Peleg, "They Shoot Prime Ministers Too, Don't They? Religious Violence in Israel: Premises, Dynamics, and Prospects," *Studies in Conflict Terrorism*, vol. 20, no. 3 (1997), pp. 228-29, 242, 243, 245.

75. David Singer, "Rav Kook's Contested Legacy," *Tradition*, vol. 30, no. 3 (Spring 1996), p. 19.

76. Eliezer Don-Yehiya, "Jewish Messianism, Religious Zionism and Israeli Politics: The Impact and Origins of Gush Emunim," *Middle Eastern Studies*, vol. 23 (April 1987), pp. 216-17.

77. Ehud Sprinzak, "When Prophesy Fails: The Crisis of Religious Fundamentalism in Israel," *Contention*, vol. 4, no. 2 (Winter 1995), p. 116.

78. Nina Gilbert, "Tekuma Weighs Porat Resignation," *Jerusalem Post* (May 23, 1999).

79. Between 1967 and 1977 the annual average of settlers was 300. During 1977-82, the first five years of Likud rule, it increased to 4,400. Giora Goldberg and Efraim Ben-Zadok, "Gush Emunim in the West Bank," *Middle Eastern Studies*, vol. 22, no. 1 (January 1986), p. 53.

80. Rafael Medoff, "Gush Emunim and the Question of Counterterror," *Middle East Review*, vol. XVII, no. 4 (Summer 1986), p. 22.

Chapter 4

Swadeshi Economics: Toward a Critical Assessment of Hindu Revivalist Economics in India

Santosh C. Saha

Discourse on economic liberalization monopolized economic discussion in India from the early 1990s. The standard line of opposition to liberalization, advanced by a stoic Left as well as by old-style and newer Hindu religious revivalists[1] (also known as the Hindu Right), was known as *swadeshi* (supporting Indian-made goods) economic nationalism, which invoked the fear of losing national economic sovereignty.[2] This nostalgic yearning for an autarkic purity was sadly diversionary. The real issue lay elsewhere: how to set an effective strategy for sustained economic growth and the reduction of poverty. The Indian historian Sunil Khilani has correctly suggested that this ambition for a self-producing community was strongly moralizing, but at the same time it dispensed entirely with the idea of a territorial nation-state.[3] In calling for *swadeshi*, religious revivalists unduly reduced the issue of national identity to a misinterpreted set of cultural norms. They tried to create something impossible: a new synthesis between religion and the secular state.

With this background, I would like to examine the following interconnected themes related to revivalist economic policies: (a) *general economic goals*, (b) *the rural-urban divide*, (c) *small-scale versus large-scale industries*, and (d) *foreign capital and firms*. It will be argued that while Hindu revivalists gave much attention to inequalities of income, and called for efficient allocation of resources through the decentralization and the "Indianization" of the means of production, their ability to adapt to new circumstances of a complex world remained inadequate. The Hindu revivalists unduly considered trust, confidence, and cooperation as economic capital. The Hindu Mahasabha theorist Nitya Narayan Banerjee claimed that "emotion and not economics is the real integrating force in the human society."[4] We need not agree with Professor John P. Powelson who argues that there is something inherently wrong with the poorer nations' social norms and economic culture,[5] and yet it may be argued that the fervor of *swadeshi* economic nationalism, based on what the noted historian Romila Thapar called "imagined" ancient culture, should not be an appropriate guide to economic success. Of Talcott Parsons's two factors—the "material" (economic) and the "ideal" (cultural)—the economic factor appears to be more relevant to growth because religions emphasize only "eternity, identity, and continuity."[6]

Revivalists' economic philosophy and strategies have been defined as a combination of anti-utilitarian values (no separation of economics from ethical considerations), market economics, nationalism, and populism. Some have called this economic order neo-Gandhian, that is, a decentralized small-scale production system that was believed to be preferable to the large-scale mechanized industrial system of production.[7] Two friendly Indian critics of the nationalist Bharatiya Janata Party (Indian People's Party—BJP), which started as a northern and urban oriented party of *Banias* (traders) and Brahmins, have characterized the Hindu Party's economic order as conservative in which the fast expanding small-scale or medium-size industrial sector was dominated by a dynamic class of entrepreneurs who preferred conservative and free enterprise oriented policies.[8] In the same vein, but with a superior analysis, the Danish historian Thomas Blom Hansen has justifiably described the BJP-RSS's (Rashtriya Swayamsevak Sangh) economic policy as corporatist and conservative. The policy favored small and middle-sized interests in trade and industry, which for decades had provided political support to Hindu parties in northern India.[9] There are hardly any systematic studies[10] about the nature of *swadeshi* economic policies. The newly mobilizing traditional dimension of the Indian economy and its accompanying political ideologies and religious movements involve the great majority of Indians, and as such, the newfound self-sufficiency of these economic principles deserves critical scrutiny.

GENERAL ECONOMIC GOALS

Religious revivalists have been gaining respectability in secular India since the 1980s. The number of registered Hindu religious buildings in Delhi, many of which illegally encroached on public land, rose from 560 to 2,000 during the years 1980 to 1987 to make "political uses of spirituality."[11] One out of two college graduates voted for the BJP in 1997; it was thought to be a sign of Hindu "modernity."[12] Even in the communist party (CPM) dominated state of Kerala, these groups and sub-groups spread their ideas to nearly all the 5,000 villages and set up RSS *shakhas* (branches) by 1986. Diverse communities such as the Nairs, Ezhaavas, and Namboodiris united on a single platform to fight for what they called the "Hindu cause." The growing popularity of all-night *jagarans* (awareness) and *yatras* (massive revivalist processions) kept alive the spirit of solidarity.[13]

Major revivalist parties included the Hindu Mahasabha (Hindu Great Council), the Jana Sangh (JS), the Vishwa Hindu Parishad (VHP), the Rastriya Swayamsevak Sangh (RSS), the BJP, the Virat Hindu Samaj, the Vishal Hindu Sammelan, the Hindu Samajotsav, sections of the Janata Party, the Bajrang Dal, the Arya Vir Dal, and above all the Swadeshi Jagaran Manch (SJM). Compositions of these Hindu parties were varied. Whereas the Rama Rajya Parishad (RRP) capitalized on the residual appeal of local notables and hereditary aristocrats in Rajasthan and Madhya Pradesh, the VHP's leading members included retired bureaucrats, former director-generals of police, and former chief judges.[14] The Shiv Sena, which had started as a nativist party claiming priority in jobs for Marathi-speakers, swung to the Hindu cause with a "Hindu united front." Other scholars have argued that Hindu socioreligious groups used Hindu nationalism as a hegemonizing ideology to replace Nehruvian socialism.[15]

Despite many differences among the revivalists, there were several general economic objectives. First, despite differences among them, most revivalists aimed at the restoration of a "perfect" but undefined national economic model. In this model, the Brahmanical "Great Tradition" (scripture-based), rather than "village Hinduism" (local spirits and festivals), was supposed to have more relevance. "Hindu economics is governed by the guidelines in Vedic books."[16] The RSS ideologue Dattopant Bapurao Thengadi an influential Maharastrian Brahmin organizer of the RSS and founder of the Hindu trade union movement Bharatiya Mazdoor Sangh (BMS), argued that the roots of India's economic problems were largely religious, and as such "the remedy must also be essentially religious."[17] In line with this ideal, the RRP, which was founded in 1948, wished to return to Rama kingdom and asked for the barter system, a ban on cow slaughter, and the introduction of the traditional Ayurvedic system of medicine.[18] Pandit Deendayal Upadhyaya, an architect of Jana Sangh's economic principles, argued in his "Integral Humanism" (1965) that in the West demand followed production while in ancient India production followed demand. Therefore, Western economic systems were incapable of grasping India's ailment in its entirety because the Western system did not consider the tiny organism as an integral part of the larger whole.[19] Shiva Chandra Jha, an interpreter of "Hindu economic thought" and a revivalist theorist, submitted that the mode of production of the Vedic Aryan society was based on the *Gana-Gotra* (gentile organization) communes which eventually got split into *varnas* (caste-based work). Here "wealth and property" belonged to the whole society.[20]

Second, economic nationalists would not accept the idea of much direct foreign investment or large-scale importation of foreign goods. In June 1995, Hindu economic nationalists organized a campaign to scrap a high profile U.S. government backed project in Maharastra, despite warnings of potential damage to foreign investors' confidence in India. Both the BJP and the militant Shiv Sena wanted to abandon not only the $2.8 billion deal with the Americans but also all fast-track power projects that foreign investors had proposed.[21] The campaign was a reaction against the possibility of sociopsychological dislocation of peasants from rural to urban areas.[22] Of course, there were differences in attitudes. Whereas the militant Swadeshi Jagaran Manch, established in 1993 as a forum of the RSS, urged Indians to consume local products only, the BJP president Lal Krishan Advani, currently home minister at the center, declared in 1993 that *swadeshi* "does not mean an exclusive use of goods" produced only in India.[23] Nevertheless, in general Hindu economic nationalists expected less contact with the global economy.

Third, most revivalists agreed that the central wealth-creating activities in the Hindu model would be neither the allocation of capital to productive uses nor machines, but labor.[24] The massive supply of unskilled labor (unemployed) in rural areas was thought to be inimical to overall progress. Thus in the 1980s the Hindu journal *Mazdur-Kisan-Niti* (Labor-Peasant Principles) theorized the split (peasant versus urban worker) described by Sharad Joshi, a social activist, between Bharat (Hindu India) and India as one between "Westernized" (*paschimkrut*) and "boycotted" (*bashishkrut*) India. Modern technology, which requires less labor, was believed to be against the "traditional" values of the village system, where there had prevailed a "socialist, decentralized, and people-oriented economy," as explained by socialist H. K. Paranjpe.[25]

Fourth, in invoking *swadeshi, swablamban, swabhivan* (indigenous production, economic self-reliance, and national self-respect), revivalists did not look for excessive capital formation and an abundance of consumer goods. A prominent Hindu Mahasabha leader in Bengal claimed that the mechanical production of goods had added "to the mundane pleasure at the cost of mental peace." The BJP called the pre-industrial Hindu model a "higher alternative."[26] The Swadeshi Jagaran Manch was vocal in its defense of *swadeshi*. A brainchild of the former RSS chief, Balasaheb Deoras, the SJM, which was founded in 1993, was conceived as a protectionist bulwark against economic liberalization by the Congress government of P. V. Narasimha Rao in 1991. It called on the BJP government in 1998 to repeal the ban order on the "manufacture of non-iodized salt," believed to be a Western luxury item.[27] With unemployed elements in cities and towns as well as social dropouts, the Virat Hindu Samaj and Vishal Hindu Sammelan, as well as the Bajrang Dal, patronized by the *sadhus*, (saints) wanted an economic order that would require the minimum use of consumer goods. After the Jana Sangh dissolved itself in 1977 to merge with other parties into a national front, the Janata Party reaffirmed the older call for "decentralized economic order" to limit the "craving for luxuries."[28] Even the Bharatiya Mazdoor Sangh (BMS), the second largest labor federation in India, looked for spirituality and not materialism.[29]

Fifth, revivalists thought of a new development alternative. They challenged both socialism and capitalism because they were foreign. In the 1950s and 1960s, in order to attract Hindu votes in the wake of communal riots in East Bengal and the Punjab, the Jana Sangh attacked the Nehruvian "socialistic pattern of the economy" with strong centralization, in religious tones. The party bemoaned the loss of ancient "values" and the absence of Hindu work culture.[30] The Ram Rajya Parishad, led by Swami Karapatri, offered the model as a largely rural economy based on the traditional *jajmani* system (feudalistic relationship with hereditary obligations between families of different castes in the same locality) with prohibition of alcohol and of cow slaughter. In this *Rama Rajya* (Rama's kingdom), powerful positions in sanitation departments should be given to untouchables, "because this is in keeping with their traditional calling as sweepers."[31] It was no wonder that the RRP's obscurantists managed to gain some support in India's most "backward areas" in Madhya Pradesh and Rajasthan.

Sixth, many revivalists favored, in the mold of social democratic philosophy, strong state intervention in the economy in the name of distributive justice. An egalitarian distribution of income had obvious ethical appeal, especially in the context of abject poverty in the country. A Hindu Mahasabha leader argued that the state should not play the role "of the trading community" but must "supervise trading operation and control the cost and quality of various commodities."[32] The Ganatantra Parishad, which had support among the socially and economically backward tribal people in Orissa, argued that large-scale industries controlled by "private hands" should be nationalized for "public benefit." The party went so far as to advocate "a ceiling on agricultural incomes." The state role was highly recommended.[33] Revivalists asked for state intervention in the economy not only on grounds of equity but also of the need to achieve Hindu social goals, which, as they claimed, were not delivered by the market mechanism. As Deendayal Upadhyaya argued, if *pranayam* (exercise) was useful for a healthy body, *arthayam* (economic control) was necessary for the regulation of the national economy and the maintenance of virtues.[34]

These Hindu economic virtues could be maintained, it was argued, by state coercion, regulations, licensing, forced savings, and compulsory procurement. No doubt, earlier manifestos and resolutions of the Jana Sangh were anti-socialist and liberal. During the late 1960s, the party envisaged state regulation of the economy. When fourteen banks were nationalized, the party did not oppose the policy, but simply proposed a more flexible method of public control under an autonomous monetary authority.[35] In defense of this stance, the ancient *Arthashastra* text was cited. Kautilya "wanted to control or regulate every aspect of life in every minute." There were government superintendents of even pasturelands of the city.[36] The Jana Sangh urged that even "ownership of property [should] be regulated."[37] Madhav Sadashiv Golwalkar, regarded since 1931 as a *guru* (leader) within the RSS, argued that even enterprise "with properly apportioned interest in the profits" should be under close supervision of the government to check the "non-virtuous mentality of self-aggrandizement." It was presumed that the state was capable of investigating the behavior, conduct, and misconduct of public officials.[38] In its National Charter of Directives, the Hindu trade union movement (the BMS) favored privatization and individual ownership of industries over state ownership, but the charter gave the state an important role to play as "the guide, superior arbiter, and controller of industrial life." All economic "relationships" had to be regulated by the government.[39]

The Jana Sangh argued that the state could foster a private-enterprise industrial economy provided that it was prepared to intervene to protect the weak from the strong. But there were ambiguities. The party suggested that the planning would be done by a cabinet subcommittee, but failed to explain how Gandhian socialism with decentralization would fit into the scheme.[40] Subramanian Swamy, a Western-educated Hindu economic nationalist, argued that the government should have the right to "correct market malfunction . . . and act as an umpire in the interaction between consumers and producers in the market place." He added that large industries should not be, in the name of privatization, handed over to the capitalists for private profits.[41] On the other hand, N. N. Banerjee, a top Hindu Mahasabha leader, had earlier defended the party's economic platform, which supported decreased state controls over the private economic sector.[42]

In 1971, the Jana Sangh stipulated that the state should "run" industries and businesses for profit. The unwillingness of the party to adopt a more *laissez-faire* economic program in this period was most apparent in its reluctance to form a pre-electoral coalition with the economically conservative Swatantra party. The Jana Sangh supported an interventionist economic policy during the early 1980s. It was only in 1991 that the party repositioned itself as a fierce critic of state intervention in the economy.[43]

Variations

An interventionist state was not favored by Thengadi who opposed the "managerial state" of the Russian variety[44] because doctrinal socialism was more disturbing for *Hindutva* (Hindu-ness) than the ideology of Islam. Mahatma Gandhi often rejected the state outright in any form because the state could not carry with it the moral value of an individual's action. The authority of the state rested on violence.[45] To Gandhi, the natural arrangement of the economy, based on family units and small-scale industries, was optimal and harmonious. Yet, he argued that the government must be held responsible, as a "matter of fact," for the economic ills of the society.[46] Vinoba Bhave, who had roots in the idealistic tradition of the *Vedanta* (Hindu Book of Knowledge), consistently denounced the state as destructive of "individual initiative." Thus, Bhave's *sarvodaya* (anarchism)[47] may be described as anti-statism. His "Constructive Programme" wished to substitute people's power for state power.[48] The Jana Sangh theoretician Balraj Madhok's *Jan-kalyan-vad* (idea of welfare for all) also opposed state control because too much control led to inefficiency, corruption, and high production costs. He called for an embargo on further nationalization and for the decentralization of economic power. This approach approximated a Gandhian rather than a Marxist path.[49]

In the 1980s and early 1990s, the BJP forged a coalition with Hindu religious groups and the middle classes. To appease these classes, the party looked for more 'laissez-faire' economic interests. During the election campaigns in 1996, the BJP campaigned for a liberalizing market economy. In this way, the party's economic policy captured the political and economic right of the political spectrum.[50] Indeed, the BJP's position on the state role was not reducible to its religious combination of *Hindu Rastra* (Hindu State) with a strong central government.[51] Thus, the party's conservative section called for the *panchayats* (village councils) to be "financially self-sufficient." Here economic decentralization was the goal. In this respect, the BJP was not any different from its parent body, the Jana Sangh.[52] The Bharatiya Mazdoor Sangh also argued that the state should assume a moral duty to prescribe working conditions, not industrial laws, for workers.[53] The Shiv Sena-BJP government in Maharastra, which had toppled the Congress government in 1995 on the American Enron electricity contract controversy, argued for detailed regulations of most areas from education to quotas of cotton and sugar released for export.[54] The party argued that government regulations must be backed by greater allocations of resources to agriculture. Thus a demand was made by the BJP for the allocation of 70 percent of the central development fund for agriculture.[55] This suggestion was based on the debatable concept that agricultural performance would exert an influence on industrial activity and thus would be a determinant to the performance of the economy overall.[56]

Assessment

Several aspects of the revivalists' general economic goals are open to criticism. First, it was unjustifiably assumed that there was a clear and ideal "Hindu economic order." Scholars have noted that the later Vedic agricultural society had "indications of the beginnings of unequal distribution of the produce of land." Social inequality was thus ritualized.[57] In fact, the "Little Tradition" (village order, local godlings) was more directly relevant to economic development than the value system of the "Great Tradition" upheld by religious revivalists. Second, when traditional "culture" was dematerialized, economic growth became the primary victim. The economic aspect of Hindu culture was ignored. Third, in the proposed Hindu model there would be virtual economic control by the middle class of the urban areas and the middle strata of the rural areas. In "sub-altern" terms, the imagined Hindu economic order was nothing but "tradition-in-use" (caste-based order) of the Hindu middle classes. Fourth, the proposed order was not innovative because the revivalists renewed the pre-independence nationalist slogan for government control of finances and industries, and for governmental involvement in the organized sector of the economy.[58] No other developing country had such an array of public controls over the private industrial sector. Of the industrial economy (10 percent of the national economy), the government controlled two-thirds,[59] and yet mass poverty persisted. Thus, the economist Jagdish Bhagwati legitimately argued that "the rise of nonsecular groups was partly to blame for the lack of economic reforms" which aimed at lesser bureaucratic interventions.[60]

Fifth, self-imposed poverty had never been the goal of the Hindu majority. In his *Artha-sastra*, the great Hindu political theorist Kautilya (fourth century B.C.) declared, "material well being is the first objective in the achievement of the other two—dharma and karma (virtue and action)—[and] is dependent on the material well-being in life."[61] The *Rig Veda* is full of prayers for long life, wealth, power, abundance of food and drink."[62] In the scriptural value system, *Artha* (wealth and power) represents one of the four major ends of life.[63] The great epic *Mahabharata* clearly declares that "he that has no wealth has neither this world nor the next."[64] Swami Vivekananda, the distinguished interpreter of Hinduism, remarked that it would be impossible "for hungry men to become spiritual, unless food is provided for them."[65] *Lakshmi* (goddess of wealth) is worshipped at least once a week. Material development and prosperity had thus been acceptable features of the Hindu economic process. Last, policy differences in economic matters revealed that the economic policies proved to be the weakest point in their strategy toward political success.

RURAL-URBAN DIVIDE

Revivalists believed that there had always been a Bharat-India divide, where Bharat (the Hindu term for India) notionally identified the oppressed rural majority, and India (the English name for India) represented the dominant urban minority. Most revivalists assumed that the survival of traditional culture was more nearly entire in villages than in towns, which had absorbed Western economic habits and social norms. In the "Bharat-India" divide, there was a gradation of demands among the peasants, which ranged from full independence to regional autonomy. There was also a very thin line between these village demands and the farmers' movements, which was based on a peasantry perceived as a distinct community (similar to the Naxalite concept of self-contained peasant community).[66] Based on this widely held misconception that peasants were isolated groups, revivalists asked for reformist economic programs to pressure the government for higher agricultural prices, loan waivers, and a better urban-rural balance in India's resource allocations.[67] They complained that 80 percent of the total outlays in social services was concentrated in urban areas.[68] The BJP argued that "over the years thousands of crores [millions] of rupees from the rural poor have been transferred" to the urban rich, resulting in "a colossal rural indebtedness."[69]

Revivalists defended the village order on several grounds. First, they contended that Indian economic factors were radically different from those in the rest of the world. Balraj Madhok, who came from an Arya Samajist family in Jammu and Kashmir, and became a Jana Sangh member of parliament, argued that India had a shortage of land and capital and an oversupply of manpower, an excess that could be absorbed by "traditional agriculture." Although land was inadequate, some concluded that the land-based economy would generate extra resources for the growth of heavy industry.[70] A Jana Sangh manifesto boasted that village-based small-scale projects would have an economic "immediate pay-off," not only for villagers, but also for city dwellers.[71]

Second, the simplicity of the village life was believed to be an economic asset. Mahatma Gandhi had frequently argued that the acquisitive spirit in modern town-based industries had already alienated man from man as well as from his products. He envisioned a peaceful life of the quaint village, where citizens meditated, spun their own thread, and churned butter in the backyard.[72] To arrive at that ideal stage of what the historian Sahasrasbudhey calls Gandhian "anti-developmentalism,"[73] Pandit Deendayal Upadhyaya, arguing through the daily newspaper *Swadeshi*, complained that huge modern projects and Western-style large-scale irrigation dams did not result in the proper utilization of water over wide areas, but created waterlogged soil. Large projects in urban areas generated only one man-day employment directly and three man-days indirectly.[74] In 1995, the Shiv Sena-BJP coalition government in Maharastra deemphasized modern industrialism. In reality, the Sena-BJP coalition stood for a "brutal and philistine" suburban petty-bourgeois vision of modernity. Bombay slum dwellers were ruthlessly cleared out.[75]

Third, revivalists declared that non-rural features, such as industrialization and urbanization, were against the ancient Hindu order. K. C. Sudarshan, a joint secretary of the RSS, reflected that the "urban orientation" of planned projects that imported "job-killing" technologies did not offer benefits to rural dwellers.[76] The Akhil Bharat Grahak Panchayat (ABGP), a farmer movement supported by the RSS, complained that Western-style industrialization/urbanization had caused pollution of the soil, water, and atmosphere, and destroyed the spirit of "self-restraint" as found in "Hindu philosophy."[77] As distributists and agrarians, they sought to reverse the trend toward large-scale industrialization, mass merchandising, and farm dispossession, which, revivalists argued, were transforming a population of property-owning small manufacturers, merchants, and farmers into servile white-collar employees and proletarians. Thus with distaste for the socialistic economy and the Soviet-style "metropolitan cities," B. D. Thengadi, the RSS ideologue, argued in 1955 that communism, being India's "number one" enemy, would bring disintegration in the "family, village, and communal life."[78] He conceived of developing medium size towns. According to this scheme, industries would be dispersed from the urban to the rural areas. Here "intermediate" technology (low cost technology) would be introduced. Automative gadgets and labor saving devices would purposely be avoided.[79] Like a cultural behaviorist, Thengadi further argued that India needed a "technology of human behaviour" instead of existing technology, which was "econocentric": that is, its aim was economic gain.[80] New technology's consumerism had failed to "avoid man's lust,"[81] and thus a moderate leader such as Atal Behari Vajpayee, a former Jana Sangh leader and great public speaker, argued that the process of urbanization would only give rise to "elitist consumerism,"[82] which would disturb the desired social equilibrium.[83] The BJP manifesto declared, "We reject unbridled consumerism and believe in adherence to sustainable consumption and growth."[84] In theorizing consumerism as an aspect of social and environmental destruction, revivalists showed a tendency to idealize subsistence-oriented tribal peoples in contrast to the cash crop oriented "caste" (higher class) Hindu peasants, presenting only the former as the victim of development.[85]

Revivalist Specifics

Revivalists offered several specific measures to improve the rural economy. First, Professor Thakurdas Bang, a Gandhian economist, noted that the vertical structure in monopoly capitalism could be transformed into a horizontal structure by the dispersal of economic enterprises. In this new order, the size of technological sector would remain smaller.[86] To prevent urbanization, the Hindu ideologue K. N. Govindachariya, a respected RSS *pracharak* (activist), proposed a "new *swadeshi*" village order, an order, that lay between orthodox Gandhianism (agriculture-based rural economy) and the notion contained within Rajiv Gandhi's *panchayat raj* (modern and managed rural sector). In the "new *swadeshi*" order, villagers would be managers as well as producers.[87]

Second, since rural public investment had been on the decline,[88] more emphasis was laid on agriculture, which was to be "laborized" by forming village-based cooperatives. According to G. S. Gokhale, the Bharatiya Mazdoor Sangh's theorist, new, mostly small cooperatives would reduce the rural conflict and give both the landless and the tenant a greater stake in rural society.[89] On the initiative of *swayamsevaks* (volunteers), individual groups of twenty-five families were formed in several extensions of Pune city to organize localized cooperatives for the collection and distribution of commodities. Two hundred Grahak Sanghs (buyers' cooperatives) were registered to centralize the demand for the entire area and to establish a direct link between producers and consumers, thereby eliminating the middleman. The organizers claimed that the Grahak Sanghs helped the families to save as much as 20 percent of the cost of production.[90] On the other hand, to woo the intermediate landholders whose support was vital for electoral successes in the 1960s, the Jana Sangh opposed cooperatives. The party urged the government to prevent economic conglomeration so that family enterprises, not large organized cooperatives, could flourish. On the other hand, the Ganatrantra Party claimed that theirs was a Burkean conservative and centrist party, which called for "co-management and profit-sharing" by management and labor both in agricultural and industrial sectors.[91]

Third, the Jana Sangh party promised individual land ownership, thus giving priority to small landholders who would be given land ownership rights.[92] Balraj Madhok asked, "Why should any man invest in agriculture if he knows that he will have to hold 25 acres of land only?" Deendayal Upadhyaya also argued against "the imposition of land ceilings."[93] Whereas the Jana Sangh called for individual ownership of land in order to enhance political support from small farmers in the Northern Hindi belt, Vinoba Bhave's *Bhoodan-Gramdan* movement in the 1950s and 1960s imagined the creation of Gandhian villages where land would be owned collectively, not individually.[94]

Fourth, revivalists advanced the hypothesis that enhanced agricultural commodity prices would not only improve the home market and stimulate economic development, but it would also reduce rural poverty. In simplistic terms, revivalists calculated that if the farmers were enriched, the non-farming community in the rural areas would then benefit through the "rural economic links."[95] The Janata Party's "new village movement" demanded better terms of trade between "agriculture/rural goods" and industrial products. During the 1980s, the BJP demanded remunerative prices, which peasant movements effectively had claimed in many parts of India.[96] To make farmers "managers of all operations," K. N. Govindacharya, an acknowledged BJP ideologue, argued that farmers' economic status would be strengthened if the fertilizer subsidy were given directly to individual farmers, not through manufacturers or producers of fertilizers.[97] The BJP promised to build new government warehouses and cold storage facilities in rural areas to empower farmers. The party supported the establishment of agro-technical networks by introducing science-based technology to small-scale industries. But it did not spell out who would pay for them.[98]

Fifth, revivalists encouraged indigenous rural projects and practices. The Deendayal Research Institute opened up an "all-round development project" in Gonda district in Uttar Pradesh. For irrigation, villagers used bamboo instead of metal pipes for the tube well. Seeds were treated in cow's urine, which added "a few fertilizers." Sowing of seeds thus processed, organizers claimed, resulted in an increase in the wheat yield of 20 to 25 percent. This method, the Hindu workers calculated, decreased fertilizer consumption by 50 percent with no need of "harmful pesticides." The project organizers calculated that operational costs were also low.[99] Likewise, the RSS *swayamsevaks* (volunteers) introduced "self-irrigation systems" in the state of Karnatak to avoid the building of Western-styled major irrigation projects. The South Kanara Agricultural Development Society persuaded the farmers to use small farm machines such as power-tillers, paddy hullers, irrigation pump sets, and sprinklers.[100]

Sixth, revivalists implemented measures to restore the old economic order. The Shiv Sena's officials organized job training for small enterprises and offered private business loans in Maharastra. One objective was to avoid industrial slums. This rural reconstruction was believed to be in line with the "Maharastrian model," which was based on the nineteenth-century model of the Shivaji myth and was clearly opposed to the Gandhian rural model.[101]

Likewise, banks were organized and managed by economic nationalists. To eliminate exploiting middlemen and to strengthen the position of farmers, the RSS set up several banking institutions. Organized by *swayamsevaks* in 1955, the Janata Sahakari Bank (JSB) in Pune, claimed to be the fifth largest in Asia, serving the needs of thousands of persons from low-income groups and small industrial units.[102] Babulal Mehere, a Brahmin associated with the RSS and a founder of the

Hindu trade union (BMS) in Ujjain in Madhya Pradesh, earned deep appreciation by setting up a workers' cooperative bank in 1955. This pioneer institution attracted savings from textile workers. The bank offered loans at low interest. This scheme helped Mehere get elected as Member of the Legislative Assembly (MLA) even though he had won no elected post before. This "Sangathanist method" (voluntary social work in teams) was a welfare tactic designed to win support among industrial workers.[103] A *swayamsevak* of Rahuri in the Ahmednagar district in Maharastra founded the Rahuri Sahakari Sakhar Karkhana (factory) to help peasants in such areas as housing and cooperative marketing. In Uttar Pradesh, the VHP-RSS-BJP combination highlighted various rural symbols that reinforced the notion of a Hindu community of producers, thus giving an impression that the new order was rural-not-urban and Hindu-not-Muslim.[104]

Assessment

The proposed revivalist village order suffered from several deficiencies. It appears that revivalists were politically motivated, with the explicit aim of gaining electoral success. Several authorities argued that most parties were politically indebted to the farmers, and as such powerless to ignore farmers' economic demands. "To resist rural demands is more difficult."[105]

Moreover, no farmers' movements in recent years desired to return to an idyllic and poor village republic. The economist S. Kuznets rightly argued that the economic growth of a firm, an industry, or a region meant the sustained increase for all areas for a long period.[106] The goal of meeting social justice by distribution of land ownership or cooperative farming should be made compatible with the long-term necessity of meeting the challenges of growing urbanization and the efficient functioning of highways linking rural with urban areas.

Agronomists and political economists have disagreed as to the viability of small individual holdings. In 1974, small farmers annually ran a per capita loss of Rs. 125 in the Punjab whereas farmers with between five and ten acres of land produced a per capita profit of Rs. 50, and farmers with more than twenty acres of land produced a per capita profit of Rs. 1,200.[107] The economist Pranab K. Bardhan has argued that modern rice and wheat varieties require more intensive farming, which could be best performed by permanent labor.[108] Given the size of the landholding and uncertain weather in India, agriculture could, at most, provide gainful employment for only half of the year.

SMALL-SCALE VERSUS LARGE-SCALE INDUSTRIES

In seeking to emphasize small-scale industry in order to revitalize the Hindu economic order, most revivalists emphasized saving rather than spending, and reconstruction and preservation rather than excessive production. They advanced various arguments to this end.

One such argument, put forward by Deendayal Upadhyaya, was that small-scale industries "are dying under the weight of this monopoly structure" of foreign industries. Vaguely believing that Western processes and technologies would greatly damage "our national spirit of science and research," Upadhyaya argued that Western-style "comprehensive industrialization" with its "international economies" would never promote locally available resources.[109]

Along this line of thinking, revivalists calculated that Western-style heavy industries did not help social development. Revivalists argued that they needed two sets of *khadi* clothing (one to wash, one to wear), a mud hut, two square meals, a glass of goat milk and thou (fermented milk) for existence and development.[110] During the 1950s and 1960s, Jana Sangh leaders propagated the idea, through the party news organ *Organiser*, that both the acquisition and the consumption of machine-made manufactured commodities were contrary to the non-materialist spirit of the ancient Hindu philosophy of life.[111] Some members of Jana Sangh, however, realized that while *ambar chakra* (hand-operated spinning unit) was useful, the government should avoid "fads" (obsession) for *ambar chakra* and *palm-gur* (local brown sugar).[112] In fact, Deendayal Upadhyaya gradually moved away from the party's earlier support for cottage industries. Referring to the Second Five Year Plan's (late 1950s) allocation, he argued that the government's subsidy should not "perpetuate some degree of disguised unemployment or under-employment in those industries" (village and cottage industries). Although he did not favor heavy industrial machineries, he pleaded that handlooms be converted into power-looms. Yet the Jana Sangh party's program clearly stated that "decentralisation, *swadeshi* and labour intensity should be the criteria for our industrial development."[113]

In its election manifesto in 1967, the Jana Sangh party asked for labor-intensive industries. While in power in Delhi, the party used propaganda to promote subsidies for the use of *ambar charkas*, *khadi* (rough clothes), and spinning to encourage small-scale producers.[114] It urged that most manufacturing should be done in the cottage sector, and heavy and large-scale industry should be given less preference.[115] It was further argued that there were 36,460 units of small factories in 1960 that held 17.5 percent of the fixed capital of all registered factories in India.[116] The BJP argued that indigenous industries could generate more employment through small-scale industries.[117] L. K. Advani of the BJP argued that foreign technology "is generally associated with capital intensive production and therefore does not provide sufficient employment."[118] Implicit in this scheme was the assumption that small factories were more appropriate and certainly in line with ideals of ancient Hindu society, for in them labor-intensive work was generally peaceful and happy. Interestingly, in representing itself as the champion of small and decentralized industries, both the BJP and the Jana Sangh adopted the language of state planning as enunciated by the Congress Party.[119]

Most important, cultural arguments were advanced in speaking against heavy industries. By the end of the 1980s, the RSS achieved social respectability. It reinforced the idea of Madhav Sadashiv Golwalkar (1906-73) by declaring in 1980 that large-scale industrial expansion was not the only road to industrialization, because Indian technology had relied "more on man than on machine."[120] Important members of the Jana Sangh party, Balraj Madhok, Deendayal Upadhyaya and P. N. Oke, who associated themselves with the RSS's economic goals of self-sufficiency, argued that industrial westernization and the use of heavy machines were inherently un-Indian. Nana Deshmukh, General Secretary of the RSS and an organizer of the Jana Sangh in Uttar Pradesh, Bihar, Assam, West Bengal, and Orissa, also claimed that industrial civilization would destroy the philosophy of plain living.[121] Some Hindu leaders claimed that Upadhyaya's integral humanism (decentralized small industries) would not give rise to "hedonism and selfishness."[122] Like the Austrian economist Joseph Schumpeter (1930s), who located sources of economic destabilization in technology and professionally managed large industries, revivalists considered the benefits of better education and skill attainment of managerial efficiency as insignificant components in the development process. In agreement with the social historian Francis Fukuyama, Hindu revivalists attributed the crisis in the traditional family (decline in "social capital") to technological forces alone and thereby ignored the most enduring material advancement.[123]

Progressive Stages

Revivalists passed through several stages in their attempts to develop small-scale industries. During the early part of the twentieth century, British textiles posed a serious threat to Indian cottage industries in Bengal and other places. During 1905-12, the *swadeshi* movement identified political nationalism with specific economic needs and demanded that homemade clothes be worn; *swadeshi* shops and small-scale industries were set up in Bengal and in parts of South India. Keshav Baliram Hedgewar (1889-1940), founder of the RSS and a physician, manufactured sugar *phedas* (made out of milk concentrate) in Nagpur to replace imported sugar from Java, and sold them at a cheap rate apparently to demonstrate that foreign goods were not needed.[124] Economic nationalists correctly argued that by protecting small industries, the independent state of India would ensure conditions under which infant industries could mature to strengthen the national economy. At this early stage, the boycott of foreign goods enabled a modest revival of artisan crafts industries.

Before independence in 1947, Gandhi defined *swadeshi* as "that spirit within us which restricts us to the use and service of our immediate surroundings to the exclusion of the remote."[125] Here Gandhi implied the use of only those goods that were produced by one's immediate neighbors and in homes.[126] The idea was to ensure that small-scale industry had enough public aid to develop into one of the major components of the economy.[127] This strategy, critics would argue, was based on the wrong notion that to protect the small-scale sector one had to restrain the large-scale sector. Also, the quality of products in village industries was not good. For instance, the liberal economist Jagdish Bhagwati appropriately argued that the soap produced by Lever Brothers could not exactly be a substitute for what passed as soap in the small-sector.[128]

Revivalist strategies and planning in favor of small-scale industries had some shortcomings. The recorded failure of the *khadi* (coarse cloth) and village industries programs, despite major state and central government subsidies, amply testified that the drive to self-sufficiency itself, through decentralization and small-scale industrialization, was inadequate.[129] The economist Jagdish Bhagwati has argued that India's disappointing record in generating growth "stems from a distrust of growth" as an instrument of poverty alleviation.[130] Moreover, offering maximum protection and government subsidies to home industries in order to curb the "unreasoning [unreasonable] passion for change" meant a strict adherence to the hereditary, rigid caste-based division of labor, with all its hierarchical implications.[131] Economically, the chances of success for widely scattered decentralized labor-intensive enterprises were limited because, as income rose, demand moved away from "inferior" traditional products toward "superior" modern products.[132]

Here again, considerations of political gains were supreme in the revivalist mind. For instance, the Jana Sangh's advocacy of a decentralized village order, small-scale mechanized industry in villages, and criticism of large urban monopolies was largely directed at the fears and insecurities of the small businessmen,[133] main pillars of political support in the 1960s and 1970s. In fact, the party's detailed programs indicated that it was more urban oriented than generally believed and did not seek the interests of specific rural groups.[134] The party realized that its role as an articulator of small business interests was a handicap to its penetration of the lower economic strata in urban areas and to its expansion into the countryside in areas where there was a conflict between the urban merchants and the peasants. Thus the party gradually became more responsive to its wider environment. A "self-conscious" attempt was made to appeal to a more general population for electoral gains.[135] The Jana Sangh thus became representatives of the "middle world" because the middle classes were threatened from above by state intervention in the economy and from below by the increasing political awareness of the "backward" classes.[136] On their part, the small industrialists' associations (FASIL) had no need for a party to mediate between them and the state because they were represented by well-knit associations called *Brooar Mandals* (committees) that could exert political pressure on state ministries.[137]

Above all, unconditional government subsidies to agricultural commodities have so far proven to be unproductive. For instance, an Integrated Rural Development Programme, a subsidized credit scheme in Gujrat, failed to reduce poverty. One of its main features was that eligibility for credit was restricted to the poor.[138]

FOREIGN CAPITAL AND FIRMS

Two related issues—foreign participation (external firms and direct foreign investments) and insurance—have changed the debate about the goals of national development in recent years. In line with the dependency school, revivalists argued that the global political economy was the outgrowth of past Western expansion.

They suggested that the economy could be cushioned from the impact of pressures emanating from Western capitalism. Because of its autarkic trade policies and government controls over the economy, revivalists claimed that economic processes in India had generally been unaffected by international markets.[139]

Revivalists vehemently opposed foreign firms and capital, because they feared that foreign companies had used political influence to change national policies. Shyama Prasad Mukherjee, the founding president of the Hindu Mahasabha, declared in 1951 that the Arabian sheikhs "pressurized the government to use petroleum instead of coal as the form of raw materials for the fertilizer plants."[140] The Akhil Bharatiya Pratinidi Sabha (RSS General Council) feared that the World Bank and the World Trade Organization would capture the resources and markets in order to hand them over to the superpowers.[141] Many nationalists argued that foreign monopolies, such as Glaxo, Phillips, Imperial Chemical Industries, Hindusthan Levers, and Brooke Bond had already used "corporative influence" in politics and economics. When Cargill Company, an American multinational, pulled out of a $300 million project to build a salt-works in 1993 in Gujrat, George Fernadez, a member of parliament, and now a cabinet minister in the BJP government, declared, "We have proved that by following Gandhi's method of concerted action, it is possible to defeat the combined power of the multinationals."[142] The BJP administration closed down the Kentucky Fried Chicken (KFC) shop in Delhi in 1995 on the ground that flies had been discovered inside the kitchen. KFC seemed to have broken certain high caste conventions regarding bodily and mental purification or pollution.[143]

Interestingly, various BJP state chief ministers calculated that there were insufficient public and private sources in India to provide the vast amount of capital needed to build infrastructure. Without an expansion of infrastructure, especially electric power, India would not grow at rates needed to satisfy demands of newly politicized groups. Thus the provincial chief ministers (BJP) largely ignored the economic nationalism espoused by the RSS and some hard-line BJP leaders. To lure investors in 1995, they went to foreign countries such as Germany and Britain and welcomed even consumer items from abroad.[144]

With great force, the Swadeshi Jagaran Manch (SJM) put political pressure on the central government to cancel its initiative of seeking 100 percent foreign direct investment in the liquor and tobacco sectors. It wanted an immediate review of the agreement between the Union government and Suzuki Motor Company on Maruti Udyog Limited, because the agreement, economic nationalists believed, had diluted the government's authority.[145] At its November 1995 national convention, the SJM identified Colgate, Pepsi Cola, and Coca Cola as the three pillars of undesirable foreign investments. The SJM argued that the foreign investment undermined national sovereignty and by extension opened India to foreign manipulation and cultural intrusion.[146]

Both foreign capital and foreign management became suspect. Revivalists opposed the $5 billion SDR (Euro currency) loan offered by the International Monetary Fund (IMF). The Shiv Sena leader, Bal Thackeray, contended that the Indian economy should adopt a new regime of "consultation with monitoring by and surveillance" of IMF authorities. He added that this would lead to an underutilization of domestic industrial capacities. He was particularly disturbed by the IMF's "adjustments" program, which he believed would negate the concept of the public sector occupying the "commanding heights of the economy."[147] Thus by means of its 24-day *chetna yatra* (awareness procession), which passed through 300 districts in September 1998, the SJM pressed for its anti-globalization program. The central 17-party coalition government was an easy target for attack. The SJM exerted pressure to roll back most of the 380 items for import proposed by Commerce Minister R. K. Hedge.[148] For example, the 1998 budget imposed a heavy tax, 262 percent, on the European Union's (EU) alcohol import to India.[149]

External adverse reactions and effects were inevitable. The EU, India's largest trading partner, called for a new Millennium Round Trade negotiations in order to seek tariff reductions.[150] The European Commission, the EU's bureaucratic branch, also complained that if foreign car makers took into account all the hidden duties and taxes imposed on foreign brands, any car maker would have to pay taxes of nearly 150 percent.[151] Strangely, the SJM lobbied for an extension of the license of cellular phone operators, despite the fact that the SJM knew that the cellular companies were all foreign corporations.[152] S. Gurumurthy, the joint convener of the *yatra*, asked for amendments to India's agreement with the WTO, because he had direct and personal interests in large domestic corporations which tended to discourage competition.[153]

Insurance Business

Direct foreign participation in Indian insurance generated intense debates among economic nationalists. Most Hindu parties denounced foreign collaboration in the insurance industry. The catalyst was the long-awaited Insurance Regulatory Bill, which earlier had sought both domestic and foreign investment in the sector. The life insurance business of 245 Indian and foreign insurers was nationalized in September 1956 when the Life Insurance Corporation (LIC) was established. Later, in January 1973, 107 insurers were nationalized and amalgamated into four subsidiaries of the General Insurance Corporation.

Revivalists feared the advent of joint ventures in the insurance business. The BJP president, Kushabhau Thakre, criticized the government for introducing the bill without first consulting the party.[154] Leaders of the SJM launched a frontal attack on the BJP's policy, dubbing it "anti-people and anti-*swadeshi*." The SJM was particularly critical of the Economic and Trade Advisory Councils.[155] Opponents of the new insurance bill in parliament, disliking foreign equity in the insurance sector, argued that foreign companies with money and muscle power would dominate joint ventures[156] and, in the course of time, Indian partners in insurance as well.[157] Uma Bharati, an ultra-conservative "firebrand" *sanyasin* (ascetic) from Khajuraho in Madhya Pradesh, along with Virendra Singh and K. R. Malkani, two senior lawmakers, opposed the bill. Dattpant Thengadi organized a sit-in protest. S. Gurumurthy, chief theoretician of the SJM, and a bitter critic of economic liberalization, wrote to the prime minister reiterating the SJM's opposition to the insurance bill. The Hindu trade union movement, Bharatiya Mazdoor Sangh (BMS), also vehemently resisted the introduction of the bill.[158] The RSS Chief Rajju Bhaiya, the general secretary of the Jana Sangh in the 1970s, and Ashok Singhal, the Vishwa Hindu Parishad leader, along with the dogmatic communist parties, opposed foreign participation in insurance businesses. The National Insurance Workers Organization, affiliated with the BMS, in the "national interest" asked for the non-inclusion of foreigners in insurance.[159] Until May 1999, foreign insurance companies were barred from doing business in India.

Evaluation of Insurance Policy

Critics of the revivalist strategy offered strong criticism of the policy on insurance. First, they cited consumers' concern because the LIC did not revise its mortality table from time to time. Although life expectancy touched 62, the LIC had not cut the premium rates. Service had been poor, and claims were never settled promptly. On the other hand, critics argued, there would be a flow of capital into the country to induct new products and maintain capital adequacy ratios.[160] Second, foreign insurance companies were offered only 26 percent equity in joint ventures with Indian partners. Third, with $2 billion worth of insurance business, India still remained one of the least insured countries in the world. Most countries, including China, have channeled insurance funds for the development of much needed basic infrastructure.[161] Fourth, distinctions between foreign subsidiaries and local enterprises began to blur when such units joined to form joint ventures, or when local enterprises established their own subsidiaries abroad in other developing countries.[162] A McKinsey Management research report, by international consultants based in the United States, showed that Indian joint ventures alliances had provided sustainable growth platforms for both local and global companies because global companies had intangibles— technology, brands, and skills—that "rise in value" over time.[163] In short, the "indigenizing" development theory as it refers to insurance businesses was frustratingly empty in both principle and prescription.

CONCLUSION

It is legitimate to conclude that the economic nationalists in India offered some deficient populist economic schemes. It was evident that the revivalists wanted to mark out for themselves a distinct path. Yet in doing so, they took up the fallible economic programs of the Gandhites, neo-Gandhites, and Congress leaders with only minor changes. The "anti-systemic movements" led by activist religious revivalists were seldom original in terms of their intellectual content. They worked within the world-system as a whole.[164]

The glorification of the old village order was a delusion. The revivalist demand for better terms for agricultural commodities was very often supported by "bullock-cart capitalists" in Indian villages.[165] The agrarian bourgeoisie had every interest in drawing the battle lines along a city *versus* countryside divide because it benefited most from attempts to modify the terms of trade.

An economic policy that focused on developing a vast network of small industries in order to reduce the cost of industrial goods, as well as generate employment, was a strategy for economic stagnation. The term 'small industry' involves an image of technical backwardness and the production of inferior products. Caste ridden and politically selfish, most Hindu parties had neither the will nor the expertise to end inequity, but they had the electoral talent to mislead the public. Immanuel Wallerstein, a theorist of world capitalism, has seen a link between a decentralist economic thrust (retaining "local" control over surpluses) and a decentralist political thrust (local order).[166] The revivalist political thrust was to gain political control rather than reorganize the social and economic order.

Economically, the revivalists' economic policy evaded the challenge posed by globalization. Its concern about foreign imports and Western technology indicated its lack of appreciation for the structural context of global trade and production. India needs foreign investment in order to acquire state-of-the-art technologies sufficient to develop a strong economy and sophisticated defense industry. As recent Chinese economic reforms proved, globalization would provide advantages to qualified low-cost labor through delocalization of production units.[167] Jayati Ghosh, a Bengali political economist, has rightly argued that "autarky cannot be a solution" mainly because "there is a need to consider the means of export expansion."[168] Thus it may be argued that the new form of cultural protection, through economic nationalism, for an inefficient system of production might create a new non-tariff barrier to international trade. Hindu culture was misused in order to advance unworkable economic policies.

Fortunately, signs of moderation and economic expediency were visible in some revivalist pragmatic quarters. Prime Minister Atal Behari Vajpayee and Home Minister L. K. Advani argued for open economic policies. In his address to the Confederation of India Industry, Advani tried to convince the radicals that with respect to the economy, the BJP was fully committed to policies of "deregulation, decontrol, and debureaucratisation." When he favored foreign participation in insurance, he spoke more like a Swatantra Party (conservative) leader than a modern-day BJP activist.[169] Likewise, a former *swadeshi* hardliner Murli Manohar Joshi, president of the BJP, attempted to soften the BJP's economic manifesto in 1996. Supported by two BJP leaders, Jaswant Singh and Pramod Mahajan, Joshi preferred a greater market-friendly tilt and more foreign investments.[170] In fact, the BJP did not reject foreign investment but refused to grant it preference against local industries.[171] It definitely accepted foreign investment in the capital goods sector.[172] *Swadeshi* was on hold when there was a transfer of 340 items of import from the restricted list to the open general license (OGL).[173] M. Venkaiah Naidu, BJP's General Secretary, declared, "I do not mind khadi towels becoming mandatory in all government houses but when it comes to skill and technology, we have to look outside."[174] Thus the BJP, despite its many faults, managed to remain somewhat free from the *swadeshi* fever. Like populists of nineteenth-century America, economic nationalists, though politically on the offensive, have so far failed to make any serious dent in the BJP government's economic policies and planning.

In sum, an alternative model of development is not easy to advance. This chapter has argued that Hindu revivalist parties did not offer a sound alternative to the Congress Party's socialistic pattern of economic order. Revivalist policies were analytically deficient because of their tendency to draw empirical conclusions from ideological and cultural premises. Many economists have concluded that there was little empirical basis for the claim that greater inequality was inevitable with higher growth rates.[175]

NOTES

1. The Bengali psychoanalyst Ashis Nandy has made a distinction between religion-as-faith (operationally plural and tolerant) and religion-as-ideology, which identifies a population of followers fighting for non-religious, usually political, and economic interests. Nandy concludes that the politics of secularism is part of the same process of formation of modern state practices, which promotes religion-as-ideology. In this context, Hindu revivalists were part of modernizers of the state, argues Partha Chatterjee, another Bengali intellectual. See Veena Das (ed.), *Mirrors of Violence: Communities, Riots and Survivors in South Asia* (Delhi: Oxford University Press, 1990), pp. 69-84; Partha Chatterjee, *A Possible India: Essays in Political Criticism* (Delhi: Oxford University Press, 1998), p. 231.

2. There are several works on early *swadeshi* economic nationalism. See B. Chandra, *The Rise and Growth of Economic Nationalism in India* (New Delhi: People's Publishing House, 1969); and Sumit Sarkar, *The Swadeshi Movement in Bengal* (New Delhi: People's Publishing House, 1977). Sumit Sarkar and others have described various strands within *swadeshi* economic activity; but there are few works on the recent movement. *Swadeshi* in earlier times was for the development of Indian goods for the sake of improving the quality of life in accordance with the means available, but in recent years revivalists have manipulated the *swadeshi* movement mostly for political gains. Thus, 'swadeshi' is "interpreted in a way that cuts India off from the rest of the world, walking out of the World

Trade Organization, saying that we will not have foreign investment except in priority areas," Subrata Chakravarty, "What Does Swadeshi Mean," *Forbes* (July 6, 1998), pp. 96-97.

3. Sunil Khilani, *The Idea of India* (New York: Farrar Straus Giroux, 1997), pp. 164-65. The centralizing and rationalizing nation-builders in India are pitted against the regional, linguistic, and cultural minorities. The state-church conflict, as modeled by Lipset and Rokhan, is irrelevant in India because of the absence of an authoritative church hierarchy in Hinduism. See Seymour Martin Lipset and Stein Rokhan (eds.), *Party System and Voter Alignments: Cross National Perspectives* (New York: Free Press, 1967), pp. 1-64. The blurring of patriotism and religion proved decisive during the Ayodhya crisis in 1990-91 and the Hindu state system gained some currency in India.

4. Nitya Narayan Banerjee, *Vedic Socialism* (New Delhi: Hindutva Publications, 1980), p. 265.

5. Santosh Saha, review of John P. Powelson, "Centuries of Economic Endeavor: Parallel Paths in Japan and Europe and Their Contrast with the Third World," *Journal of Third World Studies* (Fall 1995), pp. 580-85; see also John P. Powelson, *Centuries of Economic Endeavor: Parallel Paths in Japan and Europe and Their Contrast with the Third World* (Ann Arbor: University of Michigan University Press, 1994), p. 339.

6. Talcott Parsons, "Preface," in Max Weber, *The Protestant Ethic and Spirit of Capitalism* (New York: Charles Scribner's Sons, 1958), p. xiv. Most theories of economic growth and development associate the idea of economic development with a discontinuity, with the emergence of a phenomenon that did not exist before. This is quite manifest in J. Schumpeter's theory of unstable growth, and certainly in W. Rostow's concept of "take off."

7. "The Bharatiya Janata Party and Globalisation of the Indian Economy," in John McGuire, Peter Reeves, and Howard Brasted (eds.), *Politics of Violence from Ayodhya to Behrampada* (New Delhi: Sage Publications, 1996), pp. 274-88; Tavleen Singh, "Fifth Column," *India Today* (October 5, 1998), p. 7. The cult of *swadeshi* promoting indigenous industrial ventures had its beginnings in 1867. The message of self-help in industry and education was spread by the "Dawn Society," Amiya Kumar Bagchi, *The Evolution of the State Bank of India*, vol. 2 (Walmut Creek: Altmira Press, CA: 1997), p. 78.

8. Yogendra K. Malik and V. B. Singh, "Bharatiya Janata Party: An Alternative to the Congress (I)?" *Asian Survey*, vol. xxxii, no. 4 (April 2, 1992), p. 335.

9. Thomas Blom Hansen, "Globalisation and Nationalist Imaginations," *Economic and Political Weekly* (March 9, 1996), p. 611.

10. BJP's economic principles and practices have been well examined in Thomas Blom Hansen and Christophe Jaffrelot (eds.), *The BJP and the Compulsions of Politics in India* (Delhi: Oxford University Press, 1998). The emphasis has been on political calculations.

11. Lise Diane McKean, *Towards a Political Spirituality: Hindu Religious Organizations and Indian Nationalism* (Ph.D. thesis, University of Sydney, Department of Anthropology, March 1992), p. 36.

12. Lise McKean, *Divine Enterprise: Gurus and the Hindu Nationalist Movement* (Chicago: Chicago University Press, 1996), p. 32; "Swadeshi as Modernity," *India Abroad* (March 23, 1998), p. 21.

13. Staff reporter, "Militant Hinduism," *India Today* (May 11, 1986), p. 34.

14. McKean, *Divine Enterprise*, p. 35.

15. Arjuna Appadurai and Carol Breckenridge, "Why Public Culture?" *Public Culture,* vol. 1 (1988), pp. 5-11; Partha Chatterjee, *Nationalist Thought and the Colonial World: A Derivative Discourse* (London: Zed Press, 1986); Achin Vanaik, *Ideology and Economics: The Case of India, Times of India* (March 28, 1988).

16. Christophe Jaffrelot, "The Idea of the Hindu Race in the Writings of Hindu Nationalist Ideologues in the 1920s and 1930s: A Concept between Two Cultures," in Peter Robb (ed.), *The Concept of Race in South Asia* (Delhi: Oxford University Press, 1995), p. 353; M. G. Bokare, *Hindu Economics: Eternal Economic Order* (New Delhi: Swadeshi Jagaran Manch, 1993), pp. 32, 55. Sources of "Hindu Economics" were believed to be *Four Vedas* (production, taxation, resources), *Shanti-Parva* (principles of pricing), *Vidur Niti* (taxation, budgeting), *Arthasastra*, and so on. See also Bani Deshpande, *The Universe of Vedanta* (Bombay: The People's Publishing House, 1974); and R. Shyamshastri (ed.), *Kautilya's Arthashastra* (Mysore: Mysore Publishing House, 1960).

17. D. B. Thengadi, *Our National Renaissance: Its Directions and Destination* (Bangalore: Sahitya Sindu, 1980), p. 73.

18. Rama Rajya Parishad, *Election Manifesto*, cited in Myron Weiner, *The Indian Paradox: Essays in Indian Politics* (New Delhi: Sage Publications, 1989), p. 174.

19. Deendayal Upadhyaya, *The Integral Approach* (New Delhi: Deendayal Research Institute, 1978), p. 60; Hansen, "Globalisation and Nationalist Imaginations," p. 603.

20. Shiva Chandra Jha, *A History of Indian Economic Thought* (Calcutta: Firma KLM Private Limited, 1981), pp. 14-15.

21. *Wall Street Journal* (July 3, 1993), p. A4. The stand taken by Hindu revivalists was not different from that of the American transcendentalists, the Russian Narodniks, or the Gandhian self-sufficiency schemers. The common theme was to return to the traditional rural life.

22. Santosh Saha, "Religious Revivalism Among the Hindus in India: Ideologies of the Fundamentalist Movements in Recent Decades," *Indian Journal of Asian Affairs*, vols. 8 and 9 (1995-96), p. 45.

23. Bharatiya Janata Party, *For a Strong and Prosperous India: Election Manifesto* (New Delhi: BJP, 1996), p. 22.

24. Bharatiya Janata Party, *Election Manifesto* (New Delhi: BJP Headquarters, 1989), p. 15.

25. Gail Omvedt, *Reinventing Revolution: New Social Movements and the Socialist Tradition in India* (New York: M. E. Sharpe, 1993), p. 145; Anil Agarwal, "Politics of Environment," in Centre for Science and Environment, *The State of India's Environment 1984-1985: The Second Citizens' Report* (New Delhi: 1985), p. 366.

26. Banerjee, *Vedic Socialism*, p. 227; Sashi Tharoor, "E Pluribus, India: Is Indian Modernity Working?" *Foreign Affairs* (January/February 1998), p. 132; Rajiv Desai, "Implications of Illiberal Governance are Examined," *India Abroad* (January 15, 1999), p. 2.

27. *India Today* (September 8, 1998), p. 14.

28. B. K. Kelkar, *Pandit Deendayal Upadhyaya: Ideology and Perception: Political Thought* (New Delhi: Suruchi Prakashan, 1988), p. 54.

29. Thenghadi, *Our National Renaissance*, p. 73.

30. Hampton Thompson Davey, Jr., "The Transformation of an Ideological Movement into an Aggregate Party " (Ph. D. dissertation, University of California, Los Angeles, 1969), p. 357.

31. Howard L. Erdman, *The Swatantra Party and Indian Conservatism* (Cambridge: Cambridge University Press, 1967), p. 52.

32. Banerjee, *Vedic Socialism*, p. 156.

33. Erdman, *The Swatantra Party*, p. 50.

34. V. V. Nene, *Pandit Deendayal Upadhyaya: Ideology and Perception: Integral Humanism* (New Delhi: Suruchi Prakashan, 1988), p. 60.

35. B. D. Graham, "The Jana Sangh and Bloc Politics, 1967-80," *The Journal of Commonwealth and Comparative Politics*, vol. 25 (1997), p. 254.

36. Jha, *A History of Indian Economic Thought*, p. 38.

37. Kelkar, *Pandit Deendayal Upadhyaya*, pp. 52, 73; D. B. Thengadi, *Pandit Deendayal Upadhyaya: Ideology and Perception: An Inquest* (New Delhi: Suruchi Prakashan, 1988), pp. 36-39.

38. Thengadi, *Our National Renaissance*, p. 72.

39. Kiran Saxsena, *Asian Survey*, vol. xxxiii, no. 7 (July 1993), p. 686.

40. Geeta Puri, *Bharatiya Jana Sangh: Organization and Ideology: A Case Study* (Delhi: Sterling, 1980), p. 17; Erdman, *The Swatantra Party*, p. 196.

41. Subramanian Swamy, *Building a New India: An Agenda for National Renaissance* (New Delhi: UBS Publishers Limited, 1992), p. 127.

42. McKean, *Divine Enterprise*, p. 99.

43. Pradeep Chhibber, "Who Voted for the Bharatiya Janata Party?" *British Journal of Political Science*, vol. 27, no. 4 (October 1997), p. 4.

44. D. B. Thengadi, *The Perspective* (Bangalore: Sahitya Sindhu, 1971), p. 71.

45. P. Parameswaran, *Gandhi, Lohia and Deendayal* (New Delhi: Deendayal Research Institute, 1978), p. 147.

46. Richard Sisson, "Culture and Democratization in India," in *Historical and Comparative Perspectives*, p. 48.

47. The *sarvodaya* workers in Gujrat state sought to uplift the lower classes by exposing them to a Sanskritic equivalent of Protestant ethic or Methodist virtues, Lloyd I. Rudolph and Susanne Hoeber Rudolph, *In Pursuit of Laksmi: The Political Economy of the Indian State* (Chicago: Chicago University Press, 1987), p. 388.

48. Michael W. Sonnleitner, *Vinoba Bhave on Self-Rule and Representative Democracy* (New Delhi: Promilla & Co., Publishers, 1988), p. 46.

49. Manga Ram Varshney, *Jana Sangha-RSS and Balraj Madhok* (Aligarh: Ajoy Printers, 1973), p. 120.

50. Chhibber, "Who Voted for the Bharatiya Janata Party?" p. 5.

51. Ibid., pp. 1-2; Amrita Basu, "Mass Movement or Elite Conspiracy? The Puzzle of Hindu Nationalism," in David Ludden, *Contesting the Nation: Religion, Community, and the Politics of Democracy in India* (Philadelphia: University of Pennsylvania Press, 1996), p. 68.

52. Christophe Jaffrelot, "The Sangh Parivar Between Sanskritization and Social Engineering," in Thomas Blom Hansen and Christophe Jaffrelot, *The BJP and the Compulsion of Politics in India* (Delhi: Oxford University Press, 1998), p. 4; BJP, *For a Strong and Prosperous India, 1996*, p. 14.

53. Bharatiya Mazdoor Sangh, *Labour Policy: Srama Niti* (Nagpur: Bharatiya Mazdoor Sangh, 1967), pp. 52, 71, 274.

54. Hansen and Jeffrelot, *The BJP*, p. 153.

55. BJP, *Kisan ka adhikar-patra* [Farmers' Rights] (New Delhi: BJP, 1987), p. 31.

56. Sugata Bose, "The World Economy and Regional Economics in South Asia: Some Comments on Linkages," in Sugata Bose (ed.), *South Asia and World Capitalism* (Delhi: Oxford University Press, 1990), pp. 357-59.

57. Stephen Fuchs, *At the Bottom of Indian Society: The Harijan and Other Low Castes* (Delhi: 1981); R. S. Sharma, *Material Culture and Social Formations in Ancient India* (Delhi: Oxford University Press, 1983), Irfan Habib, "Moghul India," in Tapan Raychaudhuri and Irfan Habib (eds.), *The Cambridge Economic History of India*, vol. 1 (New Delhi: 1984). See also Jim Masselos (ed.), *India: Creating a Modern Nation* (New Delhi: Sterling Publishers, 1990), p. 290.

58. A. Vaidyanathan, *The Indian Economy: Crisis, Responses and Prospects* (New Delhi: Sangam Books, 1997), p. 51.

59. Achin Vanaik, *The Painful Transition: Bourgeois Democracy in India* (London: Verso, 1990), p. 32.

60. Amartya Sen, cited in *India Today* (October 26, 1998), p. 20; Bal Krishna, "Post-Independence Economic Policy Failed: Bhagwati," *India Abroad* (May 3, 1999), p. 28.

61. S. D. Kulkarni (ed.), *Economic History of India* (Bombay: Shri Bhagavan Vedavyasa Itihasa Mandira, 1996), p. 37.

62. *Rig Veda*, xix-xxv, pp. 36, 42; xcii, p. 11; xxiii, p. 12. See also R. C. Majumdar, *The Vedic Age* (Bombay: Bharatiya Vidya Bhawan, 1965), p. 386.

63. Arvind Sharma, *Hindu Scriptural Value System and the Economic Development* (Delhi: Heritage, 1980), p. 56.

64. Inder P. Nijhawan, "Sociopolitical Institutions, Cultural Values and Attitudes: Their Impact on Indian Economic Development," in J. S. Uppal (ed.), *India's Economic Problems: An Analytical Approach* (New York: St. Martin's Press, 1978), pp. 72-73; Ajit DasGupta, "India's Cultural Values and Economic Development: A Comment," *Economic Development and Cultural Change* (October 1958), p. 101.

65. Charles H. Heimsath, *Indian Nationalism and Hindu Social Reform* (Princeton: Princeton University Press, 1964), pp. 325-27.

66. Omvedt, *Reinventing Revolution*, p. 115.

67. Ashutosh Varshney, *Democracy, Development, and the Countryside: Urban-rural Struggles in India* (Cambridge: Cambridge University Press, 1995), p. 114.

68. Gurudas M. Ahuja, *BJP and Indian Politics: Policies and Progress* (New Delhi: Ram Group, 1995), p. 121.

69. BJP, *Election Manifesto,* 1989, p. 15.

70. Balraj Madhok, *Indianisation* (Delhi: S. Chand and Company, 1970), p. 14.

71. Jana Sangh, *Election Manifesto, 1962* (Delhi: Bharatiya Jana Sang), p. 14.

72. Atal Behari Vajpayee, *Dynamics of an Open Society* (New Delhi: Ministry of External Affairs, 1977), p. 21.

73. Sunil Saharasabudhe, "Peasant Movement and the Quest for Development," in M. N. Karna, *Peasant and Protest in India* (New Delhi: Intellectual Publishing House, 1989), p. 152.

74. Sharad A. Kulkarni, *Pandit Deendayal Upadhyaya: Ideology and Perception: Integral Economic Policy* (New Delhi: Suruchi Prakashan, 1989), pp. 69-70.

75. Sikata Banerjee, "Political Secularization and the Future of Secular Democracy in India," *Asian Survey*, vol.xxxvi, no. 10 (October 1998), pp. 910-12; Hansen, p. 153.

76. Reporter, "The Rampage," *India Today* (September 28, 1998), p. 14.

77. H. V. Seshadri (ed.), *A Vision in Action* (Bangalore: Jagaran Prakashana, 1988), p. 171.

78. *Organiser* (August 1, 1955), p. 13; Dina Nath Mishra, *RSS: Myth and Reality* (Sahibad, U.P.: Vikas Publishers, 1980), p. 25.

79. D. B. Thengadi, *Focus: On the Socio-Economic Problems* (New Delhi: Suruchi Sahitya, 1987), p. 67.

80. Thengadi, *Our National Renaissance*, p. 72.

81. Kelkar, *Pandit Deendayal Upadhyaya*, p. 113.

82. Atal Behari Vajpayee, *New Dimensions of India's Foreign Policy* (Delhi: Vision Book, 1979), p. 21.

83. BJP, *For a Strong and Prosperous India*, p. 22.

84. BJP, *Election Manifesto*, New Delhi, 1996, p. 18.

85. This tendency has been described as an opposite version of Marxism that asked for liberation through struggle. Omvedt, *Reinventing Revolution*, p. 147.

86. M. G. Bokare, *Hindu Economics*, p. 153.

87. Ibid.

88. Nilkantha Rath, "A Budget for Farmers," *Economic and Political Weekly*, vol. 23, 1996, pp. 739-44.

89. Walter K. Anderson and Shridhar D. Dample, *The Brotherhood in Saffron: The Rastriya Swayamsevak Sangh and Hindu Revolution* (Boulder, Colo: Westview Press, 1987), pp. 130-31.

90. H. V. Seshadri, *RSS: A Vision in Action* (Bangalore: Jagaran Prakashana, 1988), pp. 197-98, 243.

91. Erdman, *The Swatantra Party*, p. 50.

92. Kelkar, *Pandit Deendayal Upadhyaya*, p. 113.

93. *Organiser* (January 29, 1962), p. 4.

94. Ishwar C. Harris, *Gandhian in Contemporary India: The Vision and Visionaries* (New York: The Edwin Mellen Press, 1998), p. 50.

95. M. V. Nadkarni, *Farmers' Movements in India* (Calcutta: Allied Publishers Limited, 1987), p. 217; Swamy, *Building a New India*, p. 129.

96. Janata Party, "Economic Survey, 1976-77" (New Delhi: Janata Party, 1977), p. 3; BJP, "National Executive Meeting," Agra, April 8-10, 1988.

97. Staff Reporter, "Is It Real?" *India Today* (March 30, 1998), p. 21.

98. Yogendra K. Malik and V.B. Singh, *Hindu Nationalists in India: The Rise of the Bharatiya Janata Party* (Boulder, Colo: Westview Press, 1994), p. 106; Bharatiya Janata Party, *Humanistic Approach to Economic Development: A Swadeshi Alternative* (New Delhi: BJP Headquarters, 1992), p. 5.

99. Seshadri, *RSS*, p. 181.

100. Ibid., pp. 198-99.

101. Gerlad Heuze, "Cultural Pluralism: The Appeal of the Shiva Sena," in Sujata Patel and Alice Thorner (eds.), *Bombay: Metaphor for Modern India* (Bombay: Oxford

University Press, 1995), pp. 238-39; Sikata Banerjee, "Political Secularization and the Future of Secular Democracy in India," *Asian Survey*, vol. xxxvi, no. 1 (October 1998), p. 916.

102. Seshadri, *RSS*, p. 196.

103. Christophe Jaffrelot, *The Hindu Nationalist Movement in India* (New York: Columbia University Press, 1998), p. 143.

104. Zoya Hassan, "Shifting Ground: Hindutva Politics and the Farmers' Movements in Uttar Pradesh," *The Journal of Peasant Studies* (April 1994), p. 288.

105. Selig Harrison, *India: The Most Dangerous Decades* (Princeton, N.J.: Princeton University Press, 1956), p. 109; Myron Weiner, *Political Changes in South Asia* (Calcutta: K. L. Mukhopadyaya, 1963), p. 214; Paul R. Brass, "The Politicisation of the Peasantry in a North Indian State," *The Journal of Peasants Studies*, vol. 7, no. 4 (July 1980), p. 31.

106. Debesh Bhattacharya, *The Role of Technological Progress in Indian Economic Development* (Calcutta: The World Press Private Limited, 1972), p. 8.

107. Vandana Shiva, *The Violence of the Green Revolution: Ecological Degradation and Political Conflict in Punjab* (Dehra Dun: Research Foundation of Science and Ecology, 1989), p. 125.

108. J. Mohan Rao and Servaas Storm, "Distribution and Growth in Indian Agriculture," in Terence J. Byres, *The Indian Economy: Major Debates Since Independence* (Delhi: Oxford University Press, 1998), p. 223; P. K. Bardhan, *Land and Rural Poverty* (New York: Columbia University Press, 1984).

109. Kelkar, *Pandit Deendayal Upadhyaya*, p. 52.

110. C. P. Bhambari, *The Janata Party: A Profile* (Delhi: National Publishers, 1980), p. 94.

111. Jagadish Shettier, "Deendayalji's Economic Thought and Its Relevance Today," *Organiser* (September 27, 1992), p. 9; S. L. Poplai (ed.), *1962 General Elections in India* (Bombay: Allied Publishers, 1962), p. 144.

112. Deendayal Upadhyaya, *The Two Plans: Promises, Performances, Prospects* (Lucknow: Jana Sangh, 1958), p. 157.

113. Ibid., p. 201; Bharatiya Jana Sangh, *Election Manifesto 1967* (Delhi: BJS, 1967), p. 22.

114. Puri, *Bharatiya Jana Sangh*, p. 47.

115. Janata Party, *The Great Janata Revolution* (New Delhi: Janata Party Office, 1977), p. 147.

116. B. D. Graham, *Hindu Nationalism and Indian Politics: The Origin and Development of the Bharatiya Jana Sangh* (Cambridge: Cambridge University Press, 1990), p. 22.

117. Basu, "Mass Movement or Elite Conspiracy?" p. 60; Madan Das, "Swadeshi Panacea for All Ills," *Organiser* (October 4, 1992), p. 9.

118. Salim Lakha, "The Bharatiya Janata Party and Globalisation of Indian Economy," in McGuire, et al. *Politics of Violence*, p. 280.

119. Graham, *Hindu Nationalism*, p. 164.

120. Dina Nath, *RSS: Myth and Reality* (Sahibad, U.P.: Vikas Publishers, 1980), p. 136.

121. Nana Deshmukh, *RSS: Victim of Slander* (New Delhi: Vision Books, 1979), p. 142.

122. Thomas Blom Hansen, "Hindutva and Capitalism," in Hansen, *The BJP* (New Delhi: Oxford University Press, 1998), pp. 294-295.

123. Francis Fukuyama, "The End of History," *The National Interest* (Summer 1989); Francis Fukuyama, *The Great Disruption: Human Nature and the Reconstitution of Social Order* (New York: Free Press, 1998).

124. H. V. Seshadri (ed.), *Dr. Hedgewar: The Epoch-Maker: A Biography* (Bangalore: Sahitya Sindu, 1981), p. 15.

125. C. F. Andrews, *Mahatma Gandhi: His Life and Ideas* (Bombay: Anmol Publications, 1987), p. 120.

126. Ujjvala Karmakar, "The Present Day Relevance of the Economic Philosophy of Mahatma Gandhi," in Kulkarni, *Economic History of India*, p. 494.

127. Puri, *Bharatiya Jana Sangh*, pp. 13, 17, 47.

128. Jagdish Bhagwati, *India in Transition: Freeing the Economy* (Oxford: Clarendon Press, 1993), p. 55.

129. Sudhamahi Regunathan, "Symbol of Freedom Struggle Makes a Fashion Statement," *India Abroad* (January 1, 1999), p. 42.

130. Ramesh Thakur, *The Government and Politics of India* (New York: St. Martin's Press, 1995), p. 324; Bhagwati, *India in Transition*.

131. Tapan Basu et al. *Khaki Shorts and Saffron Flags: A Critique of the Hindu Right* (Delhi: Orient Longman, 1993), p. 70; Vincent Sheean, *Nehru: The Years of Power* (New York: Random House, 1960), pp. 51-52; Erdman, *The Swatantra Party*, p. 88.

132. P. N. Dhar, "Some Observations on Small-Scale Enterprise Development," in C. H. Hanumantha Rao and P. C. Joshi (eds.), *Reflections on Economic Development and Social Change* (New Delhi: Allied Publishers, 1979), p. 172. This village-based economic strategy was basically opposite of that developed by P. Mahalanobis. John Mellor, *The New Economics of Growth: A Strategy for India and Developing World* (Ithaca: Cornell University Press, 1976), p. 125.

133. Davey, Jr., "The Transformation," pp. 36-38. The Jana Sangh party was regarded as a *bania* (traders) party.

134. Ibid., p. 364.

135. Ibid., p. 371.

136. Ibid., pp. 364, 374; *Organiser* (January 29, 1962), p. 4.

137. Graham, *Hindu Nationalism*, p. 169.

138. Jean Dreze, "Poverty in India and the IRDP Delusions," *Economic and Political Weekly* (September 29, 1990), p. A-95.

139. Jayati Ghosh, in Sugata Bose (ed.), *South Asia and World Capitalism*, pp. 354-56.

140. Graham, *Hindu Nationalism*, p. 170.

141. Hansen and Jeffrelot, *The BJP*, p. 305. Both left and right wings of the farmers' movements feared American agro-business in India, Lakha Salim in J. McGuire et al., *Politics of Violence*, pp. 278-79.

142. *India Abroad* (December 25, 1998), p. 24.

143. "For Gandhi or for Growth?" *The Economist* (October 16, 1993), p. 35; Hansen, "Globalisation and Nationalist Imaginations," *Economic and Political Weekly* (March 9, 1996), p. 611.

144. Walter K. Anderson, "Bharatiya Janata Party: Searching for the Hindu Nationalist Face," in Hans-Georg Betz and Stefan Immerfall (eds.), *The New Politics of the Rights: Neo-Populist Parties and Movements in Established Democracies* (New York: St. Martin's Press, 1998), p. 228.

145. "The Rampage," *India Today* (September 28, 1998), p. 13.

146. *The Telegraph* (Calcutta) (November 11, 1995), p. 12.

147. Bal Thackeray, "Internal Economic Order," *Economic and Political Weekly* (November 1981), p. 1723.

148. "The Rampage," p. 14.

149. *India Abroad* (September 28, 1998), p. 14.

150. "Is It for Real?" *India Abroad* (March 30, 1998), p. 13.

151. *India Abroad* (December 25, 1998), p. 24.

152. Ibid., p. 25.

153. Ibid.

154. *India Abroad* (December 11, 1998), p. 25.

155. *India Abroad* (September 11, 1998), p. 4.

156. The Insurance Regulatory Authority Bill envisaged foreign investment of up to 40 percent in joint venture.

157. D. S. Mehta, "Opening Up Insurance Sector Will Help Consumers," *India Abroad* (December 25, 1998), p. 2.

158. I. Gopalakrishnan, "Insurance Opened up to Foreign Investment," *India Abroad* (December 4, 1998), p. 28.

159. Ibid.

160. *India Abroad* (December 25, 1998), p. 2.

161. Ibid.

162. Dennis J. Encarnation, *Dislodging Multinationals: India's Strategy in Comparative Perspectives* (Ithaca, N.Y: Cornell University Press, 1989), p. 81; Claude Markovits, *Indian Business and Nationalist Politics, 1931-1939* (Cambridge: Cambridge University Press, 1985), pp. 10-11.

163. "Joint Ventures," *India Abroad* (April 16, 1999), p. 30.

164. Gerald James Larson, *India's Agony Over Religion* (Albany: State University of New York Press, 1995), p. 40.

165. Lloyd I. Rudolph and Sussane Hoeber Rudolph, *In Pursuit of Lakshmi: The Political Economy of the Indian State* (Chicago: Chicago University Press, 1987).

166. Immanuel Wallerstein, *The Politics of the World Economy: The States, the Movements, and the Civilizations* (Cambridge: Cambridge University Press, 1984).

167. Many such as Gerry Mander and Ralph Nader have shown that the global economy could not be the panacea. Basic infrastructures would need to be built before globalization would yield good results. See James H. Mittelman and Mustapha Kamal Pasha, *Out from Underdevelopment Revisited* (New York: St. Martin's Press, 1996).

168. Ghosh, p. 356.

169. Hansen, "Globalisation and Nationalist Imaginations," p. 612.

170. S. N. Bhaumik, "BJP's Changing Colour," *India Today* (February 19, 1998), p. 13.

171. L. K. Advani, "Presidential Address," BJP, National Council Session, Bangalore, June 18-20, 1993, p. 11.

172. *Organiser* (New Delhi), vol. xliv, no. 38 (April 25, 1993), p. 3.

173. *India Abroad* (April 24, 1998), p. 26.

174. Sandy Gordon, "Indian Security Policy and the Rise of the Hindu Right," in McGuire et al. *Politics of Violence*, pp. 264-65.

175. Hollis B. Chenery et al., *Redistribution with Growth* (New York: Oxford University Press, 1974).

Chapter 5

The Rise of Neo-Fundamentalism in Egypt

Rudolf T. Zarzar

This chapter presents a theoretical investigation of the rise of neo-fundamentalism in Egypt.[1] Its main thesis is that Islamic neo-fundamentalism can be understood best as a response to the challenge posed by Westernization and modernization that the Egyptian elites sponsored since the reign of Muhammad Ali. More specifically, I argue that Westernization and modernization have, directly or indirectly, precipitated a series of crises, real or imagined, to which the bodies social, economic, and political have been unable to respond. Neo-fundamentalism, which is merely the most recent variant of a series of fundamentalist movements in Egypt during the last two hundred years, therefore, arose as an alternative attempt to cope with these crises.

Before starting the analysis, a few general remarks on the fundamentalist movement itself are in order. First, the movement is characterized by intellectual or ideological diversity. While all neo-fundamentalists share the political goal of establishing an Islamic order,[2] they disagree on the nature of such an order, how to bring it about, and its relationship to modernity. They have yet, as Butterworth observed, "to set forth clear ideas about how Islamic government should function. Their [referring to the ideologues of the movement] rhetoric, addressed now more than ever to the . . . masses of citizens, speaks . . . of what might be and ignores the practical, procedural issues of how these goals are to be reached without harming citizens along the way."[3] Second, while most Muslims can be considered fundamentalists in the broadest sense the term, that is, in their acceptance of the basic tenets of the faith, only a small number of movements among them are *actively* involved in a crusade against the state, seeking to act on their religious-ideological convictions to bring about an authentic Islamic order in their respective countries at first but ultimately on the international level as well. In this chapter, we are concerned primarily with the politicized wings of the movement. Third, all Islamist groups "are symptomatic of a crisis [that is occurring] in the Muslim world"[4] today. As we shall see below, such a crisis is multifaceted and complex. It has many dimensions: individual, social, political, economic, and moral, to mention a few. It is also not unique to Egypt for it exists in practically every Third World country. What does make it unique is the fact that Muslim neo-fundamentalists resort to religiosity and religious answers in confronting, defining, interpreting, and offering solutions to these crises. Fourth, except for the militants among them, these groups, far from being fanatical or violent, are generally moderate in their views and orientations and so prefer non-violence to violence as the means to bring about desired change. As Ibrahim puts it, today's neo-fundamentalists are "quite moderate in both word and deed. . . . On the rare occasions that these groups urged the use of force, this was often directed against Western imperialism or against Zionism. While vigorous in the advocacy of their vision, they do not, as a rule, resort to violence."[5] Again, the method of choice for the majority of these groups is to bring about change through "consciousness-raising, teaching and peaceful pressure on rulers to heed the call of Islam,"[6] and we might add, not infrequently, through methods of civil disobedience such as peaceful demonstrations, boycotts, protests, and non-cooperation with the powers that be. Finally, the movement, as pointed out earlier, is not politically or socially monolithic: many groups in Egypt fit the label of neo-fundamentalist.[7]

EXPECTATIONS OF THE RISE OF NEO-FUNDAMENTALISM IN EGYPT

Many theories have been advanced to explain the contemporary neo-fundamentalist phenomenon in Egypt. While these theories may differ in their emphases, orientations, conclusions, and causal attributions, they all rely on the concept of crisis, whether explicitly or implicitly, to explain the malaise that is afflicting Egyptian society and politics.[8] Accordingly, one finds in the literature on Islamic fundamentalism, both by Western and Egyptian commentators, repeated references to and usage of the term *crisis*. Where they all differ is in how they define the nature of that crisis. Is it a crisis of modernization or modernity? Westernization? Secularism? Identity? Authenticity? Legitimacy? Ideology? Islam? Culture? Morality? Is it a crisis of the individual or the collectivity? Is it a crisis of the body social, economic, or political or all of these? Or is it essentially a psychological crisis? Is it all of the above? No consensus exists as to the answers to these questions nor, perhaps, is one needed. In this chapter, I take the position that the crisis is multidimensional and that Islamic neo-fundamentalism is the product of a series of factors and events, some contemporary and some that have their roots deep in the past.

One of the oldest and most prevalent explanations for the rise of neo-fundamentalism throughout the Arab world postulates that the phenomenon emerged, ironically, as a product of modernization and Westernization, or, more accurately, as a reaction and challenge to modernization and Westernization.[9] It should be emphasized that the two terms *modernization* and Westernization, which are often used synonymously, are indeed quite different. Modernization implies building viable social, economic, political, and military institutions in order to build strong "modern" states. Westernization, on the other hand, implies adoption of certain patterns or activities of Western civilization: its ideas, its culture, and its institutions. Muslims generally accept modernization, at least its scientific and technical manifestations, not only because it helps them build viable states and improved standards of living but also because there are very few components in modernization that are inherently incompatible with Muslim law or culture. Most Muslim neo-fundamentalists too claim that they are not inimical to what Lawrence calls "instrumental modernity,"[10] only those facets of it they perceive to be incompatible with Islam. However, their literature sometimes suggests a confusion of modernization and Westernization, which makes it very difficult at times to determine what their actual attitude towards these phenomena really is. Nonetheless, it is accurate to suggest that they accept the scientific and technical aspects of modernization but they reject Westernization altogether. No one among them that I am aware of is proposing that we return to the horse or the camel as a means of transportation, nor are they (except perhaps the most die-hard among them such as the Taliban in Afghanistan) calling for the banning of radio, television, telephone, or other similar products of modernization. It is interesting to point out in this context that many of the leaders and members that belong to militant Islamic groups in Egypt come from the faculties of science and technology in Egyptian universities. With limited opportunities available to them after they graduate, they become the most alienated in Egyptian society. At any rate, at least theoretically and ideologically, they are virtually unanimous in their condemnation and rejection of Western civilization. To the old and new Islamists, it is decadent and as such constitutes a mortal threat to Islam and the Islamic way of life. They will concede nothing to defenders of Western civilization because they see a zero-sum relationship between Western and Islamic civilizations: a gain for one constitutes a loss for the other. Even small concessions will undermine the purity of the faith and ultimately lead to its destruction. Such an attitude explains in part their aversion to and antipathy towards other Muslims who seek even limited accommodation with Westernization. Perpetual struggle between Westerners and Muslims, therefore, is all but inevitable. This is reminiscent of the hypothesis of Huntington who argued that future conflicts would not be driven by ideological or economic animosities but by antagonisms over culture and cultural authenticity and identity. In a word, the future struggle will involve not so much the clash of nation-states as the "clash of civilizations" and cultures.[11] At any rate, according to Islamists, any attempt at Westernization will ultimately fail. Should it succeed, it can only lead at best to the fossilization of Islam and at worst to its demise as a civilization and to the cultural enslavement of Muslims. It is not surprising, given these views, that Muslim neo-fundamentalists have made their hostility to Western civilization almost an article of faith.

More specifically, then, why do neo-fundamentalists, the anti-modern modernists as Lawrence likes to call them,[12] manifest such deep hostility and fear towards some aspects of modernity and specifically towards Western civilization? It is tempting to blame such antagonism on stereotypical images of the West, on misunderstanding of Western culture, on the confusion that exists regarding modernity and Westernization, on the fear of everything modern, on religious bigotry and fanaticism, on one-dimensional modes of thought, on alleged irrationalism, and even on paranoia. Such explanations are popular not only in the Western world, which often succumbs to its own brand of stereotyping of Muslims,[13] but also among secular groups and ruling elites in the Arab world who have a vested interest in portraying Islamists, whom they consider to be their main adversaries and competitors in the political arena, as deranged, irrational, and misguided souls. There is perhaps some truth in such accusations, especially when applied to Islamic true believers. To accept them unequivocally, however, is to divert attention from the root causes that give rise to Islamic neo-fundamentalism and Islamic movements in general and to focus instead on its negative symptoms and outward manifestations. Furthermore, to taint neo-fundamentalists all over the world with such labels does not explain why neo-fundamentalism is so appealing to millions of Muslims all over the world. To uncover the root causes one needs to take a closer look at some of the forces unleashed by modernization and Westernization to understand how these led to the emergence of neo-fundamentalism both historically and contemporaneously.

Egypt was the first Arab country to come in touch with modernity. Egyptian ruling hierarchies, from Muhammad Ali to Hosni Mubarak, embraced modernity, or, more accurately, certain aspects of it including technology, industrialization, mass education, Western legal codes, and so on. This was done for a variety of reasons: to overcome "backwardness," to help in the economic and social development the country, to strengthen the state, to consolidate the power of the ruling hierarchies, and to resist Western encroachment. Initially, this embrace was largely a preoccupation of the ruling oligarchies and Muslim Westernizers who believed that Egypt had to adopt modernity if it was to cope with the challenges and problems it faced as a nation. These constituencies accepted and continue to accept most aspects of modernity despite the fact that they couched such acceptance in Islamic terms. They saw no major contradictions between Islam and modernity's secularist underpinnings. Islam, they argued, is a dynamic, progressive, and adaptable religion suitable for all times and places. If Islam fell into hard times and became stagnant, it is because it came under the spell of the traditional or "reactionary" elements such as the traditional anti-progressive *ulama* (experts in Islamic jurisprudence). If Islam is to succeed in meeting the challenges and forces generated by modernity, it has to be reinterpreted and made adaptable to changing conditions in order to survive, and this it can do only by coming to terms with modernity.

Such views ultimately set the stage for the emergence of secularism or semi-secularism in Egypt—a development that was instrumental in the emergence of neo-fundamentalism, then and now. However, not every group in Egypt at the time saw a positive correlation between Islam and modernization. Traditionalists rejected the Westernizers' views outright as a contaminant of Islam while others took the middle of the road by accepting some aspects of modernization while rejecting others.[14] At any case, these varying responses to modernization and Westernization are expressions of divisions within the Islamic movement today.

Once the modernization process began in the nineteenth century, it unleashed forces that precipitated a series of crises, real or imagined, that in turn played a prominent role in the creation of Islamic fundamentalist movements in nineteenth- and twentieth-century Egypt. According to Vatikiotis,[15] modernization brought about many conditions that were seen by contemporary Islamists as constituting a mortal danger to Islam. These included the fragmentation of the Muslim community into separate territorial states, the introduction of secularism and other "alien" ideologies, and rapid economic and social change that contributed to the "disruptions, dislocations, disorientations, and disaffection."

Very few of these developments were palatable to the traditional or contemporary fundamentalists. The rise of the nation-state in the Arab world, which they saw as a machination of the Western imperialists and proponents of modernization in the Arab world, not only fragmented the Muslim and Arab worlds but it also undermined the Muslim ideal of a worldly moral and spiritual community of believers linked together by faith and brotherhood and guided by the principles of the *Qur'an* and the teachings of the Prophet. Essentially, modernization became synonymous with the twin "absolute" evils of nationalism and secularism.

Neo-fundamentalists oppose nationalism for a variety of reasons: first, because it is an "alien" ideology; second, because it is responsible for breaking up the Muslim community into separate entities; and finally and most important, because it calls upon Muslims to forsake the worship of God for the worship of the state. This latter point means in effect that believers are asked to submit to the will of men (rulers) rather than the will of God. Islam, according to these Muslims, does not recognize worship of any human organization, unless it conforms to God's commands. Clearly, a secular state, such as the one that allegedly exists in Egypt today, does not meet these criteria. Nationalism and its organizational manifestation, the state, therefore, are forms of idolatry and apostasy because they alienate man from his Creator.[16]

Secularism,[17] which Kepel designates as one of the "four horsemen of the apocalypse" (the others being the Jewry, the Crusade, and communism) is one of the four deadly enemies of Islam.[18] Secularism brought about an even greater calamity to Egypt and the Muslim world because it undermined one of the basic principles of Islam, namely, the separation of religion and politics and religion and the state. On a more general level, it violated the quintessential principle of Islam, that of *tawhid* (unity)—the unity or oneness of God; the unity of the social, economic and political orders; the unity of the individual and the collectivity; and the unity of the whole cosmos. To practically all Muslim neo-fundamentalists Islam is an all-encompassing, self-sufficient and holistic religious system.[19] It regulates and informs all facets of life—that of the individual, community, and public authority. Any attempt to compartmentalize Islam, to separate private and public space, is contrary to God's design and intent. Worse still, the introduction of secularism and other manifestations of the Western model in Egyptian politics implies that Islam as a belief system has failed, that it is no longer relevant to the modern world, and that it is incapable of dealing with the monumental problems that Egypt is facing. By relegating Islam to the realm of private space, it ceases to be relevant to larger entities such as the state, society, or the international community; it ceases to have collective relevance. It becomes, in effect, marginalized and trivialized. This in turn makes it impossible to establish a moral, let alone a political, order that is consistent with Islamic values and principles.[20]

The fear of losing, incrementally, Islam and the Islamic way of life to Western culture is the essence of the psychological crisis (anxiety) crisis that not only Islamic neo-fundamentalists in Egypt but Muslims generally, are facing. Whatever its shortcomings, Islam gives the faithful a degree of predictability, stability, comfort, and guidance in their lives. It makes them tolerate their existence in that it promises rewards in the hereafter and hope for this world if only they lead pious lives. It enables them to accept stoically their wretched existence because of their belief that this must be God's will. It also gives them solace, comfort, and a degree of security in a world that is increasingly harsh, uncertain, and unpredictable. This abiding faith in Islam is working to the advantage of Islamic activists today. Their battle cries that "Islam is the way!" and "Islam is the solution!" have fallen on sympathetic ears. Islam has all the answers to the contemporary malaise, psychological or otherwise, afflicting Egyptians; all they have to do is embrace it and support the establishment of a truly Islamic state.

The Muslim neo-fundamentalists' argument that the answer to the psychological anxieties of the Egyptian people and the only answer to their social, economic, and political problems is Islam, has drawn much support among the Egyptians particularly in the last three decades or so. They never tire of preaching that the other systems that have been tried by the Egyptian state, such as nationalism, pan-Arabism, socialism, communism, liberalism, and capitalism, have "failed." This is proof to them that imported ideologies do not work in Egypt precisely because they are inimical to Islamic culture and praxis.

Their message is clear: if these systems imported from the West have failed, is it not time to give Islam (the only authentic system that can lead to salvation, individual and collective, because its prescriptions emanate from Allah) another chance? Certainly there is a power and logic in this message that cannot be brushed aside easily. To ignore it is to ignore the persistent appeal of those who speak of Allah to the rank and file Egyptians. Even Muslim militants elicit sympathy from the disadvantaged Egyptians no matter how much the latter may disagree with their methods.

The general feeling among Muslim neo-fundamentalists is that since the Crusades, the Western world was engaged in an unremitting campaign to destroy Islam and Islamic civilization and to humiliate Muslims everywhere.[21] In the past, The West tried to destroy Islam by force. Today the West purportedly is using more subtle and sinister ways to undermine Islam, namely, through globalization, cultural imperialism, and acculturation.[22] They see globalization as a euphemism for a new sort of economic imperialism that is contributing to the impoverishment and utter dependence of the Muslim world on the West, particularly on the United States, which in Ayatollah Khomeini's imagery constitutes the "great Satan." Western hatred of and persistent animosity towards Islam are accepted as incontestable facts. In addition, many others share this view of the West. Such imagery appeals to and is accepted by most Egyptians whatever their philosophical orientations. At any rate, the adoption of these alien ideologies and Western lifestyles is said to explain the Muslim decline and many other calamities that have befallen the Arab world in the last two centuries. These include the fragmentation and enervation of the Arab world, its subservience to the West, its disempowerment, and its impoverishment through the exploitation of its natural resources. Perhaps the greatest disaster to afflict the Arab world was the creation of the "little Satan" Israel (a dagger thrust into the heart of the Arab world by the conniving and duplicitous West), and the loss of Jerusalem (the third holiest city in Islam) and other Arab lands to Israel after the Six-Day War.

Most Muslim neo-fundamentalists are not opposed to modernization in its entirety. After all, in many respects, they are products of this process. What they are opposed to is Westernization that is forced on the Arab world in the guise of modernization. While a few are willing to concede that there are some facets of Western civilization that are positive, most see it as an anathema and the foremost threat to Islamic civilization today. They outwardly reject, always allowing for exceptions, its political, economic, and social systems; its incessant drive to subjugate and exploit other peoples; its secular and materialistic ideologies; its alleged decadence; its tendency to put materialistic values above spiritual and moral values; and its seeming indifference to the decline in society's most important unit, the family. They oppose Western liberal democracy because, according to their ideologues, it (a) vests sovereignty in men or their institutions rather than in God; (b) emphasizes the interests of the individual at the expense the collectivity; (c) puts individual rights ahead of individual obligations, which leads to licentious and immoral behavior that corrupts and perverts man's basic humanity; (d) fragments the community because it encourages the formation of fractious interest groups and parties; and (e) puts the interests of the privileged and the affluent ahead of those of the deprived and the disadvantaged which, in effect, purportedly transforms its government into little more than an instrument of the propertied class, by the propertied class, and for the propertied class. The experience of Egyptians with the quasi-liberal democratic experiment under the Wafd during the inter-war period did little to dispel such beliefs. The Wafd government was corrupt, nepotistic, indifferent to people's needs, and used the symbols of democracy (not its substance) to gain legitimacy for a ruling class of the landowners and wealthy capitalists.

Neo-fundamentalists also reject all materialistic philosophies imported from the West, whether they are capitalist, communist, or nationalist. [23] They are not opposed to private ownership per se (Islam recognizes the right of every Muslim to his fairly acquired wealth), but they reject *Western* or bourgeois capitalism because it fosters an economic system characterized by greed, exploitation, and crass materialism—one that allows the rich to prey on the poor and hence ensures the latter's perpetual deprivation and misery. It rejects communism, also a materialistic philosophy of Western vintage, not only because it denies the existence of God but also because it despoils every country it rules, directly or indirectly (such as, allegedly, Egypt under Nasser). Neo-fundamentalists are most uncomfortable with the social systems prevalent in the West because they are based on pluralism, which they see as divisive of the community and as a prescription for endless dissension and conflict. They deride Western civilization for its lax morality and spirituality as evidenced by the existence of such problems as alcoholism, drug addiction, crime and violence, homelessness, broken families, and prostitution, all of which add up to the devaluation of moral and spiritual values. What makes these maladies of the West particularly disturbing, aside from the fact that they violate all the sacrosanct principles laid in the Holy Book, is that they have become standard fixtures in the Egyptian landscape. One needs only to take a ride through Pyramid Street in Cairo (with its plush hotels, nightclubs, casinos, etc.) to experience the "degradation" that has befallen Egypt because of its blind emulation of the West. A truly Islamic state, it is argued, would have none of these immoralities, abnormalities, and perversities. It will be guided by God's commands expressed through the formation of a moral community where Islamic values and morality will be strictly enforced. This can only be brought about by a revolution from above, hence the imperative of taking over control of the state.

Yet another aspect of the emergence of modernization needs to be addressed: the development of the modern authoritarian-bureaucratic state. Modernization, as such, is not responsible for this development. Modernization is a politically neutral phenomenon in that it can work to the benefit of an authoritarian-totalitarian regime (e.g., Nazi Germany or Fascist Italy) or a more democratic one. But more often than not, modernization has acted as a catalyst in the transition from the old despotic systems to the rise of liberal democratic systems in much of Europe and subsequently other parts of the world. Unfortunately, modernization had the opposite effect on Egypt. This is not to suggest that modernization was responsible for the emergence of authoritarianism in Egypt, merely that it exacerbated this condition by enhancing the power of the traditional patriarchal and patrimonial state at the expense of both civil society and the Egyptian people. Authoritarianism in one form or another has existed in that country almost continually since the time of the pharaohs. Therefore, the authoritarian tradition has been in Egypt for some time—a tradition that even modernization could not reverse, at least not so far. Modernization might still bring about liberalization and democratization in the future as a result of mounting domestic and international pressures and the emergence of what traditionally has been considered preconditions of democracy, namely, a large middle class, an educated public, a viable economy, and a vibrant civil society. Let us hope that this indeed will materialize for this seems to be the only means by which the state can resolve what has been an endemic problem for Egypt, namely, the lack of legitimacy of its political system. Despite the periodic manipulation by the ruling elite of liberal and democratic symbols to co-opt opposition groups and to defuse the "crisis of hegemony," Egypt remains an authoritarian state. It is likely to remain so in the foreseeable future, liberal and democratic pretensions of its ruling elite notwithstanding.

As indicated above, the lack of legitimacy of the ruling elite is the essence of the political "crisis of legitimacy" in modern Egypt and the Arab countries.[24] Modernization has accentuated this crisis not only because it has made it easier for rulers to consolidate their control over the state (by strengthening the mechanisms of control, coercion, and intimidation) but also because it has called into question the traditional sources of legitimacy on which the authority of the rulers was based, such as charisma, custom, coercion, ideology, consent, and religion. For years, Egyptian rulers tried to establish their legitimacy by relying on one or more of these sources with at best partial success. Today, the issue of legitimacy is yet to be resolved. For neo-fundamentalists the legitimacy crisis can only be resolved if the state is Islamized and the *shari`ah* becomes the *only* source of legislation.[25] For many, perhaps most, secularists democratization is the answer.[26] On this point, however, both mainstream left and right agree, namely, that the current regime of coercion and repression in Egypt is illegitimate and that it can become legitimate only if it opens the gates of power to all groups in Egyptian society. The long-standing wall of separation and hostility between civil society and the state must come to an end if the political system is to become acceptable to the various constituencies who challenge its legitimacy. Legitimization through genuine political pluralization and cooperation between civil society and the state will go a long way towards improving the prospects that the state will be able to cope effectively with the plethora of problems that plague Egypt today and are likely to continue to haunt it in the future.

The selective modernization that Egyptian rulers followed had an opposite effect to that in the West. The rulers were selective in the sense that they chose only those features of modernization that would not only strengthen the state but, importantly, their own positions. Had they adopted the modernization ethos in its entirety (for example, respect for human rights, civic participation, the introduction of democratic institutions, etc.) and had they succeeded in cultivating this ethos in the masses, its effects on the Egyptian body politic might have been different altogether. As it turned out, selective modernization and its insulation from the masses led to the entrenchment of the state and the concentration of power in the hands of whichever power elite happened to be in control of the authoritarian-bureaucratic state at the time. Modern means of control and coercion, the revolution in transportation and communication and so on worked to the benefit of the state.[27] These developments gave the ruling elite a monopoly over power that they have not relinquished to this day. At the same time, as the state grew stronger, civil society grew weaker and became marginalized. Where civil society did exist, it was closely supervised and overshadowed by the state. In many cases, voluntary groups were dependent on the state for survival. Today, the difficulties that the state is encountering, domestic and foreign, have forced it to seek help from the private associations or organizations in dealing with the problems it is facing. As a result, civil society is showing signs of vibrancy and rejuvenation and is becoming more assertive in its demands vis-à-vis the state. But despite this positive development, civil society continues to be subservient to the state and under its control. Tensions between the two are likely to continue in the near future with the greatest challenges coming from Islamic societies, organizations, and movements whether peaceful or militant. Their secular counterparts, those that seek political pluralization, liberalization, and democratization, remain comparatively weak and out of touch with the Egyptian masses who find it easier to understand the messages of the neo-fundamentalists, precisely because it is couched in familiar Islamic terminology.

Egypt's ruling oligarchy continues to practice the politics of civic exclusion to the detriment of stability, order, and legitimization. Opposition groups are tolerated and allowed to participate symbolically in the political system only to the extent that they pose no threat to the status quo. The regime in power, ever on the lookout for encroachments on its prerogatives, precludes other groups from any meaningful sharing of power, from freely contesting elections, or from finding an outlet for their legitimate grievances. In dealing with threats from opposition groups (secular or non-secular), the regime always responds in a predictable way: it criminalizes their organizations; arrests, jails or executes their leaders; suspends civil and political liberties; declares national emergencies, and engages ex post facto in a massive and manipulative propaganda effort to justify its actions. Another favorite technique is to play one group against another: offer the carrot to those who cooperate, the stick to those who do not.[28] In short, the regime in power resorts to more oppression, repression, and violence of its own against civil society. Under these circumstances, it is easy to understand how and why Islamists, especially the young among them, have come to experience themselves as the victims of the state. That Islamists have become estranged and nihilistic as a result of years of repression by the Egyptian state should not surprise anyone. Nor should it surprise anyone to learn that these conditions help explain why young Islamists often resort to illegal, extralegal, and often violent methods to the problems they perceive as being caused by the state. Islamic militancy in Egypt, therefore, may be seen in part as a product of and a response to institutional violence, which neo-fundamentalists have termed "state terrorism." A symbiotic relationship now exists in Egypt between state and group violence with tragic consequences for both and for society at large.

It is fashionable today to call Islamic militants extremists, irrationalists, or fanatics because they support the use of force. Many commentators, journalists, and government officials in the United States and Egypt are quick to condemn these individuals as terrorists, the implication being that these people have no just cause or legitimate grievances, only deranged minds that impel them to perform barbaric acts. To a certain extent, this charge is perhaps true. *All* forms of violence, from the perspective of moral absolutism, are unjustifiable. Unfortunately, we live in a world that is informed by such "modern" philosophies as political realism, utilitarianism, and pragmatism. Each of these philosophies, arguably products of the modernization ethos, contributes to a climate of violence in one way or another. Political realism calls for the separation of ethics and politics and the pursuit of state interest by whatever means, including the use of force. As the name implies, utilitarianism underscores the importance of utility: anything and any action is judged useful if it promotes certain values (such as happiness, contentment, etc.); it is considered dysfunctional if it does not. Pragmatism measures the value of any act by its practical consequences, not by its morality. Such doctrines, albeit unwittingly, have come to be accepted and used as rationalizations by opposition groups in Egypt to undermine the existing regime. If one approach fails, why not try a different approach? If the state uses violence to *perpetuate* the status quo, why cannot the opposition do the same to *change* the status quo, especially in the absence of other ways of effecting change? If those who control the state choose to disregard moral, ethical, or spiritual considerations in the pursuit of their interests, why can't the dissidents? The point here is simply that the ideological systems (i.e., realism, utilitarianism, and pragmatism) have informed, or should we say contaminated, not only the state but also opposition groups as well. Two implications of this analysis bear special mention. First, Islamic opposition groups, not unlike the ruling elite, may be seen as products of the international state system ethos and the philosophies that undergird it. Second, Islamic militancy in Egypt may be conceived as a reaction to and a product of state violence. When government officials in Egypt, therefore, denounce Islamists as terrorists, the latter can justifiably accuse the former of hypocrisy since they themselves resort to institutional violence whenever they feel threatened by other groups.

Modernization in Egypt has also brought with it an identity crisis. As indicated above, modernization, or more appropriately quasi-modernization, was and to a very large extent remains restricted to few groups in society. It is accepted, both as an idea and as praxis, by the governing elite along with leftist groups, Muslim modernizers, and a substantial segment of the intelligentsia. They subscribe to former President Sadat's dictum that there "is no politics in religion and no religion in politics," which in its essence reflects the secularist impulse. Accordingly, they tend to identify with modernity and with the nation-state: they are Egyptians or Egyptian Arabs first and foremost. This cannot be said of the public at large who still continue to embrace, be guided to a large extent by, and identify with Islam. This is not to suggest that the Egyptian masses have not been touched by, or affected by some aspects of modernity, or have not benefited from it. It is simply to state that modernization, let alone Westernization, as an idea, has not become ingrained in the psyche of the average Egyptian who still leads a traditional life and continues to identify with Islam. Part of the explanation for this is the fact that successive ruling elites in Egypt made no serious effort, until the Nasser era, to install in the Egyptian masses a secularizing and modernizing spirit, with what Bassam Tibi calls "intellectual modernity."[29] Nasser might have succeeded in this endeavor had he been able to improve the lot of the Egyptian people, and therefore, show them the blessings of modernization. However, the 1967 war with Israel and his premature death put an end to this project. After that, many Egyptians, especially the young, looked beyond secularism in the direction of Islam. These two tendencies remained essentially the domains of the governing elite and their few supporters. On the other hand, that the state in Egypt failed to get the Muslim masses to identify with the idea of modernity is in part why the dichotomy between the state and Muslim neo-fundamentalists continues to exist today and why the latter, who continue to insist that the only true and meaningful identity is one that is religion-based, continues to appeal to the Egyptian masses. The dualism between those who call for an Islamic identity and those who call for a national (Egyptian or Arab) identity is the essence of the identity crisis.[30] Egyptians find themselves torn between these two currents. The identity crisis in essence is also a crisis of conflicting values: Islamic-based and Western-based. For the Muslim neo-fundamentalists, true authenticity derives from total identification with Islam and its ethos. True believers cannot be authentic Muslims and nationalists-secularists at the same time. The former accept God's word and live by it. The latter do not; they merely use God's word to cover up their un-Islamic behavior and policies. A secularized Islam is an oxymoron. Secular Muslims cannot be true Muslims because they have forsaken their religiosity and alienated themselves from their true identity in favor of an imported one. To neo-fundamentalists, Arab rulers feign their commitment to Islam but in fact are doing everything to destroy it. Therefore, elimination of these "impostors" *(munafiqin)* is the sine qua non of restoring Muslim identity. As we shall see later, this is one of the rationalizations that Muslim neo-fundamentalists give for their critique of and rebellion against the "impious" oligarchic-bureaucratic leadership in Egypt.

One other effect of modernization must be mentioned. Arguably, modernization brings with it the potential for the acceleration in the rate of social and economic change. Normally, such change is viewed as desirable because it is associated with social and economic development, and hence an improvement in the standard of living of the population. Before World War II, Egypt's development, while substantial, did not markedly improve the quality of life for the majority of the Egyptian people, who remained poor compared to even some of the Third World countries. Some improvements in the lot of the Egyptian people did take place under the regime of President Nasser—a fact that brought with it the promise of a better life, better future, greater equality, justice and dignity, and in due course, a more humane and more democratic political system. This contributed, in turn, not only to increased hope and optimism but also to raised expectations. Unfortunately, the subsequent privatization and economic liberalization policies pursued by Nasser's successors worsened Egypt's economic situation. The crisis generated by unrealized expectations has forced many Egyptians, almost by default, to turn towards neo-fundamentalism for salvation, both spiritual and economic.

FACTORS SPECIFIC TO THE RISE OF NEO-FUNDAMENTALISM IN EGYPT

Let us now turn our attention to the most recent "wave" of fundamentalism in Egypt and address the immediate factors that gave rise to it. Commentators generally agree that the defeat of Egypt by Israel in 1967 marks the beginning of this wave. The Six-Day War came as a severe shock not only to Egyptians but to other Arabs as well. It brought with it a crisis of confidence, disruption, shame, anxiety, and despair. But more important, it brought about further alienation, estrangement, and humiliation to Egyptian youth. Many of the neo-fundamentalists of the 1970s and 1980s were the sons and daughters of the nationalists and socialists of the 1950s and 1960s. The trauma brought about by the war led Egyptians to do what people often do in times of crisis, namely, fall back on religion for solace.

Muslim neo-fundamentalists were quick to blame the defeat in the 1967 war on the *jahiliyyah* (literally the ignorant state but in practical terms the secular un-Islamic and uncivilized state) with its embrace of secularism, nationalism, and socialism and on Western and Zionist machinations to humiliate and to undermine Islam. Even President Nasser resorted to religious explanations to account for the disaster (*nakbah*) that had befallen Egypt. It was God's will and Egypt's destiny to suffer such a fate, he told his fellow Egyptians. Muslim neo-fundamentalists interpreted the event, less benignly, as God's punishment for the Egyptians' abandoning the straight path (*al-Tariq al-Mustaqim*) and their alienation from true Islam and from God. Only through a return to Islam could Egypt prevent future disasters and meet the challenges posed by its enemies, domestic or foreign. What the defeat did was reinforce the Muslim neo-fundamentalist belief that Islam is the only solution left for the Egyptians. But more important, they saw in Islam a protective shield against Western domination and a mechanism with which Muslims, especially the youth among them, could "carve out a new future and seek a place of respect and honor in the world" for themselves.[31] Two decades under Nasser proved that Western ideas, systems, and solutions failed to address Egypt's basic socioeconomic and political problems; only an Islamic order can do so.

The decades of the 1970s and 1980s also witnessed several events that gave impetus and encouragement to Islamic movements everywhere including Egypt. These included, among other things, the "success" of Egypt against Israel in the 1973 war—a war that Sadat tried to justify in religious terms so as to appeal to Egyptian Muslims who had hitherto opposed him. The war was code named Operation Badr and took place in the holy month of Ramadan. (The battle of al-Badr was a minor but significant battle fought in 624 A.D. by the Prophet Muhammad against his enemies). Furthermore, the Arab oil embargo became indicative to the Muslim neo-fundamentalists of what the Muslims can achieve if only they can act in unison. The convening of an Islamic Conference in Saudi Arabia signaled renewed interest in Islam. Other encouraging developments included Zia al-Haqq's assumption of power in Pakistan, the start of the Afghanistan war against the Soviet Union, the Juhaiman group takeover of the Holy Mosque in Mecca, the success of the Islamic Revolution in Iran, and the increasing manifestations of "Islamic symbolism" (such as the wearing of traditional dress by men and women, the growing of beards by the latter, increased attendance in mosques, broadening religious instruction in schools, airing of religious programs on television, etc.).

Sadat's policies gave impetus to the neo-fundamentalist movement in Egypt in a variety of ways.[32] His desire to consolidate his regime after the death of Nasser led him to forge alliances with groups that had been opposed to Nasser and his policies. In the forefront of these groups were the Muslim neo-fundamentalists who had suffered probably more than any other group under Nasser's regime. Sadat's wooing of Islamic groups may have helped him achieve his objective of neutralizing his leftist opponents, but it also resulted in increased visibility, exposure, and assertiveness on the part of the neo-fundamentalists themselves. Sadat's policy of "retraditionalization,"[33] whereby the state sought the help of the traditional elite to bring about political stability, had the direct effect of strengthening the traditional Islamic groups, foremost among whom were the Muslim Brotherhood, and the indirect effect of encouraging the formation of many new Islamic groups. This resulted in the strengthening and emboldenment of the Islamic movements in Egypt considerably.

Egypt's pressing and "formidable"[34] economic problems for the populace on the whole and the worsening of the situation for most Egyptians constituted yet another factor (I believe the most important one) that contributed to the rise of neo-fundamentalism in Egypt. According to Ibrahim M. Oweiss,[35] the Egyptian economy suffers from a variety of problems that the Egyptian regimes under Sadat and Mubarak have been and are unable or unwilling to deal with. These include the following: "inadequate agricultural production . . ., balance of payments deficits . . ., a population explosion, high rates of unemployment and disguised unemployment, a crushing debt service burden, high rates of inflation, substantial budget deficits, widespread price-cost distortions, low productivity and acute external imbalance." Nasser tried to cope with these problems through the socialization of the Egyptian economy, planning, and distributive policies. By most estimates, his socialist policies and his "developmental vision"[36] failed because of the tensions that existed between the imperatives of economic growth and those of welfarism. Sadat followed this with a new "miracle formula" or "grand plan"[37] with which he hoped to end the worsening crisis, namely, through a policy of *al- Infitah* (opening, open door policy). He believed and hoped that a degree of economic liberalization would stimulate economic growth and development through privatization, economic liberalization, and increased investments (domestic and foreign) into the private sector[38] and "rationalization of the public sector."[39] Largely, this policy reflected pressures from outside, particularly the International Monetary Fund and the World Bank, to abandon the socialist economy and to introduce austerity measures. Sadat and Mubarak had little choice but to comply with these demands as Egypt found itself increasingly dependent on the West for economic, technical, and military aid. But here again, Sadat's policy, which remained basically unchanged under his successor Mubarak,[40] failed because they put too much faith in the power of private enterprise as a mechanism of growth and the improvement of the condition of the Egyptian masses. At the same time, Sadat's economic liberalization marked an important retreat from Nasser's egalitarianism, welfarism, and distributive justice. Sadat's policies led to a marked deterioration in the condition of the Egyptian masses, particularly that of the young among them, who became even more frustrated, alienated, and rebellious. As Dessouki sums it up, "Sadat's policies on the younger generations [were] devastating."[41]

The Muslim Brotherhood denounced the *infitah*, in a critique worthy of Karl Marx, as creating "false needs"[42] that would bring about lifestyles and tastes similar to those of the West. These policies had little appeal because they largely benefited the bourgeoisie but did little to alleviate the plight of the average Egyptian or to offer any hope and promise for the burgeoning young population. Worse still, such policies fell hard on the middle class whose condition continued to deteriorate through the Mubarak era. It is not surprising, therefore, to see why the young and a substantial segment of the middle class in Egypt turned to Islam, though not necessarily Islamic militancy, for redemption. In the confusion that was generated by Sadat's abandonment of Nasser's political ideology and economic policy, the young found in Islam a "yardstick, a compass, a comprehensive set of values and norms," and "the certainty that young people search for."[43] It is among these alienated young people that neo-fundamentalists of all persuasions found fertile ground from which to recruit members for their organizations and energize their movements.

Other policies of Sadat also contributed to the alienation of many Egyptians. The two most significant ones were his alignment with the United States and his peace treaty with Israel—policies that were continued by Mubarak. Both policies were resented by neo-fundamentalists and nationalists alike because the former made Egypt economically dependent on the United States and because the latter was seen as a betrayal of Palestinians in particular and Muslims in general. In effect, the peace treaty with Israel, as they saw it, gave legitimacy to Israel's continued occupation of Jerusalem. In the words of Hinnebusch, "the Israeli-American connection has generated a profound crisis of nationalist legitimacy which deprives the regime of the support needed to really confront Egypt's problems."[44] The fact that Sadat and Mubarak pursued policies that were extremely unpopular with Egyptians seemingly demonstrates yet again the willingness of Egypt's ruling elite to pursue a course of action that is out of touch with the sentiments of their own people, thereby reinforcing the popular belief at least among the Muslim neo-fundamentalists that the nationalist-secularist elite will ally themselves with the devil if they have to protect their monopoly over power.

Today, the increasing destitution of the Egyptian masses has resulted in mass immigration of rural inhabitants to the cities in search of relief from their misery and deprivation. They have found neither. What they have found is an already serious urban crisis: congestion, serious shortage in housing, urban squalor, pollution, lack of electricity, water, telephone, service in the slums, unemployment and underemployment, abject poverty, inadequate health services, and so on. The cities, not surprisingly, have become recruiting grounds for Islamic neo-fundamentalists, or here, the immigrants experience sharply the contrasts in lifestyles between the haves and the have-nots. Through contacts with their fellow Muslims in the mosques, Islamic societies, schools, and universities and through their subjection to Islamic education or propaganda or both, they have become, generally speaking, more bitter, radicalized, and rebellious.

In summary, the effect of Sadat's and Mubarak's economic and political policies has been to further fragment the political order[45] and to deepen the economic and legitimacy crises—crises manifested, as Roy points out, in the "weak legitimacy of regimes and states, even in the very idea of a nation." It is also manifested in the "permanence of autocratic regimes . . ., [uncontrolled] population growth, the destitution of the middle classes, the unemployment of the educated, [and] the growing ranks of the masses who live in cities but are poorly integrated there."[46] It is these crises and the failure of the state to deal with them, more than anything else that have led to the emergence of neo-fundamentalism in Egypt. The crisis in Egypt is not so much a religious one as a socioeconomic-political-cultural one. Neo-fundamentalists offer Islam, as ideology and program, as the answer to all of Egypt's ills.

PROSPECTS FOR NEO-FUNDAMENTALISM IN EGYPT

Whither Islamic neo-fundamentalism in Egypt? Will the movement succeed in leaving its mark on Egypt's social, economic, and political institutions? Will its crusade result in the complete Islamization of Egyptian culture? More important, will neo-fundamentalists be able to take over the reins of government in Egypt? Finally, what are their prospects for survival given the unrelenting repression of the state against them? These questions are difficult to answer. The answers that follow are speculative at best.[47]

That a crisis has been brewing in Egypt (and in the Arab political order) for decades is not a matter of dispute between Arab or Western scholars. The view that this order is "rotten to the core" or requires an almost complete repair has probably come to dominate the thinking of probably most intellectuals in the Arab world. This crisis is multi-dimensional and quilt-like in its outward manifestations. It is at once a political, social, economic, cultural, confidence, leadership, as well as an identity crisis. In a rapidly changing world, the existing order seems trivial, atomized, paralyzed, ineffective, inefficient, and increasingly irrational, abnormal, and pathological. In a world increasingly being engulfed by democratic forces and movements, the Arab political order continues to be an anomaly. The West has done little to exert the same pressure it does elsewhere to bear on Arab regimes to move in the direction of democratization. To be sure, democratic forces do exist in the Arab world, albeit in embryonic forms. So far, however, they have not been successful in bringing about the democratization of any Arab regime.

The emergence of Islamic neo-fundamentalism has been interpreted here as a manifestation of a series of crises, generated directly or indirectly, by modernization. Two "solutions" are offered for this malaise: the democratic and Islamic solutions. These are not mutually exclusive because an Islamic solution within a democratic framework is a possibility. Indeed, neo-fundamentalists, as the "new" Muslim Brotherhood discovered in Egypt, have a much better chance of attaining their objectives within a liberal-democratic framework. Moderate and "centrist" fundamentalists in Egypt have come to realize that operating within such a framework eschewing violence would generate greater respectability not only to their programs, but to their organizations as well. If reason were their guide, a possibility though by no means a certainty, they will recognize the value of cooperation with other anti-governmental forces in pushing for liberalization and democratization. In the last analysis, their success will depend less on divine intervention than on the actualization of these conditions. Islam will bring with it partial legitimization to any group or party aspiring for political power, whereas democracy produces a broad-based legitimacy that is essential for the survival and effectiveness of any regime that happens to be in power.

In general, the Islamic movement in Egypt as a whole has many reasons to be pleased about its recent successes in Egypt. Manifestations of an Islamic revival are visible everywhere. These include the return to Islamic symbolism; increased religiosity on the part of the populace; the doubling of the number of mosques; the integration of Islamic teaching into the curricula of schools and universities; the success of Islamic groups in penetrating society and its institutions, such as labor unions, student unions at the universities, and economic and financial institutions; increased sympathy for Islamic movements among the lower echelons of the armed forces; governmental wooing of mainstream Islamic groups; the proliferation of Islamic voluntary associations; and increased representation in the parliament.[48] These are but a few of the successes that mainstream neo-fundamentalists have achieved in recent years. It remains to be seen whether mainstream neo-fundamentalists will be satisfied with these gains and with their role as a mere "interest group," or whether they will continue to agitate for exclusive control of the state. One thing is clear: mainstream neo-fundamentalism is not likely to wither away any time soon, at least not as long as Egypt continues to be plagued by all kinds of problems that the regime seems unable or unwilling to solve. It is likely to remain a fixture in the Egyptian political scene for some time to come.

Even the militants have left their mark on Egyptian society and the political system albeit in negative ways. Militancy symbolizes the multi-faceted crisis that has come to plague the bodies social and political. It is symptomatic of the deep alienation of many Egyptians, particularly the young among them, from their government and all that it stands for. It is also symptomatic of the government's failure to deal effectively with the problems that often result in increasing desperation and destitution of the Egyptian masses, but especially those of the middle class. It suggests that the traditional passivity of the Egyptians is no longer to be taken for granted by the regime in power and that now some of them, at least, consider violence to be a legitimate option as a means of removing what they consider to be illegitimate regimes. The costs of Islamic-initiated violence, human and material, in the last two decades, but particularly in the early to the mid-1990s, have increased dramatically, thereby aggravating the ability of the state to deal with pressing problems facing Egypt today. Finally, Islamic militancy weakens the regime in at least two other respects. First, it forces the latter to overreact and resort to more repression of the Islamists, militant or not, thereby creating more sympathy for the Islamists. Second, it makes it virtually impossible for the regime in power to claim legitimacy for itself. This *may* lead the weakened state to seek partnership with civil society as a way of dealing with these problems and as a means of diffusing the responsibility for any failures to other segments of civil society. This in turn *may* move Egypt into the direction of liberalization, pluralization, and ultimately democratization. The opening *(infitah)* of the political system for all groups willing to abide by the democratic rules of the game would have the effect of legitimizing the regime, creating a partnership between civil society and the state, gradually ending or corroding the patriarchal and patrimonial state, undermining the rationale for recourse to violence, ensuring stability, and creating an environment more conducive to the resolution of problems that have given rise to neo-fundamentalist violence in the first place.

Despite the successes of neo-fundamentalism, there is little reason to believe that Islamic militancy will succeed in overthrowing the state. Egypt is not yet ripe for theocracy nor is it likely to be in the near future. The state may not be able to eradicate militant groups entirely, but it can contain them and withstand their assaults. The state has many resources at its disposal not the least of which is the support it gets from secular and other forces, domestic and foreign (particularly the United States), who fear Islamic militancy and its concomitant, an Islamic dictatorship. Although Islamists are represented vertically and horizontally in the armed forces, this representation is insignificant especially among the upper echelons; the likelihood of an Islamic coup initiated by the armed forces remains virtually nil. In addition, resorting to violence and terror has cost Islamic militants support among many constituencies in the population at large since many of the atrocities committed in the name of Islam have been directed against innocent bystanders: women for refusing to wear traditional dress, tourists and other foreigners, and literary and artistic figures who dared criticize them or their stance on various issues.

Finally, Islamic militants suffer from many problems common to revolutionaries everywhere, namely, disunity, poor organizational skills (although they have improved considerably in the last decade or so), leadership attrition (from imprisonment or executions, or simply death by natural causes), ideological disputes, inadequate resources, and inflexibility. Many of these groups, therefore, lack the experience necessary to wage a successful campaign against the state.[49] In the final analysis, the future of Islamic militancy in Egypt will depend on whether Egypt moves in the direction of democratization or continues with its authoritarian edifice. If it opts for the former course, there is reason to believe, as Ryan has demonstrated in his empirical study of revolutionary movements, that it will succeed in reducing the capacity of the Islamic militants' capacity to overthrow the government.[50]

Democratization of the political system may be the only option that can resolve the political crisis that has plagued Egypt for decades.[51] "The demand for democracy, the growth of prodemocracy movements," observe Esposito and Voll, "is now evident throughout the Muslim world."[52] Of course, democracy is not a panacea, a cure-all for all the problems facing any country. But if it fails, at least there will be shared responsibility for the failure. The failure cannot be blamed simply on autocratic leaders because potentially all groups will be involved in legislative decision making. Ironically, democratization, which many Islamists continue to anathematize, is the only hope for them to acquire organizational legitimacy and bring about the changes they so desperately seek. Many mainstream Islamic groups such as the Muslim Brotherhood have come to realize this. Violence will not bring them success let alone power. They have become aware that the state is simply too strong to be undermined by revolutionary violence or terrorism. They know that the state still commands resources that its opposition does not have, such as the military, coercive machinery, bureaucracy, and support from groups who fear an Islamic take-over such as nationalists, socialists, Nasserites, feminists, and labor unions, to mention a few. Hence, they have chosen to sacrifice some ideological rigidity in favor of a more realistic approach to the question of power.

Democratization is only one determinant, albeit the most important one, that will determine the success or failure of mainstream neo-fundamentalism in Egypt. There are other factors as well. These include the following: whether the crises that gave rise to the movement will continue to fester; whether the state will be able to deal with them effectively; whether Muslim neo-fundamentalists can resolve their differences and forge a united front with other groups, which will help strengthen them as a social and political force; whether they will have to compete at some future time with revitalized or rejuvenated liberal, socialist, and other secular-oriented parties; whether they can shed their image of being factious, intolerant, one-dimensional, emotional, unreasonable, and extremist; whether they can continue to appeal to the Egyptian masses and especially to the intelligentsia; whether they can reconcile themselves to modernity or not, that is, whether they can create a meaningful synthesis between modernity and Islam (the former obviously cannot be wished away or abolished by Islamic laws; fundamentalists will have to realize that two hundred years of modernity in Egypt cannot be undone unless they want to follow the example of the Taliban and take their country back into the dark ages); and whether it can convince Egyptians that Islam indeed is the solution to all the problems facing Egypt. It is difficult to predict whether the neo-fundamentalists can address any or all of these questions. It is clear, however, that they are facing, like their secular counterparts, formidable obstacles. Unless and until they can convince Egyptians that they can indeed solve their problems (sloganeering is not enough) it is very dubious that they can undermine the existing regime "with anything like the revolution in Iran."[53]

CONCLUSION

This chapter provides general as well as specific and contextual explications for the rise of neo-fundamentalism in Egypt. It focuses on modernization and its effects (the crises it generated) to describe and analyze the neo-fundamentalist phenomenon. It examines the most recent "wave" of fundamentalism that emerged roughly in the early 1970s. In general, I try to show that the Islamic neo-fundamentalist movement(s) was both a product of and a response to modernization. Modernization brought with it disruptions, dislocations, and disorientations in society and the state, which in turn produced the several crises that are discussed here. Among these were the crises of identity, authenticity, culture, and legitimacy. As to the most recent wave, I hypothesize that the primary factors that led to the rise of Islamic neo-fundamentalism are the failure of the state to deal with basic economic problems that hit the lower, lower-middle, and the middle classes hardest and the failure of the last three regimes to move in the direction of pluralization, liberalization, and democratization of the political system to resolve the crisis of legitimacy which has become Egypt's quintessential political problem. These problems, unfortunately, are likely to continue into the near future at least. Neo-fundamentalism, therefore, will continue to pose a serious challenge to the state and will continue to serve as a viable model to many disgruntled Egyptians. But if, and this is a big if, the state manages somehow to solve or alleviate these problems, neo-fundamentalism will lose much of its appeal.

One underlying hypothesis of this chapter is that genuine democratization offers the best hope of dealing with Egypt's current political and economic problems. Democracy expands participation in the political system, leads to cooperation between civil society and government in dealing with problems, offers disgruntled groups the opportunity to express their grievances without resorting to violence, ensures respect for human rights, empowers people thereby helping them overcome their sense of powerlessness and alienation, and contributes to the stability of the political order without which economic growth and development would be difficult if not impossible. There are reasons to believe, based on observations of the *mainstream* Islamists in Egypt and some Arab countries, that these groups are willing to engage in electoral politics and to respect the democratic process. After years of repression and oppression, the leaders of many of these mainstream movements have learned an important lesson, namely, that jail is not a very effective or efficient place from which to conduct a crusade on behalf of Islam. These observations, of course, do not apply to the militant groups to whom democracy continues to be an anathema. But these constitute but a tiny minority of Islamic neo-fundamentalists. What matters in the long run is whether the majority of Muslims will come to accept or reject democracy. If they accept it, then there is every reason to believe that the democratic experiment in Egypt can succeed to the benefit of most political groups in the body politic.

NOTES

1. In this chapter, we use the term *neo-fundamentalism* to describe the most recent wave of fundamentalism in Egypt. Fundamentalism is defined here as a philosophy of life, an ideology, and a movement that seeks the establishment of a political and social order in Egypt along Islamic lines, as interpreted by its leaders. On the problems of defining the term, see Bruce B. Lawrence, "Muslim Fundamentalist Movements: Reflections Toward a New Approach," in Barbara Freyer Stowasser (ed.), *The Islamic Impulse* (Washington, D.C.: Center for Contemporary Arab Studies, 1987), pp. 18-19.

2. Mark Jurgensmeyer attributes this characteristic to all fundamentalist movements. See his "The New Religious State," *Comparative Politics,* vol. 27, no. 4 (July 1995), p. 379.

3. Charles Butterworth, "Political Islam: The Origins," *The Annals* (November 1992), pp. 36-37.

4. Saad Eddin Ibrahim, *Egypt, Islam and Democracy: Twelve Critical Essays* (Cairo, Egypt: American University in Cairo Press, 1996), p. 55.

5. Ibid.

6. Ibid.

7. Mohammed Ayoob (ed.), "Introduction: The Myth of the Monolith," *The Politics of Islamic Reassertion* (New York: St. Martin's Press, 1981), p. 4.

8. See for example, Ibrahim Ibrahim, "Religion and Politics Under Nassar and Sadat," in Stowasser, *The Islamic Impulse,* p. 121. Ibrahim, *Egypt, Islam and Democracy,* p. 56.

9. Bruce B. Lawrence, *Defenders of God: The Fundamentalist Revolt Against the Modern Age* (Columbia, S.C.: The University of South Carolina Press, 1995), p. xiv; Alan R. Taylor, *The Islamic Question in the Middle East* (Boulder, Colo: Westview Press, 1988), p. 53.

10. Lawrence, *Defenders of God.*

11. Samuel P. Huntington, "Islamic Civilization Will Clash with Western Civilization," in Paul A. Winters (ed.), *Islam: Opposing Viewpoints,* pp. 205-12. Reprinted from *Foreign Affairs* (Summer 1993), where it originally appeared as "The Clash of Civilizations?"

12. Lawrence, *Defenders of God,* p. xiv.

13. Edward W. Said, *Covering Islam: How the Media and the Experts Determine How We See the Rest of the World* (New York: Pantheon Books, 1981). See also Edward W. Said, *Orientalism* (New York: Vintage Books, 1979).

14. On early reactions to modernization, see Charles Adams, *Islam and Modernism in Egypt* (New York: Russell and Russell, 1993, Reprint edition); and Nadav Safran, *Egypt*

in Search of a Political Community (Cambridge, Mass.: Cambridge University Press, 1961).

15. P. J. Vatikiotis, "Islamic Resurgence: A Critical View," in Alexander S. Cudsi and Ali E. Hillal Dessouki (eds.), *Islam and Power* (Baltimore, MD.: The Johns Hopkins University Press, 1981), pp. 169-96.

16. Muhammad Al-Ghazzali, *Our Beginning in Wisdom*, translated by Isma'il al-Faruqi (New York: Octagon Books, 1975), pp. 34-39 and passim.

17. For a brief historical treatment of the development of secularism in Egypt see Daniel Crecelius, "The Course of Secularization in Egypt," in John L. Esposito, *Islam and Development: Religion and Sociopolitical Change* (Syracuse, N.Y.: Syracuse University Press, 1980), pp. 49-70. Bassam Tibi, *The Crisis of Modern Islam: A Preindustrial Culture in the Scientific and Technological Age* (Salt Lake City: Utah University Press, 1988), pp. 45-46, 108-9, 128-34. Habib Boulares, *Islam: The Fear and the Hope* (London: Zed Books, 1990), translation of *L'islam,* pp. 85-94. Halim Barakat, *The Arab World: Society, Culture and State* (Berkeley and Los Angeles: The University of California Press, 1993), pp. 127-43.

18. Gilles Kepel, *Muslim Extremism in Egypt: the Prophet and Pharaoh*, translated from the French by John Rothschild (Berkeley: University of California Press, 1985), p. 111.

19. Ziauddin Sardar, *Islamic Fundamentalism: The Shape of Things to Come* (London: Mansell Publishing, 1985), p. 11. Boulares, *Islam*, pp. 44-60.

20. Youssef M. Choueiri, *Islamic Fundamentalism* (Boston: Twayne Publishers, 1994), p. 105.

21. Michel Youssef, *Revolt Against Modernity: Muslim Zealots and the West* (Leiden: Brill, 1985).

22. Lawrence, *Defenders of God,* p. 50.

23. Choueiri, *Islamic Fundamentalism,* pp. 105-19.

24. Michael C. Hudson, *Arab Politics: The Search for Legitimacy* (New Haven, Conn.: Yale University Press, 1977); Michael C. Hudson, "States, Society, and Legitimacy: An Essay on Arab Political Prospects for the 1990s," in Hisham Sharabi (ed.), *The Next Arab Decade: Alternative Futures* (Boulder, Colo.: Westview Press, 1991), pp. 22-37. See also Tamara Sonn, *Between Qur'an and Crown: The Challenge of Political Legitimacy in the Arab World* (Boulder, Colo.: Westview Press, 1990).

25. The *shari'ah* has always been an important source of legislation in Egypt. However, neo-fundamentalists seek to make it the *only* source.

26. In *The Passing of Traditional Society: Modernization in the Middle East* (New York: Free Press, 1956). Daniel Lerner found strong support for modernization in many countries in the Middle East. It is dubious, however, whether a similar study would come to the same conclusions today.

27. Manfred Halpern, *The Politics of Social Change in the Middle East and North Africa* (Princeton, NJ: Princeton University Press, 1963), p. 135.

28. Kepel, *Muslim Extremism,* pp. 241-57. Kepel thinks that this strategy has worked well for the regimes in Egypt.

29. Tibi, *The Crisis of Modern Islam,* passim.

30. John J. Donahue, "Islam and the Search for Identity in the Arab World," in Esposito, *Voices,* pp. 54-55. See also Ozay Mehmet, *Islamic Identity and Development: Studies of the Islamic Periphery* (London: Routledge, 1990), especially pp. 9-33.

31. Ahmad Khurshid, "The Nature of the Islamic Resurgence," in Esposito, *Voices*, p. 221.

32. Saad Eddin Ibrahim, "An Islamic Alternative in Egypt: The Muslim Brotherhood and Sadat," in Ibrahim, *Egypt, Islam and Democracy,* pp. 35-51.

33. Hamied Ansari, *Egypt: The Stalled Society* (Albany: State University of New York Press, 1986), p. 12.

34. Robert Springborg, *Mubarak's Egypt: Fragmentation of the Political Order* (Boulder, Colo.: Westview Press, 1989).

35. Ibrahim M. Oweiss, "Egypt's Economy: The Pressing Issues," in Ibrahim M. Oweiss (ed.), *The Political Economy of Contemporary Egypt* (Washington, DC: Center for Contemporary Arab Studies, 1990), pp. 3-49.

36. William Baker, "Afraid for Islam: Egypt's Centrists between Pharaohs and Fundamentalists," *Daedalus* (Summer 1991), p. 47.

37. Raphael Israeli, *Man of Defiance: A Political Biography of Anwar Sadat* (Totown, N.J.: Barnes & Noble Books, 1985), p. 200.

38. Iliya Harik and Denis J. Sullivan (eds.), *Privatization and Liberalization in the Middle East* (Bloomington: Indiana University Press, 1992), pp. 24-105.

39. Ansari, *Egypt*, p. 235.

40. Charles Tripp and Roger Owen, *Egypt Under Mubarak* (London: Routledge, 1989).

41. Ali E. Hillal Dessouki, "The Resurgence of Islamic Organizations in Egypt: An Interpretation," in Cudsi, *Islam and Power*, p. 115.

42. Baker, "Afraid for Islam," p. 259.

43. Dessouki, "The Resurgence of Islamic Organizations in Egypt," p. 115.

44. Raymond A. Hinnebusch, "The Formation of the Contemporary Egyptian State from Nasser and Sadat to Mubarak," cited in Oweiss, "Egypt's Economy," p. 207.

45. Springborg, *Mubarak's Egypt.*

46. Olivier Roy, *The Failure of Political Islam*, translated by Carol Volk (Cambridge, Mass.: Harvard University Press, 1994), p. x.

47. Springborg, *Mubarak's Egypt*, pp. 215-45.

48. Baker, "Afraid for Islam," p. 52.

49. G. H. Jansen, "Militant Islam: Strengths and Weaknesses," *Middle East International* (February 7, 1991), p. 18.

50. Jeffrey Ryan, "The Impact of Democratization on Revolutionary Movements," *Comparative Politics,* vol. 27, no. 1 (October 1994), pp. 27-44.

51. Muhammad Muslih and Augustus Norton, "The Need for Arab Democracy," *Foreign Policy* (Summer 1991), pp. 3-19.

52. Esposito, *Islam and Development,* p. 193.

53. Mark Juergensmeyer, "The Islamic Revolution is Taking Root in Egypt," in Winters, *Islam*, p. 266. Excerpted from his *The New Cold War? Religious Nationalism Confronts the Secular State* (Berkeley and Los Angeles: University of California Press, 1993).

Chapter 6

Mission UK:
Black Pentecostals in London

Harriet A. Harris

A JUDGMENT ON THE NATION

The United Kingdom is not a developing country, though with irony it is sometimes described as a Third World country in disguise because of the gulf between rich and poor. However, from the point of view of the pentecostals considered here, the impoverishment suffered in Britain is spiritual. They are first-, second-, and third-generation immigrants from Africa, the Caribbean, and the Indian sub-continent. A few are short-term residents in Britain from African countries or Pakistan, working as pastors or as students to gain skills to take to their churches back home. The story they tell of themselves is as people responsive to God in a nation that is no longer responsive. One explanation they have for Britain's current spiritual demise is its relative material comfort: the citizens of this country have become too comfortable to know their need of God. They blame the Welfare State for this because it steps in to relieve people of poverty, and they criticize the churches for allowing their work to be overtaken by social services. Their remedy is threefold: to locate the needs of people in British society;[1] out of those needs, to make people aware of their need of God; and, by being church (living as the community of God's people), to show how God is able to meet those needs.

More generally, members of black-led churches[2] in Britain have claimed to have kept "spiritual barrenness" at bay for British blacks (churched or unchurched), and even for Christian whites.[3] Black-led pentecostal churches in Britain are numerous and diverse, fissiparous, and too busy to get to know one another, yet still they share this common diagnosis for society's ills: that White, wealthy Westerners have forgotten their need of God. It is no surprise to them at all that Christianity is growing in Africa, South America, and Asia more than it is in Europe. The fastest growing form of Christianity in the world today is pentecostal or charismatic. The American pentecostal religious historian Vinson Synan gives an approximate figure of 540 million pentecostal and charismatic

Christians in the world in 1999 (out of 1,990,018,000 Christians overall).[4] Currently the biggest church in Britain is the Kingsway International Christian Centre in East London, which is largely black and was founded in 1992 by a Nigerian, Pastor Matthew Ashimolowo, who came out of the pentecostal Four-Square Gospel Church. KICC boasts a congregation of 6,500, which includes those who meet at its new 5,000-seat church and office complex and at its 8 satellites in the London area.

More established, mainstream churches find new pentecostal churches threatening. The rapid growth of KICC in the 1990s and its vigorous publicizing drive in and around Hackney, East London, have drawn actual and potential worshippers away from longer-serving churches in the area. At the Lambeth Conference in 1998, Anglican bishops from around the world voiced concern about the burgeoning pentecostal congregations in their dioceses. Resolutions were passed at that conference to explore the possibility of conversations and relationships between the Anglican Communion and the pentecostal churches, New Churches, and Independent Christian Groups.[5] In attempting to implement these resolutions, Anglicans have discovered that black pentecostal energy is channelled into ministry to the poor and is not readily diverted into fostering inter-church relations. Black pentecostalism is a means for people not to be the recipients of mission but to engage in mission themselves; to have the freedom to minister to their own people and to be a channel of grace for others.[6] It is racially conscious,[7] and it counteracts the tendency, keenly felt by all non-established churches in Britain, of the Church of England to take a presidential role in its relations with them. Burgeoning new black-led pentecostal churches are numerically successful, racially aware, and "have done it themselves without you," as a black pentecostal bishop of the International Ministerial Council for Great Britain said to me.[8] In these terms they pronounce judgment on the white mainstream's failure to meet people's needs, to welcome black people,[9] and to know Christian humility. The national church, the Church of England, must feel this judgment most acutely.

I feel uncomfortable, as a white theologian and Anglican ordained, hearing this critique of mainstream churches and British society by black pentecostals. The challenge naturally requires self-examination of my own church and theological tradition. It is difficult deciding how to write about the challenge. Black theologians are frustrated and angered by white theologians who appropriate aspects of their thinking. Paul Grant and Raj Patel lament the "colonizing of Black hearts" when people look to learn from black Christianity for the sake of "street credibility" or the salvaging of their own consciences.[10] Bishop Joe Aldred, of the Church of God of Prophecy and director of the Centre for Black and White Partnership, insists that only blacks can do black theology because it must be written from black experience.[11] These concerns limit what will be attempted here. I do not discuss black theology, but attempt to speak in the gap that exists between the perceptions and judgments of black pentecostals and the sense of threat felt by the white churches. This chapter is an articulation of dissonance, in that while Anglicans feel threatened by burgeoning new churches, these churches themselves regard Anglicans as inadequate in meeting people's spiritual and practical needs.

The various bishops and pastors I have met from very different pentecostal churches have emphasized that they are not "segregationist." They are polite about the Church of England, but critical of it. They have certain images of its present condition: big church buildings standing empty or being sold off; "dignified" church services and restrained worshippers. They accuse the church of moral compromise over sexuality, particularly homosexuality and teachings on marriage and divorce. They say that Britain was once a great missionary country but that it has become "backslidden" and is now a mission field served by others. They regard Britain as a nation that is too comfortable and self-satisfied, and whose churches have themselves become comfortable and failed to call the people to acknowledge their need of God.

In this chapter I present an account of the black pentecostal mission to Britain as I have been told it. I find story-telling an appropriate model for recounting their words because it reflects their own practise and their particular style of theology. At the same time, I am struck by how their very clear ideas about mission and Britain's spiritual decline contrast with their lack of clarity about theology.[12] Church of England clergy seem to be in the opposite situation, being well acquainted with their theological heritage but unsure what to do about mission, as manifest in their reluctance to give a Christ-centered message for the millennium.[13] The intention of the Lambeth Resolutions is to move beyond the level of threat and problematizing to constructive engagement with pentecostal and new churches. But at present there is dissonance, in the sense of confusion rather than of conflict. Anglicans respond by vetting the theology of these groups because it is endemic amongst Anglicans to regard themselves as guardians of the faith. They therefore have not heard these churches' own explanations for their relative success: that they recognize and address people's needs as needs to which God would have us respond.

The black pentecostal narrative and rhetoric should be appraised and not simply taken at face value. For example, the Welfare State is being pruned back, and Anglican churches do respond to the needs that are created by running homeless shelters, employment agencies, and the like. Also, Anglicans are, like black pentecostals, immensely diverse so that generalizations about their moral stance or spiritual health can be distorting. David Holloway, vicar of a large Anglican-evangelical church in Newcastle, berates the Church of England for compromise over homosexuality whilst Richard Holloway, Bishop of Edinburgh, welcomes homosexuals into the full life of the church as an enactment of Gospel principles, and would vociferously deny that he was "compromising." But critique of the ensuing story and an Anglican response are topics for another essay. First of all the story needs to be heard so that the religious establishment and black-led pentecostal churches can move into a clearer understanding of one another.

A FUNDAMENTALIST THREAT?

In my research I specialize in white evangelicalism and fundamentalism. I have argued elsewhere that the lived evangelical faith is far richer than fundamentalist articulations of the Christian faith, and I have come to see pentecostal forms of Christianity as powerful in subverting fundamentalism.[14] Over a period of time I became aware that black pentecostalism transcends many of the tensions that arise between evangelical faith and fundamentalist expression. This was despite the fact that most of the black pentecostals interviewed for this study were happy to identify with "fundamentalism" because they want to implement and maintain biblical standards in their own lives and in society. They see their commitment to scripture as the inspired Word of God as underlying their commitment to mission, and they judge that churches that become unclear about the Bible go into spiritual decline.[15] A student group, whom I shall introduce shortly, quizzed me over the Church of England's attitudes on the matter of gay and lesbian clergy, and shook their heads in despair at the church's "compromises." One man responded: "Fundamentalism is your equipment, armament, to the flourishing of faith." The students said that the Church of England tolerated gays, lesbians, and single mothers, whereas "the Bible doesn't allow that." Nonetheless, neither their use of scripture nor their mission activity was fundamentalist.

By *fundamentalism* I mean a strongly foundationalist attitude towards the Bible. Those who have this attitude require scripture to be the factually reliable foundation for faith, and ask that it be wholly accurate and perspicuous in that capacity. Although they mostly experience scripture as a means through which they develop a relationship with God, their doctrine of scripture says something quite different: that unless the Bible is 100 % reliable we have nothing upon which to rest our faith. Fundamentalist patterns of thought present evangelicals with uncomfortable dichotomies: between Word and Spirit, reason and feeling, religion and politics, church and world, private and public, individual and social, and so on. Since black pentecostals transcend these dichotomies, a study that asks how "fundamentalist" they are would be distorting. Let me give two examples of this transcending ability.

1.   Pentecostals disagree amongst themselves over whether to embrace fundamentalist doctrine or not, but even where they do formally endorse it, their practice subverts it. They use scripture very directly, making immediate parallels with their own situations, but they do not use it rigidly. They are led more by their experience than by grammatico-historical attention to the text. They are not biblical foundationalists in the sense that their very faith depends on an error-free Bible. They ground their faith first and foremost in what they take to be God's Spirit working within them, rather than in the factual accuracy of biblical narratives. Therefore they are less vulnerable than fundamentalists to textual dilemmas. Black pentecostals, in particular, find in scripture immediate justification for liberative theology. Their readings of scripture involve mapping their own lives onto the story of God's work as unfolded in scripture. Israel as a liberated people and Christ as "the suffering liberator"[16] are crucial motifs. Because their reading of

the biblical story is liberative, they see the Bible as a divided text rather than assuming, as do fundamentalists, that it is unified.[17] They discard portions of scripture that seem to support injustices or that, judging from their experience, the Holy Spirit has overridden, such as slavery and the silencing of women in churches. They might well call themselves "bibliocentric,"[18] in that the Bible is their primary reference and its story is the central story by which they understand their lives. More specifically, they genuinely practice a circular rather than foundationalist hermeneutic; that is to say, rather than believing that they construct faith on a biblical foundation by means of linear reasoning, they know that their faith grows in a circular or interactive way, as Bible-reading and lived experience interact.

2.   For black pentecostals, Christian mission is wholly compatible with social and political action, and salvation pertains to physical as well as spiritual redemption and to the well being of the community as well as of the individual. The white evangelical-fundamentalist world, by contrast, has been divided over how to spend its missionary energy: entirely on the saving of souls, or partly on social and political engagement. It has understood salvation as a matter for individual souls, not for bodies, communities, or the world. It has tended to regard the world as that from which people need saving. Ronald Nathan, a black pentecostal minister of an Elim church, says:

Historically, Black people have never been able to create the great divide between the supernatural and the natural, the spiritual and the secular, that seems so easy for many white Evangelicals to maintain. It is therefore not surprising that my sermons would be punctuated with social issues. Discussions on morals and ethics would always be aligned to employment policies, racism, and sexism, without neglecting personal salvation, righteousness, and spiritual growth.[19]

These two ways in which black pentecostals transcend fundamentalist dichotomies, could be expressed in terms of pentecostalism's democratic and holistic nature (democratic in that it has neither an intellectualist nor a priestly elite; holistic in attending to human well-being in every aspect of life). Both democratization and holism are experienced as healing for marginalized peoples, which may be why so many of the world's marginalized are attracted to pentecostalism.[20] Such an explanation would accord well with the self-understanding of pentecostals I have spoken with: that they meet people where they are, and meet their whole need.

SOME LONDON GROUPS

The reflections given in this chapter grew out of meetings in 1999 with black pentecostal worshippers, students, pastors and bishops and attendance at services and at courses. They are enhanced by reading the works of British black pentecostal theologians,[21] but the primary shape and content of what follows emerged not from literary sources but from interactions with four very different black pentecostal groups in London. I do not identify any interviewees by name.

I use initials, which I have changed, for those who have had the most input into this study.

1. The Institute for Community Development, organized by Bishop JI of the International Ministerial Council for Great Britain, runs courses in community development. They use an old community building in Barking, East London, for teaching space. They have minimal teaching resources. The students whom I met were pastors and lay people from Africa (Sierra Leone, Ghana, Zambia) and from Pakistan. A few live permanently in the UK, but most come from abroad and intend to go home to implement community projects. They are currently members of various pentecostal churches in London

2. The Cherubim & Seraphim Church (UK) meets on Sunday afternoons in an old Anglican church building, which they rent from a parish church in Hackney. There are numerous small pentecostal congregations in Britain who rent church buildings for worship. This is perhaps the greatest area of cooperation between pentecostal and mainstream churches, but it does not often go beyond a financial arrangement: the congregations who share a building rarely come to know one another. This particular congregation is the English branch of the C&S, the only other branch being in Nigeria. In Nigeria, C&S is one of the Aladura churches (the term coming from the Yoruba *al adua* meaning the praying people or owners of prayer). Aladura churches emerged in the 1920s in an initiative to make Christianity a religion in which Nigerians felt at home. They have been accused of syncretism for merging too much with Yoruba culture, and have been criticized for their use of charismatic gifts. They themselves have sought to cleanse established churches of spiritual bankruptcy.[22] In London, C&S is a small church, numbering about twenty members, all of Nigerian origin. Their services are in a mixture of English and Yoruba, with much additional speaking in tongues and with ritual and ceremony from Yoruba culture. Instead of taking Holy Communion at the end of the service they have a ritual of cleansing and marking: they drink a cup of blessed water to cleanse them on the inside, and have a cross marked on their foreheads with oil as a sign to others that God has touched them. Their purist nature is apparent in their apparel: they wear white from head to toe—white robes over their normal clothes, and bonnets for the women. They disrobe in the church after the service, but the symbolism is of being washed clean and set apart. The C&S Church (UK) celebrated its twenty-first anniversary in August 1999.

3. Built on the Rock International Ministries have their London base in the East End. Bishop Dr. KDP is pastor of this church. He was born in Jamaica and came to Britain in 1962 when he was 21. He started his ministry in the Bible Way Church, which began in Washington, D.C., in 1957. There are ninety-five churches under the umbrella of Built on the Rock International Ministries: eight in England, six of which are in London, one in Chatham, Kent, and one in Doncaster; two in Ghana, one in Kenya, fifty-three in Mozambique and Malawi, three in Pakistan, fourteen in South Africa, two in St. Lucia, one in Zaire and eleven in Zambia. In a Third World country, Bishop KDP explains, if your ministry has a link with the First World it helps it to grow, through visiting preachers, donations of clothes, and financial help with building. This ministry does not have much money, and all the money they do have comes from congregational giving. Their building is an old warehouse in a back street. It is clearly not that of a wealthy congregation. Downstairs there is a brightly

colored room, yellow walls and red chairs, and odd bits of red carpet. This is where the services are held. About 200 people come, most but not all of them black.

4. Kingsway International Christian Centre is a mega-church in London, as already mentioned. It began in Holloway Boy's School in 1992, then moved to Darnley Road in Hackney, and now occupies an eight-acre site of old offices and warehouses between Hackney and Stratford. The site is in an isolated spot, on a road that contains other warehouses, a bus depot, and a cash 'n' carry. It is not well served by public transport, and is difficult for people to reach without a car, especially for the Friday evening Bible studies and other evening activities. It is the fulfilment of "the church's vision to build a 5,000 seater church and office complex," and is regarded as tangible evidence of God's blessing and the power of prayer, especially since KICC was "successful over corporate giants" in beating more competitive bidders.[23] KICC have a "Target attendance of 25,000 by the year 2000." Publicity brochures in summer 1999 advertised attendance at 5,000, though I am told that, including satellite congregations, attendance is 6,500. The congregation is largely but not exclusively black. The church emphasizes its international profile. The pastors are Nigerian, Caribbean and Ghanaian. The welcome packet given out to newcomers explains: "In our 'melting pot,' we have 30 nations of the world represented, yet we are truly a 'United Nation,' with a United Effort. No matter what your culture or background, we have a place for you here at KICC."[24]

KICC broadcasts on Premier Radio, London's Christian radio station, and on the "God Channel" on Sky television network. Their radio and television programs are known as Winning Ways, and this is also the title of a magazine produce between four and six times a year. The television program "is transmitted across 21 European nations and has a potential viewing audience of 65 million," as well as reaching "40 million Africans and when Ghana TV opens, it will hit 50 million." Their other forms of evangelism include preaching in the local outdoor market and giving out tracts, posting fliers through people's doors, and putting up posters. But the best form of evangelism, as Pastor M said to me, is when people bring their friends to church.

The diversity of these four groups cuts across the question of whether pentecostalism is a religion of the proud poor or of upwardly mobile blacks.[25] They represent both the "pentecostal elite" and the "pentecostal poor."[26] They all meet in borrowed buildings or back streets, which is quite typical of black pentecostal churches, reflecting their relative material poverty and social marginalization compared with mainstream churches and other socially established institutions. It is both a cause and a confirmation of the pentecostal conviction that "Revival is *outside* the churches today. . . . Revival is in Pentecost—not in the gorgeous temples where the ritual of Pentecost is travestied still, but in the back street upper rooms where the power of the Spirit of God is mightily distributed in soul-satisfying Spiritual Gifts and outpourings."[27] Even KICC meets off the beaten track, despite being fairly wealthy and displaying its wealth in the form of sharp-looking buildings and the latest technology as a sign of God's blessings and of the power of prayer. Their media and internet presence are likewise out workings of the conviction that revival is happening outside the mainstream churches, a conviction that is voiced in various ways by the black pentecostals represented here. I soon got the story of Christianity in decline in Britain as they, in all their diversity, tell it.

THE MORAL OF THE STORY: KNOW YOUR NEED

The story goes like this: If you are comfortable and do not have financial needs, your spiritual sense is dulled. You stop looking for God, and the churches become ineffective in mission because they do not know what needs to address in people. They lose their ability to minister. They become comfortable themselves, and then become slack and start to compromise morally. Not surprisingly, people stop coming to church, and church buildings stand empty. The Church then fails further in its Christian witness by selling off its buildings, and it makes yet more compromises by selling the buildings to Muslims, Sikhs, and others who do not recognize Christ.

The hardening of hearts in the people of Britain is how the pastors of C&S explain the small size of their UK congregation. It is also how Bishop KDP accounts for the small fruits of his ministry in Britain relative to African countries. People are more responsive to God in Third World countries, he explains, for they have nothing else to depend on. In Britain there is so much luxury, and instead of giving God thanks we turn away from God. So "it is too much blessings of the Lord in this country that makes people fail to respond. Many of the missionaries that are coming [to this country] are pointing out the blessings." Still, African and Afro-Caribbean churches grow quickly in Britain relative to white churches because Africans and Afro-Carribeans remember their cultural background (their Christian heritage). In British culture, Bishop KDP notes, instead of giving credit to God, people give credit to luck.

Such a critique is most fully articulated by students at the Institute for Community Development who concentrate on church work in the community. One woman said:

In a Third World context, we're looking at hunger, deprivation, etc. In Europe, the welfare system is taking care of these things, acting as the church would in a Third World country. So we have to identify communities in Britain, for example, communities of people who are abused, or drug addicts. So there is not hunger for food, but there is hunger for knowledge. The Church has to be relevant.

To be relevant the Church needs to identify people's needs and find niches in which to work. The students used as evidence of people's "hunger" the establishment of website communities, where people create relationships over the internet while having no physical interaction with one another. Churches should be praying for communities that go unrecognized. Lamenting on the gap between the Church and community, another woman proclaimed:

The only way for the gap to close is for the Church to go out to the community. Look at Nehemiah, when he built the wall, he involved the whole community. Look at Daniel, he became a prime minister, to be a light. We are to bring the community to the altar, to go to their level and to bring their level to the altar. . . . Christ was a man of community. If we look to Matthew, Jesus preached to community forty-one times [the woman then enumerated how many times Jesus preached to community in the other gospels], so Jesus was outside. He was breaking the barriers. . . . The Bible is saying, the community workers are saying, we can touch people wherever we are.

KICC explains its very success in Britain along similar lines: it catches the hearts of people because the British churches have let them down. Pastor M was brought up in the Anglican church in Nigeria. At 15 or 16 he was born again and began attending a pentecostal church. He is now a full-time pastor with KICC. He regards African people in London as more responsive to the Gospel than whites. The Western world, he says, has become artificialized. Westerners "won't receive what they're offered from the Bible, because they say they are Christian already." But, he argues, "there is a difference between having Christian ancestors and personally committing your life to Christ."

KICC thinks in terms of church growth, individual piety, and the accessing of God's power. Its slogan is "Raising Champions, Fulfilling Dreams," and its approach is to bring more and more people into its church so that there they can pray for and receive God's blessings. The first three items in the KICC Vision 2000 proclaim the intention:

- to be a place where the hurting, the depressed, the frustrated and the confused can find love, acceptance, help, hope, forgiveness and encouragement.
- to share the Good News of Jesus Christ with the 11 million people resident in London.
- to welcome 25,000 members into the fellowship of our church family, growing, glowing, going all out for Jesus.

Rather than bringing people into the church, students at the Institute emphasize moving out into the community as a demonstration of God's power. They describe the church as "a holy organisation established for its non-members." They speak of Jesus' ministry continuing in the work of His followers and flowing like rivers into people's lives. One student said that people will see the power of Christians from the fact that "it was Christians that supported [Bill] Clinton in prayer when he got into trouble."

These divergent orientations reflect significantly different views of God's Kingdom and power, and of human responsibility, as we shall see. For the moment, however, let us note that while their emphases differ from one another, the Institute and the mega-church, as well as the small C&S congregation and Built on the Rock Ministries, understand themselves to be responding to those needs of people in Britain that have gone unrecognized by white mainstream churches. Crucial in their response to people's needs is their shared conviction that God's blessings are intended for every aspect of human life.

BODY, MIND, AND SPIRIT: ADDRESSING PEOPLE'S NEEDS

Pentecostals speak of a God who is interested in all three aspects of human being: body, mind, and spirit. This God expects believers to engage with others at all three levels, hence the onus on believers to reach out to people in ways that affect their material existence.

The students at the Institute for Community Development describe this as a "holistic approach"—a description often used of pentecostal and of African theologies. They are developing a theology of praxis to express their community work. One woman put it like this: "The theology that we practise . . . we end up with the answer that God is love. God loved us so much that he gave . . ." the woman did not finish the verse; the reference to John 3:16 was to be understood. She continued: "We are to give. When the Welfare system gives, it is not doing it out of love. . . . The welfare system meets only the physical aspect. We want to meet every side of man. This is what Jesus did . . . ," the point being that Jesus did not only preach the kingdom but met people's hunger and other physical needs. Love is not truly practiced where people's needs are not fully recognized and addressed: "When you love somebody, you are thinking how best to relate to that person. When we go out to community we are thinking how best to get these people to think about God, by relating to them." This group understands themselves to be God's agents on earth: "God is trying to reach man. We are the ones who know about God's love, so we have to go out to reach man . . . in all three aspects, body, soul, spirit." They repeatedly emphasized: "There is an emotional side of a man, a spiritual side of a man, and a physical side of a man."

The tripartite nature of human being is often stated in pentecostal discourse. It underlay Bishop. KDP's accounts of ministry: "The whole man is spirit, soul and body. The soul is the emotional part, the thinking part, the part that can be tempted and that reacts. You can't minister to it without ministering to the body. . . . It [the soul] tends to want to do things that please the flesh." I asked the bishop where this tripartite emphasis comes from, which I intended as a question about the influences on pentecostal thought. He said it comes from the Bible: "All through the Bible there is body, soul, and spirit. The Spirit is like the breath or wind. The body houses the spirit. If the spirit goes, the body drops." He answered with biblical consciousness rather than historical consciousness, as when I asked him how old his particular church was, and he responded that it was the oldest church because it goes right back to the first pentecostal experience. Others have suggested that in African spirituality the whole congregation moves as one body-mind-spirit, and that charismatic gifts such as speaking in tongues remind us of the interaction between the spirit and the physical and corporate body.[28] Calls for justice and equality also undergird the impetus black-led churches place on bringing the Gospel to bear on "the needs of the whole person."[29]

One way of promoting the total application of Christians and their full engagement with the needs of others is to create a full network of Christian firms and services. The broader evangelical world has come under some criticism for creating an evangelical "sub-culture" in this way.[30] However, the Institute for

Community Development likes this practice. One student, a pastor from Ghana, argued that "ministry should flow like rivers into where these [poor] people live," and he asked "why can't there be Christian firms of accountancy and agriculturists, coming out of the church working for secular systems?" The group explained that with Christian banking, housing projects, and the like, people put the whole of themselves, body, soul, and spirit, into their work, and because this is part of Christian witness, everybody would see the benefit. Thinking along the same lines, KICC has a community division for reaching out "beyond our congregants to those in the neighbourhood to demonstrate the love of God in practical ways."[31] It includes legal counsel and career counselling services, a Hope line telephone counselling service, and drop-in counselling. A small groups division has groups for Christians in medicine, in legal practice, and in business. This is in tune with KICC's vision to be "A place for the total healing of the total man and the total nation."[32]

This holism pronounces judgment on Western churches and Western theology in two main ways. First, it judges the way that in the West, spiritual or religious concerns have been separated from material and social concerns. It is well known that in African Christianity, salvation pertains to the whole of life, including physical and social well being. Healing includes the healing of the "body," corporately in terms of relationships in the community, and physically in terms of particular ailments. The idea that Christian healing be narrowed to the realm of spiritual wholeness, or the idea that spiritual wholeness be separated from physical and corporate considerations, is anathema to this way of thinking. Second, it is critical of the way in which Western churches and Western theology are so mind-orientated. Not only are they inattentive to bodily matters, but they also lack spirit.[33]

When Pastor M of KICC describes his Anglican experience, he speaks of going to church and not "getting much out of it": "It gives you 'religion' rather than a relationship with God. He acknowledges that some Anglican churches are on fire for God." "We know about Holy Trinity Brompton," he said, which indicates KICC's point of reference with the Church of England. Holy Trinity Brompton (HTB, as it is affectionately known) is a big evangelical church in London, which has been much affected by charismatic renewal. Nicky Gumbel, an ordained minister at HTB, designed the *Alpha* course, which is a widely used, highly successful course in evangelism and Christian basics. "But many Anglican churches," Pastor M continued, "don't relate to life," and he contrasted this with Jesus in the gospels, who did relate to the whole of life. The message, he said, "is a wholesome message, not 'one-track.'" It affects people's emotions, bodies, and minds. It is not trying to focus on one particular thing. It concerns marriage, material possessions. The all-encompassing nature of the Gospel message is communicated in KICC publicity material, which proclaims success in all areas of life: "you will be supplied with wisdom and power to reach out to the sick, the unsaved and the needy, so that God's church will grow big in our day." "Our vision for the year 2000 is to be a place for the total healing of the total man and the total nation."[34]

Bishop KDP told two stories about pentecostals and Anglican churches, which gently and with good humor criticize the Anglican lack of spirit.[35] He adapted them from stories he usually tells about Methodists, with whom he has more interaction, but as he said, they could be applied to any "toned-down, dignified church."

1.   A mother takes her son to a toned-down dignified, Anglican church where only the minister speaks. When the minister is preaching, the whole congregation is quiet, but something touches the boy and he cries out "Amen." The minister asks him to be quiet. So the boy resolves to sit quietly, but it happens again that he feels moved, and he cries out "Praise the Lord." The minister sends him to the back of the church, and he tries to keep quiet. But the minister is preaching the Word of the Lord, and it is affecting the boy. He cries, "Amen, Praise the lord." The minister sends him outside, where there is a field of horses. One horse comes and hangs his head over the fence by the boy's shoulder. The boy strokes the horse down the nose and says, "You must be a good Christian because your face is so long."

2.   A big Anglican church with one hundred of people meets every week and never makes a sound. The minister is the only one who speaks. Opposite is a small pentecostal congregation with only a handful of people, making a big noise. The pentecostal pastor thinks he must do something about the Anglican church, so he puts a sign outside saying: "A body with no Spirit is dead." The Anglican priest sees this and thinks up a way to get back at the Pentecostal. He puts up a sign saying: "A spirit with no body is a spook."

Bishop KDP told the second story to say that we need spirit, but that this is not all we need. He was making a point about the relation between pentecostals and quieter worshippers. "If we toned everyone down," he said, "it wouldn't be biblical." We should be allowed to be who God wants us to be: a quiet person should not be made to be loud or vice versa. But he is unconvinced that white British people, by virtue of being white and British, want to be quiet in church. People in England, he mused, say they are not trained to show their emotions, but they do show them at football matches: "Why? Because they love football. So why don't they let it out in church to God? When the woman washed Jesus feet with her tears, those tears represented all that she is, her good times, bad times and everything. And she was saying 'Lord, I'm pouring it out to you.'" The bishop invokes people to be all that they are, to be fully engaged, before God.

THE KINGDOM AND THE POWER: MEETING PEOPLE'S NEEDS

Some studies of pentecostalism seek to correct the perception that pentecostals are orientated to the after-life and neglectful of worldly concerns, allowing their religion to work as an opiate.[36] Meanwhile, the growing popularity around the world of such churches as KICC gives rise to a contrary perception: that pentecostals are too focused on material improvement in this life. In South Korea, for example, Minjung Christians have been leaving their liberationist churches for Paul Yonggi Cho's Yoiddo Full Gospel Church in Seoul. This church claims to be the biggest in the world, with 750,000 members. At least part of its attraction seems to be, like KICC, its optimistic, prosperity-style gospel. (The KICC Vision statement ends with a financial acronym: "THE VISION IS STILL ALIVE.") Under either perception, a European observer might be inclined to see black pentecostalism as a religious mechanism of adaptation: either by consoling believers for what they cannot have in this world or by enabling believers to gain some rewards in this world. Either way, Black pentecostalism can be made to look like the opposite of black power as a political protest movement. However, this is deceptive.[37]

We have seen that pentecostals do not make the division between this-worldly and otherworldly concerns that has characterized much of Western Christianity in the modern world. Moreover, black pentecostals have undergone a political awakening, and reject the white pentecostal assumption that political commitment is a matter best left to the individual Christian.[38] Even in earlier days, when they tended to ignore politics, they were counter-culturally subversive, in prioritizing the poor, mixing races and having women ministers.[39] Pentecostals profess Jesus' imminent Second Coming—that Jesus will return to earth very soon to establish his Kingdom—which gives them a sense of urgency. But their urgency is not only to proclaim the Gospel to people's souls, to prepare them spiritually for their Lord's return, as millions of fundamentalist evangelicals have understood the Christian mission. Pentecostal spirituality replaces resignation with hope, and hope is actively expressed.[40] Therefore pentecostals work for salvation here and now, and do not only await it in the next world. They minister to the spirit, soul, and body, and relate the command to "be watchful" to the responsibility to be socially vigilant.[41] Black pentecostals remind us that making the kingdom real involves affirming blackness, because it requires us to challenge racial injustice and to reclaim what God has revealed from the hands of white westerners.[42] Nonetheless, a pertinent question for the new century is whether the mega-churches that preach a prosperity Gospel will cause black pentecostals to withdraw again from political engagement.[43]

The extent to which the Kingdom (God's reign) is claimed as a present reality differs among pentecostals, as does the sense of social responsibility in bringing about the Kingdom. Of the groups considered here, C&S are the least socially empowered and the most introverted. Here is an exception of a typical sermon preached at the church. This particular sermon was prefaced with a warning that greed and power create problems in the world. Bible references were shouted out, and sometimes (male) members of the congregation would look them up and read them aloud:

Ps 22:2f, we can't even look after ourselves. God is the one who looks after us. Jer. 17: 7, when we look unto God for help, help will come. Ps 20:7, as children of God, we just have to put our hope and trust in God. . . . If you are looking for a job, trust in God. If you are looking for a wife, trust in God. . . . If you go to the Bible you will see the power of God. That power won't change. You have to tap it. Proverbs 16:20, just trust and obey. If God says "stop," you stay there, when God says "go" you go. God is the only one who won't let us down.

Bishop JI's students are more outward looking, concerned with the hard work of developing community projects. They see this as part of their role as God's agents on earth. Theirs is a social Gospel expressed in terms of both human and divine agency. One male student said that rather than sending down manna today, God was equipping and sending people to do this work. Does this mean that God no longer works miracles? The student was a bit subdued by the logic of his own argument, and others added that they do believe in miracles: "God is sovereign, and chooses where to do a miracle;" "We need to acknowledge that God is able to do it." Nevertheless, while the Institute's members believe firmly in miraculous divine interventions (one woman gave testimony about being healed that morning so that she was able to come to the session), their community development work involves long-term planning and perseverance. Mission schools where "children are brought up properly, to become good people in society" (by which they mean socially responsible and not addicted to drugs) exemplify for them the sort of lengthy nurturing work involved in building God's Kingdom.

KICC's outlook is more immediate: the Kingdom is established through the power of prayer and positive thinking. KICC pastors claim that "We have been commissioned by God to help raise His people as Champions and help them to fulfil their God-given dreams." Part of their vision is "to equip every believer for a significant ministry by helping them **discover**, **develop**, and **deploy** the gifts and talents God gave them."[44] They do not find the world oppressive but full of boundless opportunities.[45] They barely mention the afterlife, and while they treat the millennium as a mark for reaching certain prayer targets,[46] they are not millenarian. That is to say, they do not preach Jesus' imminent return to mark the end of the age. Rather they preach ways of moving powerfully in God's Spirit, which involves claiming the power of the Holy Spirit to secure certain blessings or benefits. "The world is not ending; for these Christians it is just beginning."[47]

KICC is influenced by the American Faith Movement, or the "Health and Wealth Gospel." This influence sets them apart from the other pentecostal groups in this study, but relates them to the "Name It, Claim It" practices of televangelists, and to Paul Yonggi Cho's methods in building up his mega-church in Seoul. The American Faith Movement originated in the 1960s with such pentecostal evangelists as Kenneth Hagin and Oral Roberts.[48] Hagin teaches that there is a spiritual principle or "law" by which we can receive from God. The law is to:

1. Say it,
2. Do it,
3. Receive it,
4. Tell it.

Hagin holds that there is power in words to effect anything that is required. These ideas derive from the evangelist E. W. Kenyon, who had pentecostal connections, and who argued that what we confess with our lips dominates our inner being. The crucial biblical verse underlying this teaching is Romans 10:10: "he confesses with his lips and so is saved." Matthew Ashimolowo has a lot to say about "the power of words," in CDs, tapes, and books on Positive Confession. He states that words can influence your perspective and affect your performance, and should be used to "build your spirit man," "paint the picture of your desired future," "re-write the negatives spoken into your life," and "lift yourself from defeat to victory." Because of the influence of the Faith Gospel on KICC, this is a church more focused on harnessing God's power and less attuned to redemption through suffering than the others featured in this study. One might think that the Faith Gospel would undermine the link noted above between material comfort and spiritual barrenness in Britain. However, KICC's judgment on the British has to do with the quality of personal relationships and care. They do not regard material gain as threatening spiritual health, but as resulting from acts of faith. Power and success have replaced simplicity and sacrifice as marks of holiness.[49]

GRACE AND INITIATIVE

In the theologies of all the groups discussed here, there is an emphasis on human initiative: in recognizing needs, responding to God out of those needs, and claiming God's power in facing one's circumstances. The flip side to the stress on human initiative is a downplaying of divine grace. A doctrine of grace is about God's gift freely given to an undeserving humanity. The undermining of this doctrine is probably not conscious and not intended. It is most apparent in the "successful" ministry of KICC, which includes a recent proposal to "enforce God's Kingdom in London."[50]

KICC constantly implies that human power and initiative determine the work of God. One of Ashimolowo's numerous tape series offers listeners "101 Truths about Divine Success: Principles to help you enter the greatest dimension of blessing and favour you have experienced." Its promotion of positive attitudes, such as self-respect, confidence, ambition, planning, determination, and discipline, may be interpreted in this light.[51] The KICC Product Catalogue opens on to an advertisement for a tape series of "The Road to Success." The "Milestones" in this series include goal-setting, unlocking your destiny, the power of a positive attitude and diligence, developing a God-centered life and Godly self-image, developing self-esteem, money miracles, walking in winning wisdom, the power of positive relationships, promoting generational blessings, and commitment to work. A three-tape series called "101 Truths about the Holy Spirit," where one might expect to find a theology of the Spirit's freedom to bless and to give, presents the truths about the Spirit as things to "help you maximize His presence in your life." The onus for having success with God is thereby placed on the believer or practitioner, "hang on until your breakthrough comes," "quitters never win and winners never quit."[52]

Grace seems to be less in the forefront of pentecostal minds than other categories such as power. This is as true of KICC as of Bishop JI's students, although their different conceptions of the outworking of divine power significantly affect their ministries: bringing people into the Church as the place where they can move powerfully in God's spirit, or going out into the community with the gentle power of love. Wherever grace is undermined, there is a danger of burdening believers with the responsibility for securing God's will, as though ultimately we humans are in control of the universe. No pentecostals intend to convey this, but rather wish to emphasize that we have a responsibility to be God's agents on earth. However, pastorally they have to deal with the consequences of unanswered prayers. KICC's teaching on illness explains failure to receive healing in terms of some short fall on the part of the sufferer: "lack of knowledge of God's Word in the area of healing (Hosiah [*sic*] 4:6);" "unforgiveness, strife and bitterness. . . (Mark 11:25);" or "fear, worry and a negative confession. . . (1 Peter 5:7);" which belittle the power of prayer or make "the Word of God of no effect (Mark 7:13)" by holding on to "the traditions of man and the lies of the devil."[53] Such an approach produces a great amount of activity, but also induces guilt and striving, and a model of God that many ex-charismatics and pentecostals try to unlearn.

THEOLOGICAL DISSONANCE

The lack of emphasis on divine grace at KICC and elsewhere is no doubt partly due to the fact that black pentecostal theology is not "systematic" in a way that western theologians recognize. In particular, the theology does not start from first principles, such as "God is necessary and self-sufficient," "we are contingent and dependent beings," "God does not need to give, but gives with perfect freedom," and so on. A theologian who reasons from such principles is likely to argue that God is free from our endeavours, otherwise God would not be sovereign. From this it follows that we cannot enforce God's will, and we cannot fail to enforce it either. Pastorally, such theology promotes neither a sense of achievement nor a conviction of failure and guilt. Arguably, it fails to motivate people sufficiently to work towards the realization of God's kingdom, and hence black pentecostals favor Kingdom principles over theological literacy.[54]

Black theologians have been described as pastoral rather than systematic theologians because they use the scriptures as "pastoral documents: intended to shape, orient, strengthen, and inspire the church in the process of addressing the whole person."[55] They do not organize God topics under particular theological headings. Rather, their theology is oral and narrative, comprised of stories of people's lives as journeys undertaken with God.[56] Scripture is used in an immediate way, quoted to build up faith, motivate action, and back up points, and all the time the stories of the Bible are understood as a mirror in which God's people today can see themselves.[57] Moreover, black-led churches are a locus for the black community, and their theologians tend to have the community rather than the church in mind as their primary audience.[58] White, Western theologians understand themselves as writing for the Church so that the Church can serve the world. By being subject to the Church they make the point that they are not subject to secular philosophies. But such a gap between Church and world has not opened up in the consciousness of black pentecostals. They might say instead that serving the world is practicing theology.

We have seen these principles at work in the way that the Community Development students talk about their theology of practice: they go out into the community, as did the people of God in the Bible. They used the term theology in our interviews only because I did, and they asked me to explain what I meant by it. (They may have come from churches that do not claim to have a theology.[59]) They then said that theology for them is interpretation of the Bible for community development, which was a very good way of describing the discussions I had attended. For example, when I asked them whether their emphasis upon community was relatively recent in their church traditions or something that had always been there (I had in mind the bias towards individualism and personal piety in evangelical religion), one woman responded, "Moses did a great community work. He liberated Israel from Egypt." The students do make theological statements, such as "God himself is a community, a three in one, so already God loves community," and "Faith without works is dead. . . .You have to lay your bridge across the water before you go into another land," but they do not name them as such. They seamlessly move between reading and interpreting scripture, commenting both socially and politically, and living out the Gospel commands. So they say: "The Bible is saying, the community workers are saying, we can touch people wherever we are;" "God wants you to be a hard-working human being;" and, as we have already heard, "The theology that we practise . . . we end up with the answer that God is love. God loved us so much that he gave. . . .[John 3:16]." Thus they achieve an immediacy between scripture, reflection, and practice.

By contrast, mainstream Western Christianity has suffered the consequences of dividing up the theological discipline and creating professionals in biblical studies, systematic theology, pastoralia, mission, spirituality, and other specialized areas. So we have to develop theories about how these fields relate to one another, and how to put our theology into practice. Walter J. Hollenweger, the great scholar of pentecostalism, noted the democratizing and therefore the revolutionary force of pentecostalism's freedom from scholarly constraints:

Pentecostalism is revolutionary because it offers alternatives to "literary" theology and thus defrosts the "frozen thinking" within literary forms of worship and committee-debate and gives the same chances to all—including the "oral" people. It allows for a process of democratization of language by dismantling the privileges of abstract, rational, propositional systems.[60]

Some black theologians portray liberation from stifling modes of theology as liberation from white Christianity, and draw parallels with black liberation from slavery.[61] A crucial part of this liberation is freedom from having to 'talk white," and hence a reclaiming of their identity.[62] Bishop KDP explained to me that the Ethiopian eunuch in Acts 8 needed a "guide" not a "'teacher." He could already read, and therefore needed not literacy but spiritual guidance. Bishop KDP said this as a statement of African dignity, and went on to emphasize the importance of

African thinkers in early Christianity: "The whole church is Africanized, because that's where it begins. The Bible was not written in Europe. It has Egyptian background. People used to have to go to Africa, to Alexandria, to train—the greatest theological university in the world."

Pentecostal theologians themselves disagree over whether pentecostal theology is adolescent and growing towards fully-fledged European literacy, or whether it is preserving an integration and a wisdom that European theology has lost.[63] I found differing attitudes towards theology among the pentecostals whom I interviewed. Bishop JI suggested that black pentecostals could learn about theological training from the Anglican Church. His students at the Institute wanted to gain a clearer sense of what theology is, but they were not to be diverted from their practical theology. Bishop KDP held in high regard clear thought and a learned approach to scripture. In this respect he came closest to the way that white evangelicals typically think: fairly oblivious of theology but with a dutiful approach to studying scripture. "We must study, the Bible tells us to," he said, quoting from II Timothy 2:15, about "rightly dividing the word of truth." Pastor M harbored some suspicion of theology, and used a derogatory tone in uttering the word. He pointed out that at KICC people are chosen to be pastors who are seen to be spiritual, and not on the grounds of theological training. This is pentecostal rhetoric, manifesting ill-grounded suspicion of how mainstream churches choose their ministers. It is part of the competition with the religious establishment whose congregation's pentecostals are not educationally qualified to lead.[64]

The matter of theology is not the only area where we have seen divergence among the pentecostals in this study, but also more broadly shared attitudes. All of the pentecostals I encountered would agree that to prioritize theology, let alone engage in a debate about theology, is to be diverted from mission. The Anglican Church feels threatened, not by the likes of C&S to whom they have been letting buildings for several decades, but by such new and burgeoning ministries as Built on the Rock and KICC, which are attracting large numbers of people. If, in trying to build relations with new pentecostal churches, Anglicans begin by trying to assess them theologically, they will remain at cross-purposes with them. Black pentecostals gauge Anglicans by their practical ministry. Their attitude, as conveyed to me, is this: if you want to cooperate in Christ's saving work in community, let us find ways of doing that; if you want to discuss how we compare as Christians, we are too busy.

A difficulty Anglicans have in trying to do anything other than repeat the story as black pentecostals tell it is that we are given no handles. We cannot respond theologically without appearing either to appropriate black theology or else to fall into abstractions that are presumed irrelevant. Nor, however, is it clear how we are to respond in a practical way because Black pentecostals draw their energy and ideas for mission from the very story they tell, which is a story Anglicans will only half recognize as depicting the problems of the nation and the state of the Church of England. Their responses to these problems seem to depend on society staying how it is rather than undergoing any deep structural change; and part of society staying the same is that the established church remains both mainstream and ineffectual, and pentecostal churches remain on the fringes meeting the needs that the social structures have created. That they operate more with a biblical consciousness than with a critical sense of their own history works against certain types of self-awareness, which in turn works against an impulse to make concessions to others. It makes it possible for them to regard themselves as biblical people in contradistinction from non-biblical "Christians." The pentecostals I interviewed were at pains to say they were not "segregationist," but they were nonetheless oppositional. They claimed an identity, a practice, and a function that they denied to white mainstream churches (with perhaps the exception of Holy Trinity Brompton, in respect of its spiritually lively worship). The sense of threat that Anglicans feel, I would suggest, comes from bewilderment at not knowing how to interact with new pentecostal churches, as much as from these churches' numerical strength. The purpose of this chapter has been to try to make some preliminary moves in advancing understanding by performing the risky task of using my own voice to report what I have learned from believers whose standpoint I can at best try to understand, and of course can never actually occupy.[65]

NOTES

1. To some extent they regard material abundance as creating emotional, social and spiritual needs, but they also see it as their Christian task to meet material needs, and they would not make sharp distinctions between types of need. For example, they use the concept of "hunger" to mean much more than physical craving.

2. The usual expression used to refer to churches led by Black ministers, and whose congregations are often predominantly black.

3. See Elaine Foster, "Out of this world: a consideration of the Development and Nature of Black-led Churches in Britain," in Paul Grant and Raj Patel (eds.), *A Time to Speak: Perspective of Black Christians in Britain* (The Racial Justice and Black Theology Working Group, 1990), p. 67.

4. Statistics given to the Eighteenth triennial Pentecostal World Conference, September 22-25, 1998, and cited by Cecil M. Robeck, Jr., *Pentecostal Report* (The Secretaries of Christian World Communions, October 21-23, 1998).

5. These are the terms used in the Lambeth Resolutions, and refer to newly founded churches, which are usually charismatic, and to churches around the world that are established in independence from the missionary churches associated with old colonial powers.

6. Foster, "Out of This World."

7. Bishop Joe Aldred, a black pentecostal bishop who sees the first task of black theology as one of "Black self-disclosure" "Paradigms for a Black Theology in Britain," *Black Theology in Britain* 2 (1999), pp. 23, 32.

8. Bishop JI who will be introduced later in the chapter.

9. White churches have been judged by their treatment of blacks, Robert Beckford, *Jesus is Dread: Black Theology and Black Culture in Britain* (London: Darton, Longman and Todd, 1998), pp. 42-43.

10. Grant and Patel, *A Time to Speak*, p. 1.

11. Aldred, "Paradigms for a Black Theology," pp. 9-32.

12. I intend, in these statements, to be comparing like with like as far as is possible: comparing pastors of black-led pentecostal churches with Anglican clergy, and not comparing the theologians (many of whom are also ministers) of either tradition.

13. For example, at the national level, Church of England prayers for the millennium, such as the prayer distributed with millennium candles, did not mention Jesus Christ.

14. See especially Harriet A. Harris, *Fundamentalism and Evangelicals* (Oxford: Clarendon, 1998).

15. Cyril C. Okorocha, "Scripture, Mission and Evangelism," in John Stott et al, *The Anglican Communion and Scripture* (Carlisle: Regnum and EFAC, 1996), pp. 65-66.

16. Aldred, " Paradigms for a Black Theology," pp. 23-32.

17. Christopher Rowland and Mark Corner, *Liberating Exegesis: The Challenge of Liberation Theology to Biblical Studies* (Louisville, Ky: Westminster/John Knox, 1989), pp. 63-67, 191. African-American Scholarship: especially Vincent L. Wimbush, "The Bible and African Americans," in Cain Hope Felder (ed.), *Stony the Road We Trod: African American Biblical Interpretation* (Minneapolis: Fortress, 1991), p. 96; which portrays fundamentalism as a white phenomenon and accuses blacks who embrace it of rejecting racial consciousness; Alice Ogden Bellis, "The Bible in African American Perspectives," *Teaching Theology and Religion*, vol. 1, no. 3 (1998), pp. 161-65.

18. Aldred, "Paradigms for a Black Theology," p. 9.

19. Grant, "Issues for the black minister," *A Time to Speak*, p. 13.

20. Jean-Jacques Suurmond, *Word and Spirit at Play: Towards a Charismatic Theology, translated* by John Bowden (London: SCM, 1994), pp. 151-52.

21. Notably Robert Beckford and Bishop Joe Aldred and Ronald Nathan. In the notes I invite occasional comparisons with black theology (British and African-American), African theology, and white pentecostal writing, to shed light on wider contexts and sets of influences.

22. Afe Adogame and Akin Omoyajowo, "Anglicanism and the Aladura Churches in Nigeria," in Andrew Wingate, Kevin Ward, Carrie Pemberton, and Wilson Sitshebo (eds.), *Anglicanism: A Global Communion* (London: Mowbray, 1998), pp. 90-97.

23. *Winning Ways*, vol. 1, no. 2 (Spring 1998), p. 14.

24. *Raising CHAMPIONS fulfilling DREAMS* (information brochure given to visitors and newcomers).

25. Walter J. Hollenweger, *The Pentecostals,* 3rd ed (Peabody, Mass.: Hendrickson, 1988), p. 460; Beckford, *Jesus Is Dread*, p. 28.

26. Walter J. Hollenweger, "The Pentecostal Elites and the Pentecostal Poor: A Missed Dialogue?" in Karla Poewe (ed.), *Charismatic Christianity as a Global Culture* (Columbia: University of South Carolina Press, 1994).

27. Harold Horton of the Church of Christ, quoted by Hollenweger, *The Pentecostals*, p. 429.

28. Steven J. Land, *Pentecostal Spirituality: A Passion for the Kingdom* (Sheffield: Sheffield Academic Press, 1993), pp. 111-14.

29. Foster, "Out of This World," pp. 67-68.

30. Dave Tomlinson, *The Post-evangelical* (London: Triangle, 1995).

31. *Raising CHAMPIONS fulfilling DREAMS*.

32. From "The KICC Vision 2000."

33. The lack of spirit was a criticism I often heard in interview, and included the sense of lacking in passion and emotion in worship and not exercising spiritual gifts such as glossolalia; healing, and prophecy.

34. *Raising CHAMPIONS fulfilling DREAMS.*

35. Beckford, *Jesus Is Dread*, p. 42. Beckford remembers as a child being "indoctrinated" that white, staid Christianity was not true Christianity. Beckford sees this dismissiveness of other Christians as a trait learned from white American Christianity.

36. For discussion see Hollenweger, *The Pentecostals*, pp. 465-72; Luther P. Gerlach, "Pentecostalism: Revolution or Counter-Revolution?" in Iwing I. Zaretsky and Mark P. Leone (eds.), *Religious Movements in Contemporary America* (Princeton, NJ: Princeton University Press, 1974).

37. Walter J. Hollenweger, *Pentecost Between Black and White: Five Case Studies on Pentecost and Politics* (Belfast: Christian Journals Ltd., 1974), pp. 25, 26.

38. Hollenweger, *The Pentecostals*, pp. 469-70; Hollenweger, *Pentecost Between Black and White*, pp. 16-18; Foster, "Out of This World," pp. 67-68.

39. Hollenweger, *The Pentecostals*, pp. 467-72; Land, *Pentecostal Spirituality*, pp. 179-81.

40. Hollenweger, *The Pentecostals*, p. 11.

41. Aldred, "Paradigms for a Black Theology," especially p. 13; Margaret M. Poloma, *The Assemblies of God at the Crossroads: Charisma and Institutional Dilemmas* (Knoxville: University of Tennessee Press, 1989), pp. 237-38; Beckford, *Jesus Is Dread*, p. 32.

42. Aldred, "Paradigms for a Black Theology;" Beckford, *Jesus Is Dread*, pp. 144-47; Foster, "Out of This World," p. 67.

43. In Latin America and South Korea pentecostal churches have been attracting liberationist Christians, but whether they have really depoliticized them remains to be seen.

44. From "The KICC Vision 2000."

45. Paul Gifford, "Gospel for champions," *The Tablet* (September 18, 1999), pp. 1256-57.

46. "The KICC Vision 2000" includes the following goals:
- to plant at least 30 satellites all over London.
- to send members on short and long term ministry projects to every continent.
- to build a 5,000-seater church building and a four floor office—a *state-of-the art* facility providing:
  (a) 5,000 seats for worship
  (b) 1,000 place children's church
  (c) 600 place teenage church
  (d) A counselling and prayer center [note the priority —secularizing]
  (e) Class rooms for Bible School
  (f) 100 place nursery
  (g) 400-seater restaurant
  (h) A fully equipped gym

47. Gifford, "Gospel for Champions," p. 1257.

48. Paul Gifford, *African Christianity: Its Public Role* (London: Hurst & Co., 1998), pp. 39-40, 337-40; D. R. McConnell, *A Different Gospel: Biblical and Historical Insights into the Word of Faith Movement* (Peabody, Mass.: Hendrickson, 1995).

49. Poloma passed this verdict in her own study, *The Assemblies of God*, pp. 232-41.

50. Publicity for the "Gathering of Champions" conference, held August 22-30, 1999, in London Arena, which also used captions "Taking Hold of the Future" and "1999 Is the Year of Prophetic Fulfilment Specific Assignment Strategic Planning."

51. This would complement sociological interpretations of the confidence pentecostal religion bestows on marginalized people and the powers it gives them to face the future; e.g., Gerlach, "Pentecostalism: Revolution or Counter-Revolution?"

52. Publicity for one of Matthew Ashimolowo's books, *It's Not Over 'Till It's Over* (Product Catalogue, p. 14).

53. *Winning Ways*, vol. 1, no. 2 (Spring 1998), pp. 4-6.

54. Aldred, "Paradigms for a Black Theology."

55. Thomas Hoyt, "Interpreting Biblical Scholarship for the Black Church Tradition," in Felder, *Stony the Road We Trod*, p. 37. Beckford's point that the text is "pharmacosmic," that is, it has the power to heal, and one reads it so as to become a better Christian, *Jesus Is Dread*, p. 169.

56. See, Hollenweger, *Pentecostalism: Origins and Developments Worldwide* (Peabody, Mass.: Hendrickson, 1997), p. 196; Land, *Pentecostal Spirituality*, pp. 80, 113, 183.

57. Wimbush, "Biblical Historical Study as Liberation," pp. 140-41, argues that the telling and retelling of biblical stories, of strength under oppressive regimes, and of hope in hopeless situations, by which black people identified with biblical heroes, represented the beginning of the "Afro-Christian tradition." He describes this tradition as a blending of (West) African "sacred-cosmos" and Euro-American Protestant evangelical Christianity.

58. Garnet Parris, "Black Theology: The US experience," in Grant, *A Time to Speak*, p. 28; and Charles H. Long, "Assessment of New Departures for a Study of Black Religion in the United States of America," in Wilmore (ed.), *African American Religious Studies*.

59. Gifford, *African Christianity*, pp. 26-27.

60. Hollenweger, *Pentecost Between Black and White*, p. 26.

61. For African American academic critique of white Western theology see Felder (ed.), *Stony the Road We Trod*, and Wilmore (ed.), *African American Religious Studies*. For African stances, see M. L. Daneel, "African Independent Church Pneumatology and the Salvation of All Creation," in Harold D. Hunter and Peter D. Hocken (eds.), *All Together in One Place: Theological Papers from the Brighton Conference on World Evangelization* (Sheffield: Sheffield Academic Press, 1993); and Bénézet Bujo, *African Theology in Its Social Context* (Maryknoll, N.Y.: Orbis, 1992), pp. 58ff.

62. Beckford, *Jesus is Dread*, p. 143; Nicole Rodriguez Toulis, *Believing Identity: Pentecostalism and the Mediation of Jamaican Ethnicity and Gender in England* (Oxford: Berg, 1997), p. 271.

63. Contrast Land, *Pentecostal Spirituality*, p. 190, and Poloma, *Assemblies of God*, pp. 232-41, with Hollenweger, *Pentecost Between Black and White*, pp. 16, 31.

64. Douglas Peterson, *Not by Might nor by Power: A Pentecostal Theology of Social Concern in Latin America* (Oxford: Regnum, 1996), p. 30.

65. My thanks to Dr. Pamela Sue Anderson, James Grenfell, and Dr. Mark Harris for their comments on this chapter.

Chapter 7

The Politics of Islam in Bangladesh

Syed Serajul Islam

One of the most important crises of the Muslim world is the use of religion for political purposes by a regime. Islam has been exploited in many of these countries as a means of extending authority and earning legitimacy rather than giving true meaning to its principles. In Abu Sulayman's words, today, "the Muslim World, which is internally weak, relatively backward, frustrated, suffering from internal tensions, full of conflicts and often controlled and abused by powers, is in a state of crisis. Its modern history is a tragedy."[1] Bangladesh, the third largest Muslim country in the world,[2] is no exception to this pattern. In Bangladesh, the regimes have used Islam as one of their most important ingredients of legitimacy because, "as a religion and a stable value system in Bangladesh, Islam has always been a guiding force for the people. Islamic traditions, customs, institutions, and beliefs are part of everyday life and are often the only familiar forms of social being and consciousness."[3] Each regime has successfully maneuvered the minds of the Muslims during periods of crisis because Islam is the predominant value system in the country. Therefore, even half a century after the end of colonial rule, religion is as much alive in Bangladesh as it was in the past. In this chapter, an attempt is made to highlight the revivalism and predominance of Islam in Bangladesh despite the commitment of the Sheikh Mujibur Rahman's (henceforth Mujib) government to secularism immediately after independence. However, before going into that analysis, it will be essential to explain briefly the connections between Islam and politics.

ISLAM AND POLITICS

In Islam, religion and politics are not considered to be two sides of a single coin. Islam is holistic, integrating religion and politics. As John Esposito points out, "the traditional Islamic world view provided a holistic approach towards life, a life in which religion was intimately and organically related to politics, law and society."[4] Similarly, Ka'b has eloquently expressed, "Islam, the government and the people are like the tent, the pole, the ropes and the pegs. The tent is Islam; the pole is the government; the ropes and pegs are the people. None will do without the others."[5]

From the Islamic point of view, the state is an institution for enforcing and implementing the fundamental principles of Islam. None is entitled to make laws on his own authority and none is obliged to abide by them. The Holy *Qur'an* says, "The authority rests with none but Allah. He commands you not to surrender to any one save Him. This is the right way" (12:40). "They ask: have we also got some authority? Say: all authority belongs to Allah alone" (3:154). "Whosoever does not establish and abide by that which Allah has revealed, such are dis-believers" (5:44).[6]

An Islamic State is supposed to be free from all traces of nationalism. It is a state built exclusively on Islamic principles. According to Abul A'la Maududi, "Nothing more than a combination of men working together as servants of God to carry out His Will and purposes and whereby each member renders his responsibilities to Allah who commands social justice, and forbids all kinds of exploitation, injustice, disorder and inequalities."[7] Consequently, in any society that is largely dominated by Muslims it is very difficult for any regime to ignore the values of Islam or to do anything that is prohibited by Islam, even though the country is not formally declared an Islamic republic. Although at some points in history a few countries with a Muslim majority[8] adopted measures to separate religion from politics, generally it is very difficult for the politicians to ignore religious values. Any serious deviation from basic Islamic tenets may endanger the very existence of the regime.

In South Asia in particular, despite 200 years of British colonialism, traditionalism pervades the villages, where the majority lives. The minorities of South Asians who are the ruling elite are secular which is the result of European colonialism. Gunner Myrdel observed that in South Asia religion is so deeply rooted that "even the communists do not dare to speak against the religion."[9] Even a nationalist leader like Gandhi said, "For me there is no distinction between politics and religion." With specific reference to Bangladesh, Rashiduzzaman comments:

When East Pakistan broke away from Pakistan to become an independent and sovereign nation of Bangladesh, many observers believed that South Asia was irrevocably on its route to a secular nationalism, beyond religious tribalism and parochialism, which purported the 1947 partition of British India. As later events proved, they were sadly mistaken. The primacy of Islamic traditions and sentiments, cast aside by the Bengalis in East Pakistan in 1971 to fight the Pakistani crackdown, and later deliberately exercised by the new Bangladesh government, subsequently returned as a resilient and widespread political phenomenon.[10]

This chapter makes an attempt to examine how and why Islam has been used in Bangladesh by every regime as a core value for earning legitimacy.

PRE-INDEPENDENT BANGLADESH

Upon the colonization of Bengal in 1757, the position of Muslims was affected adversely by the policy of British East Indian Company. During the late 1930s and early 1940s, the Muslims of Bengal realized that they were relatively behind the Hindus economically, politically, and educationally, and that they would continue to be so if they did not support the Muslim League, which championed the cause of Islam and Muslims in India. The Muslim League, on the other hand, mainly counting on the support of Muslims in East Bengal (now Bangladesh), eventually succeeded in bringing about the existence of Pakistan in 1947 on the basis of the "two nation theory." East Bengali Muslims supported the theory and joined Pakistan. The Objective Resolution was adopted in 1949, which declared, "In Pakistan the Muslims shall be able to order their lives in the individual and collective spheres in accord with the teachings and requirements of Islam as set out in the Holy Qur'an and Sunnah."[12] It was further stated in the Resolution that the state would establish "the principles of democracy, freedom, equality, tolerance, and social justice as enunciated by Islam."[13] Subsequently a constitution was adopted in 1956 that declared Pakistan an Islamic Republic. It was stated, "Sovereignty over the entire universe belongs to Allah Almighty alone and the authority to be exercised by the people of Pakistan within the limits prescribed by Him is a sacred trust."[14] The Constitution of the Islamic Republic of Pakistan emphasized the importance of maintaining unity with Muslim countries. After the declaration of martial law in 1958, the constitution was abrogated and a second constitution was adopted in 1962, which also included many Islamic provisions.

However, soon after the creation of Pakistan the country became politically unstable due to the growing conflict between the two wings of the country over the sharing of political power and economic resources. East and West Pakistan were separated from each other by more than a thousand miles. In fact, according to Richard Weeks, Pakistan was a "double country."[15] The ruling elite of Pakistan had to identify Islam with the Pakistani state in order to maintain the legitimacy and integrity of the state. Islam was the only bond of unity between the two wings of Pakistan.[16] However, the frustration of the East Pakistani Muslims increased due to a growing feeling of sociocultural, economic, and political domination by the minority Muslim elite of West Pakistan. The disparity between the two wings of Pakistan grew, and very little attempt was made by the West Pakistani ruling elite to decrease the frustrations of the Bengalis. The Awami League, which had already emerged as a result of the Language Movement of 1952, epitomized the feeling of Bengalis when it demanded regional autonomy as a solution to their problems, announcing its firm commitment to secularism. This movement eventually culminated in the 1971 War of National Liberation that led to the emergence of a separate independent state called Bangladesh.[17]

THE MUJIB REGIME (1972-75)

After independence, the Awami League, which had led the nationalist movement of Bangladesh in 1971, formed a government under the leadership of Sheik Mujibur Rahman. The regime's stand on religion was clearly enunciated in Bangladesh's constitution. Secularism was declared one of the fundamental principles of state policy. The constitution abolished all kinds of communalism, political recognition of any religion by the state and the exploitation of religion for political ends. It was stated, in article 12 of the constitution, "Every citizen shall have the right to form associations or unions, subject to any reasonable restrictions imposed by law in the interest of morality or public order; provided that no person shall have the right to form or be a member of any communal or other association or union which in the name of or on the basis of any religion has for its object, or purposes, a political purpose."[18]

In order to implement the principle of secularism, the Mujib government took a few steps. First, school textbooks were revised. All Islamic stories in the primary and secondary school textbooks were removed. Second, the subject Islamiat (Islamic studies) was withdrawn from the secondary school syllabus. Third, though *Madrassah* (religious schools) education was not abolished, no attempt was taken to upgrade them. In fact, government grants were cut. Fourth, all Islamic names of public places were changed. The Islamic Intermediate College of Dhaka, for example, was renamed Kazi Nazrul College. The Dhaka University students' residence names were changed from Fazlul Huq Muslim Hall to Fazlul Huq Hall, Salimullah Muslim Hall to Salimullah Hall, Allama Iqbal (famous Pakistani poet and leader of the Pakistan movement) Hall to Zahurul Huq (a Bengali police sergeant who was killed in the late 1960s autonomy movement) Hall, Jinnah (founder of Pakistan) Hall to Surjasen (a Bengali Hindu hero during the nationalist movement in British India) Hall. Fifth, the government renamed and changed the logo/monogram of Dhaka University, removing the *Qur'anic* words *rabbi zidni ilma* (O) lord increase my knowledge). Sixth, the tradition in Bangladesh of initiating public gatherings or ceremonies with a recitation from the Holy *Qur'an* was eliminated by the regime. Even the radio and television station openings had to stop the reciting from the *Qur'an*. Finally and most importantly, by virtue of Article 12 of the Constitution of 1972, the Mujib regime prohibited any religious activities that had a political agenda. By this token, all political parties that had religious names were banned on the plea that religion should no longer be used as a political weapon as it had been used during united Pakistan.[19]

Despite the government's commitment to eliminate the influence of Islam, Islamic sentiment was running high in the minds of the people. In a survey, the Education Commission found that, while about 21 percent supported secular education, about 75 percent were in favor of having religious education as an integral part of general education.[20] In another survey, it was found that 50.6 percent and 62.1 percent of rural and urban respondents respectively held orthodox Islamic beliefs.[21] It is true that Bangladesh was constitutionally secularized, but the deep-seated Islamic culture of the society could not be altered. Within two years of Mujib's rule many of the Bangladeshis started openly criticizing the government's secularization programs. Many people felt that in the name of secularism the regime was particularly hostile to Islam rather than to all religions in Bangladesh. As Hashmi observed, "not a single Hindu, Christian, or Buddhist organization having religious identity or name was affected by the Mujib government's secularization program."[22] Many began to call the Mujib government a "puppet regime" of Hindu India.

By 1974, also as a consequence of Mujib's development policy, Bangladesh's economy faced a grave crisis. As heavily dependent upon the Indian economy, it maintained a low rate of production, an excessive money supply, deficit financing, and a high rate of unemployment. Meanwhile, leftist parties, especially the underground parties, challenged the existence of the regime.[23] According to them, the independence of Bangladesh had not brought about the emancipation of peasants and workers; rather, a puppet government of the Awami League—"representative of exploiting classes of Bangladesh, agents of Indian expansionists, Soviet and American imperialists"—had come to power.[24] The puppet government had, therefore, to be uprooted by the proletariat through an armed struggle under the leadership of a communist party that would complete the "unfinished" revolution of Bangladesh started in March 1971.[25] With this ideological orientation, the underground parties began training their political cadres in the spirit of a "second revolution" in Bangladesh, launching three types of violent activities. First, they started killing leaders of the Awami League on a large scale. Second, they attacked the houses of rich farmers. Third, in addition to the secret killing and looting the property of Awami League leaders, revolutionary cadres attacked the local law and enforcement machinery —police outposts and police stations. The revolutionaries thus posed a serious and direct challenge to the authority and security of the state.

In response to the challenge, the government declared a state of emergency and banned the activities of all political parties. Several ordinances were promulgated, which included establishing special tribunals exclusively for trying persons charged with offenses such as the acquisition of arms and ammunition, providing of firing squads for the execution of persons found guilty by the tribunals, arresting without warrant those suspected of having committed crimes, and voiding any challenge by those persons in the court of law.

In order to convince the majority that the regime, despite its adherence to secularism, was neither pro-Indian nor anti-Muslim, Mujib declared that in Bangladesh, "the favored religion of the vast majority of the population is Islam. No law will be formulated or enforced in Bangladesh contrary to the laws of Islam well stabilised in the Holy Qur'an and Sunnah."[26] Mujib's first manifestation toward Islamic sentiment was the release and declaration of general amnesty for all politicians who collaborated with the Pakistani army during the 1971 liberation war. Second, the government declared its confirmation to make the study of *Islamiat* and Arabic compulsory in secondary schools. Third, the government released more funds for *Madrassah* education.

In 1971, the allocation of Islamic education was Taka 2.5 million, which went up to Taka 7.2 million in 1973. Fourth, the practice of beginning radio and television broadcasts and state functions with recitations from the *Qur'an*, which had been discontinued, was reintroduced. Fifth, the government formed *Sirat* Committees (celebrating committees) for the observance of *Eid-e-Milad-un Nabi* (Prophet Muhammad's birthday) throughout the country. Sixth, the Islamic Academy that had been abolished in 1972 was revived; and in March 1975, five months before Mujib's assassination, it was upgraded to a Foundation. Finally, and most importantly, Mujib himself Islamized his speeches by using Islamic terms such as *Insha Allah* (if God wishes). He started attending Islamic gatherings and began to conclude his speeches with *Khuda Hafiz* (God is all-conscious), instead of the secular slogan *Joi Bangla* (victory of Bengal). Mujib also participated in the Summit of Organization of Islamic Conference (OIC)[27] held in Lahore, Pakistan, in 1975 to gain the support of the Muslim world.

All the above steps, however, did not mean that the Mujib regime was Islamicizing Bangladesh; rather, he was trying to earn the loyalty of the masses in order to prolong his rule. In fact, all this proved to be too late because the masses were already disenchanted with his corruption, inefficiency, dictatorial disposition, and pro-Indian stand, which culminated in his assassination in August 1975 in a military *coup d'etat*.

THE ZIA REGIME (1976-81)

The young majors who masterminded the August coup proclaimed Bangladesh as an Islamic republic, but to this announcement there was no official follow-up. Khondakar Mustaq Ahmad, a former member in Mujib's cabinet, believed to be anti-Indian and pro-Islamic, was declared the president of Bangladesh. After a very brief interlude of the Ahmad government, the chief of staff of the army, General Ziaur Rahman, became the president of Bangladesh in April 1976. Although there was no resentment in the public for Mujib's assassination, the Zia regime did not have any electoral legitimacy. Since Zia usurped power through non-electoral means he was suffering from a lack of legitimacy.[28] Therefore, besides adopting many political strategies for earning legitimacy, he tried to gain popularity by resorting to Islamic slogans. He stated that, "religious belief and love for religion are great and imperishable characteristics of the Bangladesh nation. The long mass struggle against the cruel and unscrupulous foreign rule and domination has given the most sublime and tolerant character to and stabilised our religion."[29]

The Zia regime adopted a number of steps towards the Islamization of Bangladesh. First, the regime declared all Islamic parties legal, allowing their activities and appointing many leaders who were allies and supporters of Islamic parties or Islamists to his cabinet. For example, Shah Azizur Rahman who had represented Pakistan at the U.N. in 1971 during the war of independence was made the prime minister. Second, in April 1977, Zia amended the constitution by dropping the word "secularism" and replacing it with "absolute trust and faith in the Almighty Allah." Third, "*Bismillahir Rahmanir Rahim*" (In the name of Allah, the Beneficial, and the Merciful) was inserted in the preamble of the constitution. Fourth, several symbolic measures were adopted, such as the hanging of wall posters in public offices with *Qur'anic* verses and Prophet Mohammad's *Hadith* (sayings); *Eid Mubarak* (happy festival); the flying of festoons beside the national flags on the *Eid* day (the largest annual festival of the Muslims); the issuance of messages by the head of the state on religious occasions; and offerings of *munajat* (prayers) on special occasions. Fifth, attempts were made to propagate the principles of *sharia* (Islamic Laws) and to introduce *Azan (*call for prayer) through radio and television five times a day. Sixth, instead of Sunday, Friday was declared the official weekly holiday in the country. Finally, Zia personally popularized the term *Bangladesh Zindabad* (Long Live Bangladesh) instead of *Joi Bangla*, which was considered to be un-Islamic.[30]

In concrete terms, the Zia government also attempted to introduce Islam into the general education system of the country. A new "syllabi committee" was formed which declared that, "Islam is a code of life, not just a sum of rituals. A Muslim has to live his personal, social, economic, and international life in accordance with Islam from childhood to death. So the acquiring of knowledge of Islam is compulsory for all Muslims—men and women."[31] The committee suggested the introduction of a compulsory course on *Islamiat* (Islamic studies) from the first to the eighth grades (with the option to the students of minority communities of having similar courses on their religion). The government accepted these recommendations and the Ministry of Education implemented the policy immediately.[32]

The government also opened a new Ministry for Religious Affairs. Moreover, the Islamic Academy was given an extensive network of research facilities. An Islamic University, along with an Islamic Research Center, was also set up. Finally, during the Zia regime, Bangladesh became an influential member of the OIC, the Al-Kuds Committee (a peace committee formed for ending the Iran-Iraq War 1980), and Islamic Solidarity Front with its constitutional declaration for "stabilizing, preserving, and strengthening fraternal ties with the Muslim states on the basis of Islamic solidarity."[33]

Every step taken by the Zia regime made the majority happy; but he did not declare Bangladesh an Islamic state. Rather, he said that Bangladesh, with a 90 % Muslim population, was a *de facto* Muslim state and therefore it was redundant to declare it an Islamic state.[34] In fact, this was nothing but a political stand of the regime in the wake of rising Islamic sentiments. Thus, Rashid comments, "as the revolutionary fever ended in August 1975, the Bangladesh polity regained its original traits and Islam which was muted, reappeared on the Bangladesh political scene."[35]

THE ERSHAD REGIME (1982-90)

President Ziaur Rahman was assassinated in 1981 in an abortive military *coup d'etat*, and therefore Vice President Abdus Sattar became acting president of Bangladesh. A fresh presidential election was held in 1981 in which Sattar won in a landslide victory. Within three months of his rule, however, the army's chief of staff, General Hossain Mohammad Ershad, demanded the participation of the armed forces in the administrative machinery of the government. President Sattar disagreed with this proposal. Consequently, on March 24, 1982, General Ershad assumed full power under Marshal Law and suspended the constitution. Immediately after capturing power, Ershad declared, "Sattar had lost sight of the Islamic nationalistic goal, previously set by Zia ur Rahman," and he stated further, "Islam will be given the highest place in the country's future constitution and Islamic provisions wherever necessary."[36]

The seizure of power by Ershad led the opposition political parties, despite their differing ideologies and orientations, to be united against the regime. They demanded "immediate withdrawal of martial law, restoration of fundamental rights, parliamentary elections preceding any other election, release of political prisoners, and the trial of persons responsible for student killings."[37] By 1988, the government made several attempts to reach a compromise with the politicians, but by then Ershad had alienated all the major sections of the community—students, professionals, intellectuals, trade unions, and so on. He therefore thought that the "Islamic slogan" might be the easiest way to gain the support of the masses. He began to appeal to the sentiment of the Muslim masses by adopting steps towards the further Islamization of Bangladesh. He declared, "Bangladeshis are good Muslims who offered their prayers five times a day and whom Allah would certainly help."[38]

First, Ershad himself began to visit *mazars* (tombs/shrines) and *masjids* (mosques) in order to show his religious commitment. He also addressed the people at *Jumma* (Friday) prayer and asked them to follow the true path of Islam. Second, the government adopted an education policy in which the study of Arabic and Islamiat was made compulsory from grade one.[39] Third, the government established a *Zakat* Fund[40] (poor fund) headed by the president himself in order to distribute money to the needy. Fourth, the regime also established a separate directorate under the Ministry of Education for *madrassah* education. One remarkable feature of these institutions was their large-scale expansion and development. In 1975-76, there were 1,830 government-approved *madrassah* in Bangladesh, which in 1988 increased to 2,700. Fifth, the government offered financial grants to many *madrassahs* and mosques for the repair, reconstruction, and beautification of their buildings. Finally, and most importantly, the Ershad government passed an amendment (Eighth Amendment) to the constitution on June 7, 1988, declaring Islam the state religion of Bangladesh.[41]

All of these steps, however, did not help General Ershad stay in power. The *Jama'at-i-Islami* (the largest Islamic party in Bangladesh) chief held that the people wanted an Islamic state, not a mere declaration of Islam as the state religion.[42] Mowlana Muhammad Ullah, the chief of *Khilafat Andolan* (Islamic leadership movement), gave a *fatwa* (religious decree) condemning Ershad as anti-Islamic since he did not rule according to the *Qur'an* and *Sunnah* (teaching of the Prophet Muhammad) and illegitimately seized power without the consent of the people.[43] In fact, there was no specific measure for the realization of state religion. Thus, General Ershad's frequent and emphatic Islamic declarations did not last long. Ultimately he had to face a violent protest movement in 1990, which resulted in his removal from the office of the presidency of Bangladesh.

THE KHALEDA ZIA REGIME (1991-96)

In the post-Ershad era, Khaleda Zia (widow of President Ziaur Rahman) came to power through achieving a majority vote in the General elections held in 1991. She pursued all the symbolic measures taken by the previous governments of Zia and Ershad. Khaleda's party, the Bangladesh Nationalist Party (BNP), had to form a coalition with the Islamic party, the *Jama'at-i-Islami* (henceforth *Jama'at*) since it did not have an absolute majority of seats in the 1991 election.[44] Consequently, she could not take any steps displeasing to the *Jama'at,* though she did not keep all the promises that she made before the formation of the alliance.[45] However, there were three challenges that forced Khaleda's government to take a stand and would not have dissatisfied the Muslims.

First, Professor Ghulam Azam, chief of the *Jama'at*, was alleged to have collaborated with the Pakistan army during the Liberation War of 1971. His party was outlawed by Mujib until the ban was lifted by Zia in 1976. Azam remained in Pakistan until he returned to Bangladesh in the mid-1970s. As soon as he came to Bangladesh on a Pakistani passport, he became the *de facto* leader of the *Jama'at*, emerging as a power broker after the 1991 election. By then, Azam did not have Bangladeshi citizenship, as it had been revoked by the Mujib government in 1972. Consequently, the opposition party, the Awami League, and a coalition of secular and liberal groups complained to the government that Azam had violated the law, since a foreigner could not be the head of a party. Under the pressure, the government sent him to jail. While Azam was in jail, there were protests and counter-protests both supporting and opposing Azam's claim to citizenship. Ultimately, the government could not go against popular demand. Public sympathy for Azam was expressed at informal gatherings, schools, mosques, and social events. In 1993, the Bangladesh High Court rendered judgment in favor of Azam, restoring his Bangladeshi citizenship (by birth), a decision that was subsequently confirmed by the Supreme Court of Bangladesh.[46]

The second issue was the case of Taslima Nasreen, a feminist writer from Bangladesh, who became the target of attacks by Muslim zealots for her controversial views on Islam. In her book *Lajja* (Shame), she made offensive comments against Islam, which included suggestions for a thorough revision of the *Qur'an*. Although she claimed that she had freedom of expression, Islamicists attacked her as an enemy of Islam and an agent of Hindu India. She was nothing but an "Indian discovery."[47] Begum Khaleda's government was compelled to order her arrest, but she fled and took asylum in a Western country, most probably in France.

The third issue that tilted the political balance in favor of the Muslim majority was the public reaction in Bangladesh to the demolition of the Babri mosque in India.[48] The government issued a press statement that condemned the barbarous action: "The government is equally concerned and deeply shocked at the demolition of the Babri Mosque along with the people of the country."[49] Thus, though the Khaleda regime did not need to take any new steps toward Islamizing Bangladesh in the wake of Islamic revivalism, the government had to side with the popular sentiments of the majority.

SHEIK HASINA REGIME (1996 TO DATE)

The departure of Khaleda in 1996 in the midst of the opposition's continued strikes and protests opened the possibility of a return of the Awami League to power. However, that was possible only if the party could use Islamic symbols. During the election campaign, therefore, the Awami League used as many symbols as possible. First, it posted its electioneering campaign banners that read *Allahu Akbar* (God is the greatest), which it had never done in the past. Some banners were written with *Qur'anic* words. Second, during her national election campaign speech given in public meetings as well as on the TV, Sheikh Hasina, the leader of the Awami League, appealed to the masses with many examples from Islamic history. Third, during the election campaign, Hasina was very careful to cover her whole body with a veil. Not only Hasina but other political leaders as well dropped their political dress, *Mujibcourt* (jacket), replacing it with traditional Muslim dress. Fourth, all the leaders addressed public meetings with recitations from the *Qur'an*, which was against the party's policy of secularism. Finally, Hasina performed her *Al-haj* (pilgrimage) just before the election and visited Saudi Arabia to show her ties with the Muslim world.[50] All these steps were taken to win the minds of the rural Muslim masses, with the result that the party was finally successful in winning the election.

After coming to power Sheikh Hasina did not take any measures to eliminate the Islamic forces despite her party's policy of secularism. Neither has she been able to bring back secularism as one of the state principles, nor eliminate the clause that which declares Islam to be the state religion of Bangladesh. Rather, by paying frequent visits to Saudi Arabia for *umra hajj* (semi pilgrimage performed not during the annual pilgrimage time), she has assured the people of Bangladesh that she is also a Muslim.

THE CAUSES OF RELIGIOUS REVIVALISM

The above discussion indicates the continuous use of Islam by Bangladeshi regimes to further their political interests. Hence, the question arises: why has Islam been dominant in the politics of Bangladesh? One possible answer is the existence of various social, charitable, economic, and political organizations that have kept Islam alive as the dominant value system in Bangladesh. During British rule in India, when the Hindus came to occupy the commanding heights of Bengal's society, Islamic institutions—*masjids, madrassahs,* and *ulema* (religious teachers)—to some extent lost their effectiveness. In order to be on par with the Hindus, Muslim upper classes began to gain a Western secular education; but the great majority stayed firmly rooted in traditional Islamic values and a *madrassah* education, and consequently, they remained religious. A large number of Islamic institutions and organizations have thus always existed in Bangladesh, training people in the teachings of the *Qur'an* and *Sunnah*. Four such institutions and organizations can be found in Bangladesh. They are: (a) religious institutions such as *masjids, madrassahs,* and *Tablighi Jama'at;* (b) the *mazars* (tombs) of famous sufis, (c) cultural-religious organizations such as the Islamic Foundation, and the Masjid Mission; and (d) political organizations based on religion, that is, those political parties that pledge to serve the cause of Islam.

In Bangladesh, the *masjids* (mosques) are the oldest Islamic institutions. They were built by the earliest *sufis* or *ulemas* in the places where they settled. In the early history of Islamic civilization in Bengal, these mosques served as centers of Islamic education. In about 65,000 Bangladeshi villages, there are 133,197 mosques, which serve as centers for daily and congregational prayers.[51] The blaring loudspeakers in the mosques are a daily reminder of the Islamic character of Bangladesh. Furthermore, in these mosques there are *waz mahfils* (meetings for religious preaching) where Islamic scholars are invited to lecture. In particular, during the month of *ramadan* (fasting), prayer meetings in the mosques are among the public activities engaged in by the Islamists and Muslim nationalists. *Eid-e-miladunnabi* is an official holiday for observing the designated birthday of the Prophet.

Existing side by side with the mosques, some 5,766 *madrassahs* and 58,126 *maktabs* have kept the Muslim tradition alive in Bangladesh.[52] These institutions offer basic lessons in the *Qur'an* and *Sunnah*. The main goal of these institutions is to train the *imams* for ministry in the mosques and the teachers of Arabic and *Islamiat* in schools and colleges. Many of these *madrassahs* are very old, as they were founded in the pre-British period. Since then, these institutions have updated their curriculum by introducing Western subjects like science and mathematics. The Bangladeshi government set up a separate directorate and a *madrassah* Education Board in 1978 for administering the *madrassahs* throughout the country. There are about 500,000 students studying in them. The government also provides a large number of financial grants to these institutions.

Tablighi Jama'at is another religious organization supporting the Islamic resurgence in Bangladesh. The primary aim of this organization is to strengthen faith among the Muslims through three means: devotion to Allah as a means of self-purification, respect for others, and missionary works.[53] The *Jama'at* invites the Muslims to separate themselves from their families for a certain period of time in order to devote themselves completely to the task of understanding, learning, and practicing Islamic rituals. The *Tablighi Jama'at* holds its regular seminars and meetings at its center in Kakrail Mosque in Dhaka and its *estema* (annual assembly) every year in Tongi, an industrial town near Dhaka, where more than one million participants come from both home and abroad.

The *mazars* (shrines) of the famous *sufis* and *pirs* (early religious preachers) are another variant of religious institution through which the ideals of Islam are upheld in Bangladesh. Most of these *sufis* and *pirs* came to South Asia from Central Asia. The local converted Muslims have a high regard for them; and, therefore after their death, most of them remained as models of Islamic men to their disciples. Their followers visit their tombs in large numbers for peace of mind. There are hundreds of *mazars* in Bangladesh; the most renowned among them are the Shah Jalal Darga of Sylhet, *Biswa Zaker Manzil* of Atrasi in Faridpur District, Shah Niamat Baizid Bostani Mazar of Chittagong, Shah Makdum Darga of Rajshahi, Khan Jahan Ali Darga of Khulna, Mirpur Mazar and High Court Mazar of Dhaka. Hundreds of people from all walks of life, including the president of Bangladesh, ministers, politicians, teachers, doctors, engineers, lawyers, industrialists, bureaucrats, army officials, peasants, and workers come to these shrines to seek solutions to their problems. The *pirshahibs* (heads) of these shrines advise the visitors to follow the true path of Allah and the Prophet and to cultivate the essential values of Islam.

In addition to the above religious institutions, there are a number of socioreligious and cultural organizations that aim at establishing a true Islamic society. The most prominent among these are the Islamic Foundation, Bangladesh *Masjid* Mission, Bangladesh Islamic Center, Qur'anic School Society, Bangladesh *Jamatul Mudderissin* (organization for religious teachers), *Islam Prachar Samity* (organization for preaching Islam)*, Ittehadul Ummah* (organization of the ulemas), the Council for Islamic Sociocultural Organization, and the World Islamic Mission. The main function of the Islamic Foundation is to train the *imams* of mosques as community leaders. It also organizes seminars, symposia, and workshops, and has published an Islamic encyclopedia. The aim of Bangladesh *Masjid* mission is to turn the mosques of the country into centers of socioreligious activities. The Bangladesh Islamic Center studies the teachings of the *Qur'an* and translates Arabic, Urdu, and Persian books into Bangla. There is a flourishing market for Islamic theological literature. The Qur'anic School Society's main objective is to provide the Muslim children with an Islamic education. The Bangladesh *Jamatul Mudderissin* explains the ideas of the

Islamic way of life and tends to generate Islamic consciousness among the Muslim community. The *Islam Prachar Samity* preaches the ideas of Islam among non-Muslims. The *Ittehadul Ummah* aims at bringing about unity among the Islamic forces in Bangladesh. The World Islamic Mission is a humanitarian organization.

While these institutions and organizations perform the task of preaching Islam, many Islam-based political parties have been born in Bangladesh with the aim of carrying out the same objective. Immediately after independence in 1972, as already mentioned, Islam-based parties were banned, but this restriction was withdrawn after the fall of Mujib. Since then many of these Islamic parties, which were founded even before the birth of Bangladesh, have become active in the country's politics. The renowned Islam-based political parties are the *Jama'at-i-Islami, Nizam-I-Islami,* Muslim League, Islamic Democratic League, Islamic Republican Party, Bangladesh Justice Party, and the *Khilafat Andolon.* Though all of them stand for the principles of the *Qur'an* and *Sunnah,* they are divided among themselves along the lines of personal interest.

Of the Islam-based parties, the most famous and organized political party is the *Jama'at-i-Islam.* In August 1941, Sayyid Abu Ala Maududi founded *Jama'at-i-Islam* in undivided India in order to offer institutional shape to his reconstruction of Muslim society based on Islamic principles. With the emergence of two independent states—India and Pakistan—in 1947, the organization had to be divided, and again with the separation of East and West Pakistan, *Jama'at-I-Islam* had to be subdivided into *Jama'at-I-Islam,* Pakistan and *Jama'at-i-Islam* of Bangladesh.[54] As an organization, the *Jama'at* has a four-point program. First, there are *tabligh* and *dawah* (propagation and call), which are thought to purify and reconstruct the thoughts of the people on the basis of the Holy *Qur'an* and *Sunnah.* Second, there are *tanzeem* and *tarbiah* (organization and training), which help organize and train Muslims through practical activities. Third, *islah al-Ijtimayee* (social reform) uplifts the condition of the people and the nation through extensive social service and welfare activities. Finally, there is *islah-al-hurumah* (the reform of the government and public administration) in the light of Islam. In order to achieve these activities the *Jama'at* has built extensive networks of members, workers, and associates.[55]

The workers in the *Jama'at* are recruited through a highly selective process. In order to become a full member one has to receive lessons in party ideology for a certain period of time. Unlike other parties, the *Jama'at* has a stable party fund collected from regular contribution of its members and supporters. Moreover, the party has a student front, *Islami Chhatra Shibir* (Islamic Student Front), which is steadily making inroads among students. It has become one of the strongest student organizations in the Universities of Dhaka, Chittagong, Rajshai, and Jahangirnagar. Since the *Jama'at* emphasizes character building and disciplined action, the front organizations are increasingly drawing the attention of people in Bangladesh.[56] The party also has contacts with people in Saudi Arabia, Pakistan, Malaysia, and Iran and other Muslim countries. In the last two elections, as well as in the current opposition movement, the *Jama'at* has played an active role.

Besides the aforementioned internal factors, external factors also have contributed for the predominance of Islam in Bangladesh. The Muslim world seriously counts on the support of Bangladesh in global affairs. Thus, one scholar says:

Since the middle of the 1970s, following the hike in oil prices, the Muslim states of West Asia and North Africa have become aware of their enhanced role on the world scene. Some of them have undertaken efforts to shape the world in their own images and, with the help of their newfound wealth, have been financing missionary programs in various Muslim countries. The proliferation of Islam-based institutions and organizations, mainly of a charitable and missionary character, and the construction of new mosques and madrassahs along with the repair, extension, and beautification of old ones are but overt manifestations of the phenomenon. The rejuvenation of some of the Islam-based political parties in Bangladesh can also be explained in terms of the enhanced role of the Muslim states in West Asia and North Africa.[57]

Overall, both internal and external factors have helped in the revitalization of Islam in Bangladesh. Religious institutions are operating in the country both at the governmental and non-governmental levels. All the institutions aim at creating Islamic consciousness and demand the implementation of Islamic principles. As a predominantly Muslim country, Bangladesh has been profoundly influenced by the activities of these institutions and organizations that are covered daily in its Islam-oriented newspapers.

CONCLUSIONS

The above analysis indicates that Islam is a dominant force in the socioeconomic life of Bangladesh. Despite the initial commitment of the government to establish secularism in Bangladesh, the Bangladeshi constitution was amended in 1976 to replace the term secularism with "absolute trust and faith in the Almighty Allah." Islamic roots are pre-existing conditions in Bangladesh, which have in recent years gained a fresh impetus. The secularist forces are in the minority and, therefore, Bangladesh has never had a truly secular society in the Western sense of the term. Although there exists conflict between religious and cultural predominance, Islam has never lost importance in the public sentiment of Bangladesh. Given the history of the development of Islamic institutions and their resistance to anti-Islamic forces, it is obvious that the majority of Bangladeshis maintain their own identity as Muslims.

There is no doubt that though Islam remains a stable value system, it has failed politically in Bangladesh. Primarily, there is no Islamic political party with a widely based organization throughout the country. The strongest Islamic party, *Jama'at-i-Islami* won only eighteen seats and three seats in 1991 and 1996 elections respectively.[58] Hashmi noted that "*Jama'at* faced a three-prong attack: from the government, secular/socialist/liberal groups, and the Ulema."[59]

A recent study shows that more Bangladeshis want to vest political power in Western-educated-cum-religious minded people rather than with purely religious leaders. In the survey, it was found that 53 % of the rural and 78 % of the urban people responded to their willingness to elect western-educated-come-religious minded people as their representatives, while only 39 % and 7 % of the rural and urban respondents respectively voted for purely religious leaders.[60] Similarly, Hashmi said that most of the Bangladeshis prefer "Islam loving western educated, the anglo-mohamedans" as their *mollahs* (spiritual leaders) and political candidates.[61] The Muslims still think that the religious leaders of Islamic parties are not capable of ruling the state, since the majority of them have no background in modern education.

Furthermore, all the Islamic political parties are still seen as collaborators with the Pakistani army in the 1971 war of liberation. Moreover, among the population in Bangladesh 13 % are non-Muslims; a majority of these are Hindus. Therefore, though each regime propagated Islamic values at the state level, each has been very careful about the sensivity of non-Muslims in Bangladesh. Thus, while Zia replaced secularism with "absolute trust and faith in Almighty Allah," he retained the clause, "no discrimination against any citizen on grounds of religion, race, caste, sex or place of birth."[62] Ershad declared Islam as the state religion but added a sub-clause that all other religions would have freedom to practice. Even *Jama'at-i-Islami* chief Golam Azam stressed that, in accordance with the tenets of Islam, all human beings are related to each other, and therefore all non-Muslims will be given their full rights in Bangladesh if the party comes to power.

Thus one could say, in conclusion, that Islam is quite successful as a social force in Bangladesh and, consequently, no regime has been able to ignore basic Islamic values. However, the strength of Islam as a social force has by no means helped the Islam-based political parties capture political power. The Islamic parties are badly fictionalized and fragmented. They have failed to translate Islamic values into a strong political force due to their lack of intellectual leadership, weak organization, and personal conflict among the Islamic leaders. It is thus true that the Islam-based parties have failed to capture political power, but it is also true that the liberal/secular political parties or regimes in Bangladesh cannot ignore the dominant Islamic values, because Islam is constantly alive as a social force and value system in the majority populace.

NOTES

1. Abdul Hamid A. Abu Sulayman, *The Islamic Theory of International Relations: New Directions for Islamic Methodology and Thought* (Herndon, Va.: International Institute of Islamic Thought, 1987), p. 1.

2. Bangladesh has a population of 130 million. Indonesia and Pakistan have a population of 202 million and 132 million people, respectively.

3. Emajuddin Ahmed and D.R.A. Nazneen, "Islam in Bangladesh, Revivalism or Power Politics,"*Asian Survey*, vol. 30, no.8 (August 1990), p. 80.

4. John L. Esposito, "Introduction: Islam and Muslim Polities," in John L. Esposito (ed.), *Voices of Resurgent Islam* (London: Oxford University Press, 1983), p. 5.

5. Cited in Abdul Rashid Moten, *Political Science: An Islamic Perspective* (London: Macmillan Press Ltd., 1995), p. 20.

6. Akhtaruddin Ahmad, *Nationalism or Islam: Indo-Pakistan Episode* (New York: Vantage Press, 1982).

7. Syed Abul A'la Maududi, *Musalman Our Maujuda Syasi Kashmakash* (Muslims and the Present Conflict) [in Urdu], vol. 3 (Pathankot, India: n.p., 1942), p. 29.

8. For example, Syria, Albania, South Yemen, Egypt under Nasser, Turkey under Kamal Ataturk, and Iran under Reza Shah Pahlavi are exceptions to the tradition.

9. Gunner Myrdel, *Asian Drama: An Abridgement* (London: Penguin Books, 1977), p. 141.

10. M. Rashiduzzaman, "Islam, Muslim Identity and Nationalism in Bangladesh," *Journal of South Asian and Middle Eastern Studies*, vol. 28 (Fall 1994), p. 55.

11. The theory suggested that Hinduism and Islam were two different civilizations. Therefore, Indian Muslims are from Indian Hindus. The only way to resolve Hindu Muslim differences was to divide the county into two sovereign states: Pakistan and India.

12. *Sunnah* means custom or tradition, comprises both the words and deeds of the Prophet Muhammad, and therefore complements the *Qur'an* as the major source of Islamic faith and practice. For Objective Resolution, see Syed Serajul Islam, *Bangladesh: State and Economic Strategy* (Dhaka: University Press Ltd., 1988), p. 32.

13. Ibid.

14. Government of Pakistan, *The Constitution of Islamic Republic of Pakistan, 1956* (Karachi: Government Press, 1956).

15. Richard Weeks, *Birth and Growth of a Muslim Nation* (Princeton, N.J.: Van Nostrand Co., 1964), p. 3.

16. M. A. Rashid, "Dharma O Rajniti: Pakistan and Bangladesh," *Samaj Nirrikhon* (September 1982), p. 15.

17. A serious controversy appeared on the issue of official language at the very inception of Pakistan. The Bengalis demanded Bengali to be the official language because it was spoken by a majority of the people of Pakistan. On the other hand, the central leadership, mainly Urdu speaking, wanted to make Urdu alone the official language of Pakistan. In January Prime Minister Khwaja Nazimuddin's announcement making Urdu alone the official language of Pakistan came as a rude shock to the Bengalis. A serious opposition movement started in East Pakistan. Students of Dhaka University organized massive demonstrations on February 21, 1952, throughout East Pakistan. The police and the military were called out to restore peace; in the process, a dozen people were killed. Thus in Bangladesh every February 21 is observed as Martyrs Day. For a detailed analysis of the liberation movement of Bangladesh, see Robin Blackburn (ed.), *Explosion in a Subcontinent* (London: Penguin Books, 1975); and Rounaq Jahan, *Pakistan: Failure in National Integration* (New York: Columbia University Press, 1972).

18. Government of Bangladesh, *The Constitution of the People's Republic of Bangladesh* (Dhaka: Ministry of Law and Parliamentary Affairs, 1972); also see Maudud Ahmed, *Era of Sheikh Mujibur Rahman* (Dhaka: University Press Ltd., 1983).

19. Friday is a special prayer day for Muslims like Sunday is for Christians. Rashiduzzaman, "Islam," p. 41.

20. U.A.B. Razia-akter Banu, *Islam in Bangladesh* (New York: E. J. Bril, 1992).

21. Ibid. Also see Syed Serajul Islam, "Islam in Bangladesh: A Dichotomy of Bengali and Muslim Identities," *Islamic Quarterly,* vol. XLI, no. 3 (1997), p. 224.

22. Tajul Islam Hashmi, "Islam in Bangladesh Politics," in Hussain Mutalib and Tajul Islam Hashmi (eds.), *Islam, Muslims and the Modern State: Case Study of Muslims in Thirteen Countries* (London: Macmillan Press, Ltd., 1994), p. 121.

23. Talukder Maniruzzaman, *The Bangladesh Revolution and Its Aftermath* (Dhaka: Bangladesh Books International, 1980), p. 217. The most famous Leftist parties were *Jatiyo Samajtantrik Dal* (JSD: National Socialist Party), Bangladesh Communist League, *Purbo Bangla Sarbohara* Party (East Bengal Proletariat Party), and *Purbo Bangla Sammobadi Dal* (East Bengal Communist Party).

24. Talukder Maniruzzaman, "Bangladesh: An Unfinished Revolution," *Journal of Asian Studies,* vol. 34, no. 4 (August 1975), p. 891.

25. Syed Serajul Islam, "The Role of the State in the Economic Development of Bangladesh, 1972-75," *Journal of Developing Areas,* vol. 19, no. 2 (January 1985), p. 185.

26. Partha S. Ghosh, "Bangladesh at the Cross Roads, Religion and Politics," *Asian Survey,* vol. 33, no. 7 (July 1993), p. 700.

27. The OIC was established in 1969 to promote Islamic solidarity and to foster political, economic, social, and cultural cooperation among the Muslim countries. The organization comprises fifty-four Muslim states. See Abdullah Ahsan, *The Organization of Islamic Conference* (Washington, D.C.: International Institute of Islamic Thought, 1990).

28. For detailed analysis of political development during this period, see Syed Serajul Islam, "The State in Bangladesh Under Zia," *Asian Survey,* vol. 24, no. 5 (May 1984), p. 556.

29. Bangladesh Nationalist Party, *Ghoshonapatra* (Manifesto), August 1978, p. 3.

30. Rashiduzzaman, "Islam," p. 38.

31. Government of Bangladesh, Ministry of Education, *Bangladesh National Syllabi and Curriculum Committee Report, Part II,* April 1977, p. 149.

32. Islam, "Islam in Bangladesh," p. 225.

33. Rashiduzzaman, "Islam," p. 38.

34. Ibid.

35. Rashid, *"Dharma,"* cited in Banu, *Islam in Bangladesh,* p. 147.

36. Syed Serajul Islam, "Bangladesh in 1986," *Asian Survey,* vol. 27, no. 2 (February 1987).

37. Talukder Maniruzzaman, "The Fall of the Military Dictator, 1991 Elections and the Prospects of Civilian Rule in Bangladesh," *Pacific Affairs* (Summer 1992), p. 203.

38. *The Bangladesh Times* (Dhaka), August 6, 1982.

39. Government of Bangladesh, Ministry of Education, *Education Suitable to Nation,* November 1982, p. 2.

40. *Zakat* is the fourth pillar of Islam in which Muslims are enjoined by their faith to annually donate 2½ percent of their wealth in alms to the poor or to charitable institutions.

41. Ahmed and Nazneen, " Islam," p. 798.

42. Ibid.

43. Syed Serajul Islam, *Rastrabijnan* (Dhaka: Hasan Book House, 1997).

44. Many *Jama'at* leaders opposed the idea of accepting a woman's leadership (Khaleda's) because it contradicted the party principle. However, at the end, looking at the long-term goal, in the context of the situation, they agreed to join the coalition. Also, the party felt that it was Khaleda's husband, General Zia, who allowed the resumption of the activities of the outlawed *Jama'at* in 1976. For the role of women in Islam, see Leila Ahmed, *Women and Gender in Islam* (New Haven: Yale University Press, 1992).

45. Rashiduzzaman, "Islam," p. 56.

46. Ghosh, "Bangladesh at the Cross Roads," p. 707.

47. Ibid.

48. The *Babri Masjid* (mosque) was built in Ayodha, India, during the rule of Mughal emperor Babur. The Bharatiya Janata Party (BJP), a Hindu fundamentalist party, propagated that the mosque was built by demolishing a temple where the Hindu God Rama was born and, therefore, the party demanded the demolition of the mosque. Eventually in 1992 the mosque was demolished by a violent mob organized by the BJP. For detailed analysis on the Babri Mosque see Syed Serajul Islam, "The Tragedy of the Babri Masjid," *Journal of Muslim Minority Affairs*, vol. 17, no. 2s (1997), p. 345.

49. Ibid.

50. Stanley Kochanek, "Bangladesh in 1997," *Asian Survey*, vol. 38, no.2 (February 1998).

51. Rashiduzzaman, "Islam," p. 56.

52. Ibid.

53. Mumtaz Ahmad, "Islamic Fundamentalism in South Asia: The Jamaat-i-Islami and the Tablighi Jamaat of South Asia," in Martin E. Marty and R. Scott Appleby (eds.), *Fundamentalisms Observed*, vol. 1 (Chicago: The University of Chicago Press, 1991), pp. 457-530.

54. Syed Abul Ala Maududi, *Nationalism and India* (Pathankot: Maktab-e-Jamaat-I-Islam, 1947), pp. 9-10. For recent subdivision of the party, see Rafiuddin Ahmed, "Redefining Muslim Identity in South Asia: The Transformation of Jamaat-i-Islam," in Matin E. Marty and R. Scott Appleby (eds.), *Accounting For Fundamentalism: The Dynamic Character of Movements,* vol. 4 (Chicago: The University of Chicago Press, 1994), pp. 669-705.

55. Mohammad Hasan, *Jamaat I Islam, Bangladesh* (Dhaka: Academic Publishers, 1993), p. 64.

56. Ibid.

57. Emajuddin, "Islam in Bangladesh," p. 806.

58. Islam, *Rastrabijnan*.

59. Hashmi, "Islam in Bangladesh Politics," p. 121.

60. U.A.B. Razia-akter Banu, "Jamaat-i-Islam in Bangladesh: Challenges and Prospects," in Mutalib and Hashmi (eds.), *Islam, Muslims and the Modern State*, pp. 80-99.

61. Hashmi, "Islam in Bangladesh Politics," p. 137.

62. Islam, "Islam in Bangladesh."

Chapter 8

The State, Moro National Liberation Front, and Islamic Resurgence in the Philippines

Vivienne SM. Angeles

On September 2, 1996, the Moro National Liberation Front (MNLF) and the government of the Republic of the Philippines signed a peace agreement. This event marked the end of almost twenty-eight years of intermittent conflict, which caused the loss of thousands of lives, millions of dollars in property damage, and the displacement of countless citizens in southern Philippines.

From its formation in 1969, the MNLF emerged as the largest and most organized Muslim movement[1] in the Philippines. Estimates of MNLF membership ranged from 15,000 to 30,000[2] at the height of the armed conflict in the mid-1970s. The MNLF described itself as a popular revolutionary movement[3] whose initial goal was to establish an independent nation out of Mindanao and other islands in southern Philippines. This nation was to be called the *Bangsa Moro Republik*. With the signing of the 1996 peace agreement, however, the MNLF, in effect, gave up their goal of establishing an independent state and accepted the sovereignty of the government of the Philippines. The Philippine government, in return, created a Special Zone of Peace and Development (SZOPAD) out of fourteen provinces[4] in Mindanao, which would be the focus of genuine peace and extensive development projects. The agreement also provided for representation in the executive, legislative, and judicial branches of the government in the autonomous[5] region, improvement of education and the integration of MNLF *mujahidin*[6] into the Philippine military and the national police. Not long after the signing of the agreement, Nur Misuari,[7] chairman of the MNLF, was elected governor of the Autonomous Region of Muslim Mindanao and appointed chair of the Southern Philippines Council for Peace and Development—the latter being the implementing agency for development programs.

Although the terms of the peace agreement provided for economic and sociopolitical benefits for Philippine Muslims, there was much more at stake than the government's relationship with Muslims. There were also issues of Muslim-Christian relations with ethnic minorities in Philippine society.

This chapter asserts that the activities of the Muslim secessionist movements, particularly the MNLF, and the reaction of Muslim countries to the situation of Muslims in the Philippines prompted the Philippine government to adopt policies that, in turn, helped to promote Islamic resurgence in the Philippines. Islamic resurgence, as used here, refers to the heightening of Islamic consciousness among the masses as manifested in various ways, like invigorated piety, increased mosque attendance, more students in Islamic schools, and an increase in the number of societies and associations for religious purposes.

In the mid-1970s, the Philippine government adopted policies and launched programs directed at improving the economic, sociopolitical lives of Muslims. However, it also implemented programs that had to do with the religious lives of Muslims. This last point is worth noting because it raises the question of whether such government programs infringe on the anti-establishment clause of the Philippine constitution.[8]

In order to understand the situation of Muslims in the Philippines, we will briefly review Muslim interactions with the Spanish from the fifteenth to the nineteenth centuries, with the Americans from 1898 to 1946, and with the independent Philippine government since 1946. This will show how colonial experience resulted in the division of Philippine society along religious lines— Christians and non-Christian tribes that include Muslims. We will then explain government policies during the period of martial law (September 1972 to January 1981), which touched on the practice of Islam and which, we believe, created an environment conducive to Islamic resurgence in the Philippines.

MUSLIMS AS "THE OTHER" IN PHILIPPINE SOCIETY

Muslims constitute the largest minority group in the Philippines bound by a single religion. Recent estimates place their number at between five to six million or 8.5 percent of a total population of 66 million.[9] They exhibit differences in ethno-linguistic characteristics, language, geographic location, economic occupations, and other cultural characteristics. They also differ in the way they have accommodated themselves to the national government. In spite of these variations, however, they share the common bond of being Muslims, which is a salient feature of their identity. Ever since their first encounter with Spanish Christian colonizers in the sixteenth century, this identity has been a critical factor for Philippine Muslims. The Spanish administration actually promoted the notion of "otherness" since Muslims generally resisted conversion to Christianity—a major aim of Spanish colonization. This notion of "otherness" permeated Muslim-Christian relations in the Philippines long after the colonial powers had left.

Spain's attempt at Christianizing the whole country met with furtive resistance from Muslims. After all, by the time Spaniards arrived, there were already established principalities in the south where Islam functioned as an official religion. While the Spanish failed in their religious, political, and economic goals[10] in southern Philippines, they were largely successful in pursuing the same goals in Luzon and the Visayas.[11] Spanish authorities and missionaries then made it a point to emphasize the wrongness of Islam and the recalcitrance of Muslims to the Christian Filipinos, thus leaving a legacy of mutual prejudice and negative feelings between Muslims and Christians. This was further aggravated by the Spanish use of Philippine soldiers in their fights against the Muslims. The Muslims felt they no longer had much in common with the Christianized peoples of the Philippines.[12] Religious affiliation thus became a determinant of each other's identity, and Muslims became "the other" in Philippine society.

In December 1898, Spain ceded the Philippines to the United States by virtue of the Treaty of Paris. In justifying the annexation of the Philippines, President McKinley explained to a group of Protestant clergymen that it had become the obligation of the United States to "educate the Filipinos and uplift and civilize and Christianize them, and, by God's grace, do the very best we could by them, as our fellow men for whom Christ also died."[13] Despite the religious tone in McKinley's statement, the United States did not officially support any move to convert Muslims to Christianity. The Christian bias of administrators was obvious, however, and Governor Pershing himself expressed the hope that their Christian teachers would influence Muslim girls.[14] It was also during the time of General Pershing (1909-13) that Muslims were discouraged from making the *haj* unless they were able to satisfy the district authorities that they could afford the expensive trip. Pershing did not like the whole idea of the *haj* because, as he said, Muslims "usually come home with exalted ideas of their own importance, notwithstanding the fact that most of them return as indigents. After the journey to Mecca, they assume the title of *haj* and are henceforth inclined to consider themselves above ordinary labor."[15] The Americans impressed upon the Muslims that the policy was being promulgated for their benefit and there was no serious objection. American administrators obviously did not pursue a religious objective as the Spanish did, but one of them, Governor Carpenter, expressed that it would have been politically and economically expedient if all peoples of the Philippines shared the same beliefs, standards, and other ideals.[16] Carpenter further added that the goal of the American government was to make the Muslims be like other Filipinos.[17] Although Americans were guided by the principles of church and state, one cannot help but infer from Carpenter's statements that he would have preferred that Muslims were Christians.

Eventually, the American governor and the sultan of Sulu entered into an agreement, which required the sultan to recognize the sovereignty of the United States. He was also required to give up his rights, as well as that of his heirs to sovereignty over Sulu, his right to collect taxes and decide lawsuits, and his reversionary rights to their lands.[18] The United States, in turn, assured the sultan of his position as head of the "Muhammedan Church" [*sic*] in the Sulu archipelago.[19] The sultan was assured of his religious freedom so long as it did not go against the basic principles of U.S. law.

The Americans, in general, pursued a policy of friendship and tolerance, but the gap between Muslims and Christians created by the Spanish policies of conquer and Christianize was not bridged. Muslims and Christians continued to identify themselves on the basis of their religion. American administrators contributed to this distinction by creating the Bureau of Non-Christian Tribes, which had jurisdiction over the Muslim areas. Negative perceptions between Muslims and Christians, which were enhanced by historical accounts, literature, and even drama,[20] persisted through time.

In 1946, the United States symbolically relinquished its control of the Philippines and declared the independence of the republic. The new government adopted the doctrine of the separation of church and state in its constitution. Although there were a few Muslims in the national government who served as congressmen and senators, Muslims generally felt alienated from and neglected by the government. This was complicated by the reality of distance between the central government in Manila and Muslim areas in southern Philippines. History textbooks that were based on Spanish records enhanced the Christian Filipino perception of Muslims as "the other." Such books portrayed Muslims as pirates and slave traders who practiced polygamy and could not be trusted because they were not Christians.[21] There were also problems of law and order in the south, largely the result of the agricultural colonization programs, which had brought Christian settlers to Muslim ancestral lands. These land disputes at times involved violent confrontations between Christian migrants and Muslims. However, Muslims were no longer fighting an invader, and their right to practice Islam was now guaranteed by the constitution. Therefore, despite their perceived neglect by the government, this situation provided for more freedom in the practice of their religion than at any time in the previous 400 years. Negative perceptions of each other, however, continued to dominate Muslim-Christian relations.

The above discussion assumes importance in light of the fact that Muslims claim that their struggle runs continuously from the time of the Spanish colonization to the post-1946 government.

THE MNLF AND THE INTERNATIONAL MUSLIM COMMUNITY

The MNLF, which was officially formed when a group of Muslims went to Sabah for military training in 1969, is but one of several Muslim groups that demanded secession from the Philippines. It was, however, the largest, most organized, and, more important, the first group to have established international linkages. The MNLF initially sought for independence, which they thought was the only way that would help improve the lives of Muslims.[22] Since Muslim areas did not enjoy the same benefits as other parts of the country in terms of education, facilities, and economic programs, they felt they had to demand independence so that they could chart their own destiny and not be left at the mercy of the Christian government. Hence, they resorted to taking up arms and the creation of its military, the Bangsa Moro Army. The MNLF received material help from various Muslim countries like Libya, Saudi Arabia, Iran, and

Pakistan. It was also recognized by the Organization of Islamic Conference (OIC) as the legitimate representative of the Muslims of the Philippines.

Although the MNLF claimed that the more than 300 years of continued oppression and persecution of Muslims had motivated them to organize an armed resistance, it was also a direct response of Muslim youth to an incident popularly known as the Jabidah massacre in March 1968. According to newspaper accounts of a lone survivor, Muslims undergoing secret military training led by Philippine military officials in the island of Corregidor were killed under suspicious circumstances.[23] In response, Muslims and other sympathizers demonstrated against the government.

In May 1968, Datu Udtog Matalam of Cotabato in the southern Philippines revealed that he had organized the Muslim Independence Movement whose goal was independence for Mindanao and Sulu. At around that same time, there were increasing reports of Christian armed bands organizing with the tacit approval and support of the Philippine constabulary forces in the Cotabato area. Conflicts erupted between Muslim and Christian groups in several places in Mindanao,[24] some of which were generated by land disputes. One of the most brutal attacks against Muslims was the Manila massacre in 1971 where men, women, and children were killed in a mosque. This incident drew the attention of the international press as well as Muslim countries that protested against the government's handling of the situation. Muammar Qadhafy called it "genocide" and directed representatives to go to Manila to confer with President Marcos and bring relief funds to Muslims in the affected areas. The Philippines situation was discussed by the Islamic Conference of Foreign Ministers by authorities of Al Azhar University in Cairo and the Organization of Islamic Conference—all of whom expressed serious concern for the plight of Muslims in the Philippines.

In 1972, President Marcos declared martial law. One of the reasons he cited for this declaration was the existence of a Muslim secessionist group. Shortly after that declaration, the government-MNLF conflict evolved into a full-scale war, resulting in the death and displacement of thousands of people. In February 1974, the MNLF attacked the airport and surrounding areas of the town of Jolo. The Philippine armed forces responded to this situation by burning the town— thus resulting in the death of thousands of people and leaving thousands more homeless. These events continued to draw the attention of the worldwide Muslim community. Libya provided sanctuary for leaders of the movement as well as war materiel to the Bangsa Moro army, while the OIC[25] pressured the Philippines government to negotiate a peaceful settlement with Muslims involved in the military conflict. In its yearly conferences, the OIC passed resolutions demanding that the Philippine government stop military operations against Muslims. At one point, Libya demanded an economic boycott of the Philippines; but later on, in 1976, Qadhafy himself brokered a peace treaty, the Tripoli Agreement. Its implementation became a bone of contention between the Philippine government and the MNLF in succeeding years. Iran, on the other hand, showed its concern for Philippine Muslims and notified the Philippine ambassador in Tehran that future relations between Iran and the Philippines depended on the Philippine treatment of Muslims. In November 1979, Iran imposed an oil embargo against the Philippines.[26]

PHILIPPINE GOVERNMENT RESPONSES AND ISLAMIC RESURGENCE

As the conflict between the MNLF and the government escalated, more lives were lost and properties destroyed. Refugees from affected Muslim areas flocked to neighboring Brunei and areas north of the island of Mindanao. Pressure from the international community grew, and the Philippine government was faced with the difficulty of explaining to the world's Muslim community its handling of the situation. It was also compelled to work for a solution to the conflict. It is important to note here that like many countries, the Philippines was dependent on Middle East countries (which were members of the OIC) for its oil supply; hence, it was important not to antagonize them.

As part of its response to the conflict, the government developed a two-pronged strategy: renewed military confrontation and economic reform. The government launched a number of economic programs in Muslim areas. These programs were guided by the belief that if Muslims enjoyed increased economic benefits, they would be less prone to rebel against the government. Among these programs was the creation of the Amanah Bank, which provided credit, commercial development, and savings facilities based on Islamic concepts of banking.[27] The traditional barter trade in the south was liberalized, and funds were appropriated for the reconstruction and development of southern Philippines.

In addition to economic development programs, the government also launched policies that were conducive to the practice of Islam. Despite priding itself as the only Catholic country in Asia, the Philippine government began officially in 1973 to acknowledge Islam as part of Filipino heritage. The government declared that the preservation and enhancement of Islamic tradition and the promotion of the well being of Muslim communities would guide their policy in Mindanao. This included the restoration of rights of Muslims to their ancestral lands.[28]

Over and against the Spanish heritage of religious intolerance, the Philippine government now sought to give Islam a rightful place in a predominantly Christian nation. President Marcos issued a number of presidential decrees to this effect. Among them was a decree that recognized Muslim holidays like *Eid al Fitr, Eid al Adha, Maulid al Nabi, Laila al Isra wa'l Miraj,* and *Ammon Jaddid* as legal Philippine holidays.[29] Even the working hours of Muslims during the month of Ramadan were regulated, and the Department of Public Information was used to disseminate information on fasting to Muslims.[30] It also sponsored a Qur'an Recitation Contest in 1975. Where previous historical materials underscored the differences between Muslims and Christians, government publications now emphasized the idea that Christians and Muslims were brothers and it was the colonial experience that separated them.[31] In many publicity pictures, First Lady Imelda Marcos took to wearing traditional Muslim women's attire and was a constant presence at Muslim festivities. She even led Filipino officials to Tripoli in the course of negotiations with Muamar Qadhafy. While many critics saw this as part of President Marcos' way of appeasing the international Muslim community, these actions, together with the decrees passed, made the public feel more accepting of Muslim cultural traditions.

The government was also involved in arranging for the *haj* (Pilgrimage). In December 1973, the government chartered a boat for the use of Philippine Muslims. This government sponsorship of the *haj*, however, was linked to government military activities. Those who contributed to the campaign in the south were given priority in boarding the chartered boat. Together with government employees, members of home defense forces, Muslim soldiers, and civilian personnel who had helped in the rehabilitation and integration efforts were granted free passage, courtesy of the Philippine government. Others had to pay for their fare.[32] While the government claimed that this was an indication of their concern for Muslims who are Philippine ethnic minorities, they had clearly used the *haj* as a reward for those who cooperated with the government. There were, however, Muslim religious leaders who claimed that government sponsorship violates the principles governing the performance of the *haj*. The Philippine government knew better than to do this again; but in 1978, it created the Philippine Pilgrimage Authority, whose role was to take care of *haj* arrangements. This time, however, Muslims had to pay for their fare. The Pilgrimage Authority helped facilitate travel documentation and arrange for chartered carriers for the trip. In 1987, this office became the Bureau of Pilgrimage and Endowment, which is part of the Office of Muslim Affairs. In 1996, this office handled *haj* arrangements for more than 5,000 Philippine Muslim pilgrims.

Although Philippine Muslims are bound by Philippine laws, they are also bound by *adat* (custom) and the *shariah*. There were conflicts between these two sets of laws; so President Marcos, upon recommendation of Muslim leaders and scholars, ordered a group of Muslim scholars to work on the codification of Muslim Personal Laws. In February 1977, he signed Presidential Decree 1083, which promulgated the Code of Muslim Personal Laws as part of the laws of the country, but which were applicable only to Muslim areas. There are also provisions in these codes for *shariah* courts.[33]

The government also sponsored the creation of a consultative council of Muslim leaders, which was composed of traditional Muslim leaders like the sultans, former members of Congress, members of the constitutional convention, retired ambassadors, and high-ranking military officers. The sultans, whose positions of political power had been long eliminated by the Commonwealth government (1936-46),[34] were recognized once more by the Marcos government. Sultan Mohammed Mahakuttah Kiram was crowned as the Sultan of Sulu. During the coronation ceremonies, he pledged his support to the government. The government also organized a Muslim conference at the Mindanao State University. In 1972, the government sponsored a trip of Muslim sultans to Baguio City in the northern part of the country in an effort to expose them to the culture of other minorities. The Office of Civil Relations organized the trip and included journalists in the entourage. The political nature of these moves is clear: President Marcos was trying to get the support of these traditional leaders against the younger MNLF members.

In the aftermath of the many battles fought between government and MNLF forces, the government realized the need to rebuild devastated areas. President Marcos created the Presidential Task Force for the Reconstruction and Development of Mindanao. There were other decrees issued by Marcos that provided for relief and welfare projects, like the resettlement of refugees. The government appropriated thirty-five hectares of Fort Bonifacio (a Philippine army camp) and constructed the Maharlika Village, as a way of helping resettle the Muslims displaced by the war. Now it has a mosque, dormitories, and a residential area for families—providing 1,000 homes for Muslims.

In 1977, First Lady Imelda Marcos ordered the construction of a mosque in the Quiapo district, in the heart of Manila. There were reports that Mrs. Marcos wanted the mosque built in time for the visit of Muamar Qadhafy, but Qadhafy never came. The mosque was built nevertheless, on land owned by the Government Service Insurance System. Since it was built on government land (like in the earlier Maharlika Village), the project put into question the propriety of the government having a place of worship built for Muslims. There were objections raised to this project on grounds of church-state separation but they were never manifested in an organized fashion. In order to prevent further objections, the government opted to refer to these structures as cultural centers, built for a Philippine ethnic minority. The building in Quiapo, however, is more popularly known as the Golden Mosque and, like the one in Maharlika Village, is used primarily for religious purposes.

All the above-mentioned presidential decrees, laws, and government projects facilitated the performance of Islamic religious duties, and at the same time brought back the sense of acceptance denied the Muslims during the period of Spanish colonization. Needless to say, this made the situation conducive to a heightened Islamic consciousness.

An important factor, which helped in Islamic resurgence, was education. The Commission on National Integration (CNI), which was created by law in 1957, was a key contributor to the education of Muslims. Created primarily as an instrument to hasten the integration of non-Christians into the body politic, the CNI also had a scholarship program which sent thousands of members of cultural minorities (predominantly Muslims) to universities. This program was certainly not a direct response to MNLF agitation, since it was already well in place by the time President Marcos imposed martial law; but the resulting increase in the number of Muslim scholars also further stimulated Muslim perceptions on Muslim-Christian and Muslim-government relations in the Philippines. Although the government intention was to hasten the integration of cultural minorities, this scholarship program turned out to have an unexpected side effect. As more Muslims went to universities in the Manila area, the more they came to realize the underdevelopment of Mindanao and the prejudice that dominated Muslim-Christian relations. Many of these students therefore got involved in the secessionist movement.[35]

It was also in 1973 when President Marcos signed a decree establishing the Philippine Center for Advanced Studies (PCAS) and within it, the Institute of Islamic Studies, at the University of the Philippines.[36] One of the purposes of the Institute is to educate Filipinos on the Islamic legacy of the Philippines. The institute has an academic degree-granting program and has received grants from Middle Eastern countries. The Egyptian government was one of the first Middle Eastern governments to grant hundreds of scholarships for Philippine Muslims. Many of those who received scholarships pursued Islamic studies at Al Azhar University. Other countries like Pakistan, Syria, Libya, Jordan, Kuwait, and Saudi Arabia also provide scholarships. In 1995, 378 Muslims left the Philippines to study in these Middle East countries. The majority of this group is registered at the University of Madinah.

INTERNATIONAL LINKAGES

International linkages and outside influence have also helped Islamic resurgence. For one, the support received by the MNLF from Muslim countries reinforced its belief that it constitutes an integral part of the worldwide Islamic community.[37]

The Iranian revolution provided a model for the MNLF for a successful Islamic revolution. Iran, which supported the MNLF in the hope of exporting its revolution, was also a major source for the religious literature that introduced *Shia* Islam to the Philippines.[38] Missionaries came from Iran, together with those from Saudi Arabia and Pakistan. Today, the *Jamiat Tableegh*, which first came to Mindanao from Pakistan in the 1970s, is actively engaged in missionary work in the villages and cities of Mindanao.

These international linkages are also evidenced by the increasing participation of Philippine Muslims in Islamic conferences and their membership in Muslim organizations like the World Muslim League. At the height of the government-MNLF conflict, these organizations sent representatives to discuss the situation of Philippine Muslims with the government and went to the field to see for themselves what was really going on in the southern Philippines. They also gave financial contributions to the mosques and other institutions serving Muslims. These increasing contacts, facilitated by the improved communications and transportation systems, have brought the Philippine Muslims closer to the greater community of Muslims. These linkages are vital, not only in terms of moral and material support, but also by an increased sense of identification among Philippine Muslims, with this greater community.

MANIFESTATIONS OF ISLAMIC RESURGENCE

There are many manifestations of Islamic resurgence in the Philippines, but among the more prominent is the astonishing number of new mosques all over the country, the equally numerous schools teaching Arabic and the *Qur'an*, invigorated piety, as well as the increased number of organizations for religious purposes.

The last decade saw a tremendous growth in the number of Islamic schools. As of 1993, there were 1,305 *madaris* (schools) in the Philippines. Some of them, like the Kamilol Islam College, started with the teaching of the *Qur'an* and Arabic and now boast of grade school to college level programs. Their courses of study include Islamic theology and science, Islamic law and Islamic history. These schools are mostly private institutions that may be attached to a mosque or financed by wealthy Muslims. The public schools, on the other hand, are mandated by the recent peace agreement to preserve Muslim culture, mores, customs, and traditions. Philippine history books no longer portray Muslims as bandits and polygamists who resisted Christianity but, rather, as a people who resisted colonialism and who wanted to preserve their own religion. Among the things encouraged by public school officials is the wearing of head covers for Muslim women teachers.[39]

While Muslim schools have increased, so has the number of mosques all over the country. The Islamic Foreign Ministers Conference sent relief aid to Muslims affected by the war. Parts of these funds were used for the construction of mosques, and by 1980, thirteen new mosques were constructed. Other mosques and *madaris* were also repaired with this relief money. Majul notes that Philippine armed forces "facilitated the construction of mosques and *madaris* by providing free transportation, materials and even labor."[40] This is rather ironic, since many of the mosques that were repaired had been destroyed earlier by the military. There were no visible objections, however, to the military's involvement in the construction of these obviously religious spaces, and there were even reports that Christians who were tired of the conflict were volunteering their services.[41] As of 1995, there were 2,010 cultural centers/mosques from the southernmost reaches of Mindanao to the northernmost part of the country. Although the government built many of these mosques, others were funded by contributions from different Muslim countries and from wealthy local Muslims. More Muslims are now going to the mosques for prayers; many are learning Arabic and openly expressing their Islamic lifestyle in different ways. One can readily observe this mosque attendance not only in Muslim areas but also in traditionally Christian towns, like in Binangonan, Rizal—a suburb of MetroManila. More Muslim women are now wearing the veil and even fighting for their right to wear it.[42] The ethnic clothes that Muslim women used to wear are now giving way to the Islamic dress worn by their counterparts in the Middle East and Malaysia. When asked why they wear the veil, several women said that doing so identifies them as Muslims. Others said it is also because their *imam* said they must do so. The wearing of the veil and Islamic dress are outward manifestations of a renewed commitment to the religion. There is now a television program on Islam that covers a variety of subjects, from the five pillars of Islam, to modes of dressing, to Islam's history in the Philippines. Where reading the *Qur'an* has been the preserve of men, particularly the *panditas* (Muslim teachers) and *imams*, contemporary Philippine Muslim women, especially the educated ones, are now reading the *Qur'an* and interpreting it for themselves.

Muslim organizations, which once focused on cultural and social activities like the Hidayat Muslim Society, Kamilol Islam, and Agama Islam, are now incorporating seminars about Islam into their programs. The Muslim Lawyers' League, Supreme Council of Islamic Affairs, and the Muslim Association of the Philippines now organize talks about Islam and invite religious leaders to speak. There are numerous Muslim organizations engaged in *da wa*[43] like the Women Fellowship Association of the Philippines.

An interesting factor that is partly responsible for Muslim resurgence and cannot be ignored is the Muslim diaspora, from southern Philippines to practically all provinces of the country. With refugees settling in areas as far north as Isabela, the need for mosques, and consequently, *madaris* became evident in what were traditionally Christian parts of the country. With government help as well as funds from Muslim countries like Libya, mosques and *madaris* were built and this Muslim presence allowed for Muslim-Christian interaction in areas where residents were primarily Christians. This situation has also contributed, albeit in a small way, to the manifestations of religious pluralism in a country that is still 93 % Christian. This growing Muslim presence in other areas of the Philippines is suggested by reports of as many as 100,000 conversions to Islam in northern Luzon in the last decade.[44]

ISLAM, MUSLIMS, AND THE STATE

As demonstrated by the discussion above, the conflict between the Spanish Catholics and the Muslims was clearly based on religious difference. There were also attendant issues—such as the slave trade and other commercial activities in Southeast Asia, as well as political control. However, because the colonizers were Christians and intent on converting peoples to Christianity, the conflict came to be defined primarily along religious lines. When the Philippines became an independent republic in 1946, the nature of the conflict began to change. The issues became centered on sociopolitical and economic inequities suffered by Muslims, including government neglect, lack of educational facilities and insufficient development programs in the southern Philippines. There were also issues related to the allocation of political power. With the separation of church and state clause in place in the Philippine constitution, and Muslims therefore able to exercise their freedom of religion, the conflict no longer remained as largely a religious conflict. Unfortunately, the colonial legacy of distinguishing peoples on the basis of religion continued to permeate Muslim-Christian relations long after the Spanish had left.

When the Philippine martial law government responded to the agitation of the MNLF, it not only sought to implement economic development policies in the Muslim areas but also found it necessary to enforce decrees assisting Muslims in the performance of their religious obligations. In light of all these government programs that have to do with Islam, a key question that comes to mind is whether the government's response to the MNLF agitation for a separate state actually infringed upon the doctrine of the separation of church and state. The violation of the constitutional provision was obvious, especially in terms of government involvement in building mosques. While there were some concerns raised by private individuals, they were not enough to generate public opposition. As the government controlled the press, opposition and objections were not played out in the newspapers. Under the situation of martial law, people who opposed government programs ran the risk of detention, not to mention torture, in military camps. When the mosques in the Maharlika Village and in Quiapo were built, there was no significant objection from the Roman Catholic church. This is probably because church leaders themselves thought that what the government was doing would help bring about peace in Mindanao, or they were simply preoccupied with other matters. Some church leaders were sympathetic to the Muslims and were involved in Muslim-Christian dialogues, but their priority was to organize meetings and make suggestions to the government in order to promote understanding and peace among Muslims and Christians.[45] Interestingly, there were a few Muslim leaders who opposed the building of the Golden Mosque because of the political nature of the project,[46] but again, this type of opposition was not organized.

When the Institute of Islamic Studies was created in the state-run University of the Philippines, there were academicians who questioned its propriety, but such opposition was also insufficient to mobilize public opinion. Again, one has to remember that this happened during the period of martial law when President Marcos ruled by decree. There was no legislative body at the time, and President Marcos was clearly responding to the conflict situation in the south. At the same time, he was trying to convince the Middle Eastern countries that it was not a religious war; that the government, in fact, recognizes Islam as part of Filipino cultural heritage. The government emphasized the fact that Muslims are simply Filipino ethnic minorities who happen to be Muslims. It therefore had the responsibility of preserving the cultural traditions of its people, and religion is one of those cultural traditions. Hence, to the government's way of thinking, there was no violation of the anti-establishment clause of the constitution.

It must be noted, however, that even though the MNLF recognized that Muslims living in the Philippines need to have a profound understanding of Islam, it did not have a concrete program for either revival or reform. Nur Misuari, chairman of the MNLF, indicated in the early 1980s that the MNLF's primary concern was for the Muslims to be able to take control of their own future. Issues of Islamic reform would be dealt with after the establishment of an independent state. He proposed, however, that Muslim youth should learn more about Islam and that more books should be donated to the local *madaris* for this purpose.[47] At the time, the MNLF's basic premise on the place and preservation of Islam hinged on their achieving independence as the Bangsa Moro Republik.

The MNLF, during its inception in 1969 and at the height of its activities in the 1970s clearly represented a Muslim mass-based revolutionary movement whose activities could not be ignored by the government. As contemporary events demonstrate, however, the MNLF does not appear to represent all Muslims[48] even though the OIC recognizes it as the legitimate representative of Philippine Muslims. In retrospect, its quest for independence may have been more of a strategy to gain political control and make the government respond to the needs of the Muslims at the time. The many presidential decrees signed by President Marcos during the period of martial law served as pragmatic responses in order to end the war (where the MNLF was the major participant) and its effects on Philippine citizens—both Muslims and non-Muslims. The government programs were also meant to assure not only the Philippine Muslims but the international Muslim community as well, of the place of Islam and the Muslims in Philippine society and culture. This was of critical importance to a country that continues to be largely dependent on Middle Eastern countries for its oil supply. This open recognition of Islam, even if it may have been motivated primarily by the need to put an end to the war, did help to make the environment conducive to Islamic resurgence during the period of martial law. Although attitudes and behavior cannot be legislated or mandated, government policies and programs have helped in paving the way for the Muslim-Christian acceptance of each other. Unfortunately, however, the current military conflict between the Moro Islamic Liberation Front (MILF) and government forces, has negatively affected not only the prospects for peace in the southern Philippines, but also the growing acceptance of Muslims by the non-Muslim Filipinos. The MILF, which was not included in the peace negotiations that resulted in the 1996 agreement, refused to recognize the provisions of that document. Instead, they are continuing their demand for an Islamic state. This situation is further complicated by the activities of the Abu Sayyaf, another Muslim group, which is also demanding for the creation of an Islamic state.[49] To the MILF and the Abu Sayyaf, the government programs and policies have not alleviated the sufferings of Muslims, nor have they provided for real religious tolerance. This situation demonstrates not only the complicated nature of Muslim-government relations but also the existence of contending groups among the Muslims whose visions of the place of Islam and Muslims in a non-Muslim society are not necessarily the same.

NOTES

1. The first Muslim group that asked for secession was the Muslim Independence Movement (MIM). Other groups like the Moro Islamic Liberation Front (MILF), Moro National Liberation Front reform Group (MNLF-RG), and Bangsa Moro Liberation Organization (BMLO) are splinter groups of the MNLF. Abu Sayyaf, which came out in

the open in 1993, and has been labeled as extremist, is better known for its kidnappings and indiscriminate raids on villages.

2. Al Haj Murad, "A Report Submitted by Al Haj Murad, General Staff of the Bangsa Moro Army to Habib Chatti, Secretary General of the Organization of Islamic Conference," cited in W. Che Man, *Muslim Separatism: The Moros of Southern Philippines and the Malays of Southern Thailand* (Quezon City: Ateneo de Manila University Press, 1990), p. 82.

3. Nur Misuari, Chairman of the MNLF, to Vivienne SM. Angeles, October 15, 1983, p. 5.

4. Basilan, Sulu, Tawi-Tawi, Zamboanga del Norte, Zamboanga del Sur, North Cotabato, Maguindanao, Sultan Kudarat, Lanao del Norte, Lanao del Sur, Davao del Sur, South Cotabato, Sarangani, and Palawan. Also included are the following cities in the above provinces: Cotabato, Dapitan, Dipolog, General Santos, Iligan, Marawi, Pagadian, Zamboanga, and Puerto Princesa.

5. Although the MNLF initially asked for independence, they had to settle for autonomy within the context of Philippine sovereignty.

6. The term used for the MNLF fighters. They claimed they were engaged in a *jihad*, hence, *mujahidin*.

7. Nur Misuari was an instructor at the Asian Center of the University of the Philippines. He was a member of Batch 90—the first group of Muslims who underwent military training in Sabah in 1969. While chairman of the MNLF, he lived in exile in Libya and Pakistan. He returned to the Philippines for the peace negotiations and was eventually elected Governor of the Autonomous Regions of Muslim Mindanao (ARMM).

8. Section 5, Article III of the Philippine Constitution of 1986 reiterates the provisions of the 1971 and 1936 constitutions on the relationship between state and religious groups, which says: "No law shall be made respecting an establishment of religion or prohibiting the free exercise thereof. The free exercise and enjoyment of religious profession and worship, without discrimination or preference, shall forever be allowed. No religious test shall be required for the exercise of civil and political rights."

9. See Cesar A. Majul, "Philippines," *Oxford Encyclopedia of the Modern Islamic World* (New York: Oxford University Press, 1995).

10. Spanish policy towards the Muslims was embodied in the instructions of Governor Sande to Esteban Rodriguez de Figueroa who led an expedition against the Muslims in 1579. These instructions called for imposition of Spanish sovereignty, establishment of trade, making the people settle as peaceful agriculturists, and converting them to Christianity. See "Accounts of the Expedition to Borneo, Jolo and Mindanao," in E. H. Blair and J. A. Robertson, *The Philippines,* IV (Ohio: Arthur Clarke, 1903), pp. 174-78.

11. There are three major groups of islands in the Philippines: Luzon, Visayas, and Mindanao.

12. Cesar A. Majul, "The Moros of the Philippines," *Conflict*, vol. V, no. 8 (1988), p. 170.

13. Cesar A. Majul, "Muslims and Christians in the Philippines," in Kail C. Ellis (ed.), *The Vatican, Islam and the Middle East* (Syracuse, N.Y.: Syracuse University Press, 1987), p. 314.

14. See *Reports of the Governor of the Moro Province (1913)*, p. 32, cited by Peter Gowing, *Mandate in Moroland: The American Government of Muslim Filipinos, 1899-1920* (Quezon City: Philippine Center for Advanced Studies, University of the Philippines, 1977), p. 216; also, G. Bentley, "Implicit Evangelism: American Education

Among Muslim Maranaos," *Pilipinas: A Journal of Philippine Studies*, vol. 12 (Spring 1989), pp. 73-96.

15. *Reports of the Governor of Moro Province (1913)*.

16. Carpenter to Secretary of Interior, January 27, 1919, p. 3.

17. Ibid., p. 4.

18. Garel A. Grunder and William E. Livesey, *The Philippines and the United States* (Norman: University of Oklahoma, 1951), pp. 141-43; also, Francis Burton Harrison, *The Cornerstone of Philippine Independence* (New York: Century Co., 1922), p. 110 and William Cameron Forbes, *The Philippine Islands* (Cambridge: Cambridge University Press, 1945), p. 289.

19. Forbes, *The Philippine Islands*, p. 289.

20. *Moro-moro* plays became the staple of town festivities. In these plays, the conflicts between Spaniards and Muslims were replayed with the Muslims ending up defeated and converting to Christianity. This was first staged under the auspices of the Jesuits after the defeat of Sultan Kudarat in Maguindanao.

21. As a grade school student in a parochial school on the island of Luzon, I remember clearly these ideas from our Social Studies textbooks and classes.

22. See Moro National Liberation Front, "Rise and Fall of Moro Statehood." n.p., n.d.

23. See *The Manila Times* (March 21, 22, 23, and 30, 1968) for full details of the massacre.

24. For full discussion of these conflicts, see Cesar A. Majul, *Contemporary Muslim Movements in the Philippines* (Berkeley: Mizan Press, 1985).

25. For the role of the Organization of Islamic Conference in the solution of this conflict, see Ralph Salmi, Cesar Majul, and George Tanham, *Islam and Conflict Resolution* (Lanham, Maryland: University Press of America, 1998), especially Appendix I.

26. Cesar A. Majul, "The Iranian Revolution and the Muslims in the Philippines," in John L. Esposito (ed.), *The Iranian Revolution: Its Global Impact* (Miami: Florida International University Press, 1990), p. 264.

27. Peter Gowing, "Resurgent Islam and the Moro Problem in the Philippines," *Southeast Asia Journal of Theology*, vol. 4, no. 1 (1962), p. 58.

28. Republic of the Philippines, Department of Public Information, "Seeking Solutions to the Philippine South" (January 1976), p. 3.

29. Presidential Decree 291, September 12, 1973.

30. Ibid.

31. See various publications of the Philippine Muslim Information Center, National Media Production Center, as well as the Office for Civil Relations of the Philippine Constabulary in the mid-1970s.

32. "Philippine Foreign Policy Reorientation," *Salaam* (March 1974), p. 7.

33. For a discussion of the codification process and its attendant problems, see G. Carter Bentley, "Islamic Law in Christian Southeast Asia: The Politics of Establishing Sharia Courts in the Philippines," *Philippine Studies*, vol. 29 (1981), pp. 45-65.

34. The sultans were the traditional leaders who exercised political control over a specific territory in the Muslim areas. When the Commonwealth government was established, President Quezon emphasized that the only persons who had authority were those duly appointed by law to hold public office. Although this was the official government position, Muslims continued to view their sultans as authority figures. See Manuel L. Quezon, "Development of Lanao," speech delivered at Camp Keithly, Lanao,

on August 28, 1938. Text in *Messages of the President*, vol. 4, pt. I (Manila: Bureau of Printing, 1939).

35. Discussions with Dr. Cesar A. Majul, San Pablo, California, November 23, 1997.

36. Presidential Decree No. 342, November 22, 1973.

37. Hussein Haqqani, "Interview with Nur Misuari," *Arabia: The Islamic World Review* (July 1982), p. 31.

38. Majul, "The Iranian Revolution," p. 262.

39. Personal interview with Muslim schoolteacher in Cotabato, July 15, 1994.

40. Majul, p. 84.

41. Ibid.

42. In September 1993, Muslims demonstrated against the Notre Dame University, which prohibited the use of *hijab* (veil) by those working in the hospital. A Muslim Youth Consultative Assembly later petitioned the Philippine Department of Health successfully to exempt Muslims from the standard uniform requirement and allowed them to wear the head cover. See Vivienne SM. Angeles, "Philippine Muslim Women: Tradition and Change," in Yvonne Haddad and John Esposito (eds.), *Islam, Gender and Social Change* (New York: Oxford University Press, 1998), p. 228.

43. *Da wa* basically means "call" but is used to refer to missionary activity.

44. U.S. Department of State, *Annual Report on International Religious Freedom for 1999: Philippines* (Washington, D.C., September 9, 1999).

45. See *Dansalan Research Center Occasional Papers*, no. 12, January 1979.

46. Telephone interview with Dr. Cesar A. Majul, June 25, 2000.

47. Nur Misuari to Vivienne SM. Angeles, October 15, 1983, p. 15.

48. In the mid-1990s, the Moro Islamic Liberation Front (MILF, a splinter group of the MNLF) started to emerge as a militarily armed Muslim movement seeking the establishment of an Islamic state in southern Philippines. Another group that has emerged is the *Abu Sayyaf*, which is also demanding the creation of an Islamic state.

49. For recent developments on the situation in Mindanao, see *Philippine Daily Inquirer* for the months of May and June 2000.

Chapter 9

Conclusion

Martin E. Marty

Fundamentalism. In the eyes of some scholars who had reasons to resist the use of a term born in the West and to see it applied globally, fundamentalism was the kind of movement that dared not speak its name. Somehow, as the years passed and we listened to testimonies of those who wanted to offer revisionist terminology or, more credibly, to keep the flavor of local and native names attached only to local and native movements, this became clear.

Whatever name they or we might use, the descripts, differentias, and phenomena that we found remarkable and remark-worthy generally matched what had come to be called fundamentalism. In our own five volume project, we settled for speaking of "fundamentalisms," "fundamentalist-like movements," or "movements bearing family-resemblances to fundamentalisms." And the emergent desire to show sensitivity also led our scholars, when dealing with specifics, to use the names people chose for themselves and not to impose the necessarily generic title fundamentalism.

For, make no mistake: there is some sort of genus here, a body of classifiable options that transect national and sectarian boundaries. During the summers of the Fundamentalism Project, after we had gone to press with a succession of annual volumes, Appleby, Gabriel Almond, emeritus at Stanford, and Emanuel Sivan from Israel, conclaved on Almond's patio and shook, sifted, and ordered common features, coming up with grids that appear in our fifth volume, *Fundamentalisms Comprehended*. These were not Procrustean beds into which everything had to fit nor straitjackets that would constrict the unwilling and misfit. They were broad general elements.

While doing that we had to do what the authors here do: pay closest attention to the local. Otherwise why make case studies, why specialize, why do close-ups, as they do here? The life of these movements is in their particulars, their idiosyncrasies, and their private narratives. The general and generic statements are heuristic devices to help scholars learn what to look for, while also helping them remain ready to be surprised, to come up with wonders, with "notice thises" and "notice thats" as the present authors do.

Since one of the absolutes for introducers of anthologies is not to give away the plot or steal all the exceptional items, I will remain distant and keep a broad perspective. While I shall take pains not simply to anticipate or repeat what the editors present by way of comment on their authors' findings, there is good reason to do some summarizing of what has been found here. Thus, one cannot help noticing, for example:

- None of the movements here described would call itself "fundamentalist" if it had the naming game to itself.
- Most of the leaders or participants have no more interest in how scholars evaluate and coordinate them than would folk-singers be interested in post-modernist critical theorists of poetry.
- Under whatever terms and with whatever features, they are all somehow reactive against modernity and modernization—even as they ingeniously and often reflexively put to work many of at least the external features associated with modernity.
- All the movements spring from prior movements that we would call conservative, traditional, orthodox, or classical.
- In all the cases in this book, as in other studies, we observe a threat, at least a perceived threat, to a way of life of a group and the hold on truth of its members.
- This means that such a group must respond vigorously not as mere critics but as people who would either withdraw, sectarian style, or attempt to overthrow existing civil and religious leadership, seeing it as compromising, seductive, deadening.
- In the West most of these movements were those of "people of the book," people who could agree on the dominating, even monopolizing, import of foundational texts and the traditions built upon them. On the basis of such, they could then disagree: intra-group conflict is constant and there are frequent attempts to purify movements and sometimes to purge the memory of leadership in the recent past.
- No consistent pattern of leadership emerges. It would be hard to read this book and come up with a job description or a personality assessment for leaders. Some are charismatic, but many are not. Some are ready to act, to react, immediately and forcefully. Others suggest that they know where history is going and are content to be patient if there is not a complete realization of the vision.

One could add many other features that a majority of the movements embody. But after having pointed to some constants and consistencies or continuities among them, scholars find it necessary to delve into particulars, as they do here. Which particulars? There is a partly random character to the choice of sites studied.

Substantively, this has meant, as the editors state in the introduction, the "editorial concern is to engage critically, within a variety of contexts, with the claims made by fundamentalist movements; and to assess the impact such claims have had, and are having, upon the cultures and societies that play host to them." They are also clear and decisive about the methodological concerns that give coherence to the book.

Within that coherence there is enough variety to satisfy most readers. Thus Mir Zohair Husain tells the story of Islamic politics in Pakistan by reference to three dominating leaders. Here the interplay of the secular and the religious suggests how viscous and volatile are the movements and how many shifts the leaders can take in the name of phenomena self-described as traditional and implicitly changeless. The fixed point for the leaders as they did their shifting was the claim that they were making all their moves in the light of Allah. As I read I found myself jotting on the margin: "God-intoxication." Thus Maududi spoke of the Almighty's "sovereignty" instead of the "popular sovereignty" of the people. Whatever else these leaders talked about, they always counted on this as the unifying reference point. Whatever happened to the universalizing depictions a century ago of a secular, post-religious, even God-less globe?

One almost has to pity the opponents of these forceful leaders if they had to use moderate, qualified, relativizing motifs to unite people. And yet, there is reason to ponder the irony to which Husain points: for all that Islamic invocation, the Islamic political parties have never won an election! We can be grateful to Husain for setting out the probable reasons that, in his eyes, account for "this amazing lack of electoral success." As focused as they may be, the uprisings do not necessarily win majority popular support. The insights at the close of his chapter might be useful to those who are trying to write scenarios or speculations about the future direction of such movements.

One of the only two chapters that concentrate on Christians, Carr's study of the Afrikaners demonstrates more than most the power of a book, a theological tradition, and practical military and political choices based upon particular interpretations of it. One might almost call the conflict between the neo-Calvinist shapers of apartheid and the forces that outlasted them and overthrew their version of regime a hermeneutical war. I was in Cape Town the year the Reformed church declared that its interpretation of biblical texts impelling "separate development" had been inaccurate, even false. We could sense then as never before that apartheid devotees lived on borrowed time. It was only a question of how much blood might be spilled before all sides realized this. This chapter differs greatly in mode from Husain's "three-leader" model and comes down to a "two interpretations" approach. Carr speaks of the moment when everything was "ripe" for change. This is a textbook case for those who want to approach "ripeness" in other cultures guided by a book, be it the Bible or Torah or the Qur'an. The attention to individual and collective senses of the self is certainly instructive.

By revisiting the Great Trek, Carr demonstrates how past events become enduring mythologies, and how exclusively they bind people who claim to be in the legacy of the events over against all outsiders. Carr's sophisticated discussion of worldviews can also inform those who would inquire into the nature of movements far from South Africa, neo-Calvinism, or the latter's opponents.

If the Pakistani leaders and the struggle over apartheid belong to the past, the religious zionism described by Jacob Abadi is very much of the present, though he also shows how movements prophesied to be long-term can dwindle and lose their energy. If anyone wants to study the uses that political parties can make of radically conservative or fundamentalist movements, he or she would do well to watch Israeli parties and governments "use" Gush Emunim to their own purposes. In this and other chapters I found myself writing, "creating a vacuum," "leaving a vacuum," or "filling a vacuum" on the margins. These citations came at points where one finds agents who exploit situations when no one can come forward with a guiding ideology for the whole polity. Watch the moves of the Labor party in respect to Gush Emunim to see both the language of "use" and the realization of "vacuum." But most dramatic is the past-tense sense that Abadi employs to treat a movement that in its prophetic fury seemed assured of a larger future than it could, in its moment, ever have realized.

Least familiar to me was the economic theme of Santosh C. Saha's chapter, and it offers surprises to those of us tempted to over-generalize about fundamentalism. Saha makes clear that the goal of setting "an effective strategy for sustained economic growth and the reduction of poverty" was the *Grund motif,* the underlying motif of the religious revivalist claims and appeals. This is an underdeveloped area in fundamentalist studies, and the essay should be welcomed and carefully studied. Saha's methods, narrative, and concerns might well help induce scholars of other movements to discern more of the meaning of economic change behind fundamentalist-like forces.

Here again is a story of failure, inadequacy, thanks to the inability of the Hindu revivalists to come up with plans and programs for the world that changed too rapidly around them. Those who fear fundamentalisms and foresee the takeover of polities will not get much short-range assurance from works like this. But if they step back and take the longer view, they will see that it is very difficult to sustain fundamentalist polities and political dominances. There is also good reason to pursue what Saha, quoting Lise Diane McKean, calls the "political uses of spirituality." And for those who would start a new movement, how is this for a disheartening beginning of the last paragraph: "In sum, an alternative model of development is not easy to advance." Even if it comes in the name of the gods. The conflict between ideology and the empirical situation remains decisive.

The Egyptian scene, as described by Rudolf T. Zarzar, is the one most dedicated to the theme of anti-Westernization and anti-modernization. While his story, like the others, holds intrinsic interest, it may also well be one of the more instructive for scholars of fundamentalisms anywhere on what happens when rich world meets poor world, when media intrude upon traditional ways of lie.

The perceptions of the fundamentalist reactionaries were not all wrong; westernization and modernization *did* precipitate the series of crises exploited by the reactionary modernists called fundamentalists there. But whenever there are "crises of identity, authenticity, culture, and legitimacy"—and where are there not, including in the rich nations?—the Egyptian example will be instructive. And there is here, as not in all other cases, an expression of some sort of hope: "democratization offers the best hope" of dealing with political and economic problems in Egypt. That is the last message the militants want to hear, and the hardest the impatient leaders and public have to learn.

Harriet A. Harris's study of black Pentecostals in London is the most significant departure from the studies of "generic fundamentalisms" because Pentecostalisms, as she observes them, are too effervescent, too "spirit-moved," to be restrained by "the letter" of texts. Yet the conditions that led to the rise of these "immigrant" movements, the quasi-political responses they make in a polity they had no role in forming or corrupting, and the perceptions of participants, parallel many of those elsewhere. This is a pioneering study, since most fundamentalism research deals with "native" populations being threatened and uprooted, not newcomer agents who are first making their way.

One welcomes the author's confession that she feels uncomfortable in her Anglican theological and clerical context, since Harris shows how the language of "threat" and what is "threatening" works both ways. The black Pentecostals are threatened by their environment, and those who have helped produced that environment do not welcome or always comprehend the criticisms and counterattacks. Yet this is a pattern that has appeared in much more dramatic form, for example among the Shah of Iran's people when the *Shi'ite* fundamentalist revolution began. The end of the twentieth century was not a time when the complacent could remain so.

The politics of Islam in Bangladesh parallels some of that observed in the chapter on Pakistan, yet Syed Serajul Islam's approach, curiosities, interests, and outcomes are quite different from those of Husain. We are instantly back to the theme of the "uses" of fundamentalisms, the language of "exploiting" religion. Here again there is a "vacuum" to be filled by ideologues and militants. In this case the use and exploitation have been longer terms, since the enduring leadership, here more than in many other places, learned to employ Islam sufficiently effectively that the movements were often frustrated. The value of particular studies comes clear when Professor Islam concentrates on the "why" concerning use and exploitation. There are different "whys" in other regions and religions, but in each case there has to be inquiry and speculation about the why, the rationale, the explanation; Islam's chapter furthers that search by example.

For all that, the final paragraphs are consistent with those in so many other of the essays: "There is no doubt that though Islam remains a stable value system, [agreed: the secularization thesis would find little confirmation here or any of the other "places" in this book] it has failed as politics in Bangladesh."

If potential revolutionary leaders would read and be convinced by works like these, they would either grow faint of heart, slow of tongue, or languid in spirit. If potential converts to their causes would see the word "failure" at the end of so many chapters and movements that once had been full of promise, would they be so ready to sign up, to offer all, to be ready to die? The realist need not be a cynic to say: learning from the failures of others rarely quenches the thirst for experiment and activity. Perhaps those most threatened by fundamentalisms, those most ready to panic, would profit most from the reassurances these stories of promise-turned-to-failure have to offer.

Finally, and once more, a variation on the Islamic theme preoccupies Vivienne SM. Angeles, in this case in respect to the Philippines. Her study of the MNLF finds it over-representing its popular appeal and bi-focal in its vision. It seems to have one eye on independence, and its other on political control. And here government policy had to make some concessions to end a war even it if made room for more Islamic resurgence. There is a glimmer of concord in reference to Muslim-Christian mutual acceptance. But there is the blight of an "unfortunately" in the summary, because new military conflicts dim the prospect for peace and compromise the moves toward seeing more acceptances of Muslims by non-Muslim fellow citizens. Here the diversity within Muslim movements both limited them and successfully kept others off balance, contributing to disturbances of the peace.

I have lifted only one or two main themes, distinctives, bases for learning and further inquiry from each of these rich works. While each author had organizing principles, theses, and clear preoccupations, none of their chapters can be reduced to a couple of paragraphs. The real satisfaction comes from the stories themselves, the paths, and bypaths through which the authors guide us through troubling places in a still troubled world.

Index

About the Contributors

JACOB ABADI is Professor of Middle Eastern History at the United States Air Force Academy in Colorado Springs. He has authored several books including *Britain's Withdrawal from the Middle East: The Economic and Strategic Imperatives, 1947-1971* and *Israel's Leadership: From Utopia to Crisis*. Professor Abadi has also written numerous articles on topics dealings with modern Middle Eastern history.

VIVIENNE SM. ANGELES is currently teaching at LaSalle University in Philadelphia. She obtained her Ph.D. from Temple University. Her recent article, "Philippine Muslim Women: Tradition and Change," has been published in *Gender and Social Change*. At present, she is engaged in research on Filipino Catholic communities in Philadelphia with a grant from the Harvard Pluralism Project.

THOMAS K. CARR serves concurrently as Assistant Professor of Religion and Philosophy at Mount Union College, Alliance, Ohio, and Visiting Research Fellow at Liverpool Hope University in Liverpool, Oxford, U.K. His D.Phil. Degree is from Oxford University in Philosophy and Religious Studies. He served three years as Junior Dean and Tutor in Philosophy at Oriel College, U.K. His books include *Newman and Gadamer: Toward a Hermeneutics of Religious Knowledge*, and the forthcoming *The Truth that We Are: Gadamerian Ethics and the Theological Task*.

HARRIET A. HARRIS is a Lecturer of Theology at the University of Exeter and former Junior Fellow of New College, Oxford, England. She received her D.Phil. degree from Oxford University in Theology. She is the author of *Fundamentalism and Evangelicals*. Her research interests are in Protestant fundamentalism and evangelical, charismatic, and post-evangelical faith.

MIR ZOHAIR HUSAIN is Associate Professor of Political Science at the University of South Alabama. He received his Ph.D. from the University of Pennsylvania. He has published one book, *Global Islamic Politics in 1995*, and is currently completing two books on Islamic revivalism in the Muslim world.

SYED SERAJUL ISLAM is Associate Professor in the Department of Political Science at the International Islamic University in Malaysia. He received his Ph.D. from McGill University in Canada. Dr. Islam was visiting Fulbright Scholar in 1988 at the University of Iowa. His articles have appeared in various journals, including *Asian Survey, Pacific Affairs, Journal of Developing Areas, Asian and African Studies, Journal of South Asia and Middle Eastern Studies, Asian Thought and Society, Islamic Quarterly of London,* and *Muslim Education Quarterly of Cambridge*.

MARTIN E. MARTY is Fairfax M. Cone Distinguished Service Professor Emeritus at the University of Chicago, where he taught for 35 years and where the Martin Marty Center has been founded to promote "public religion" endeavors. He is also George B. Caldwell Senior Scholar-in-Residence at the Park Ridge Center for the Study of Health, Faith, and Ethics, where he is editor of *Second Opinion*. He is contributing editor of the *Christian Century*; editor of the fortnightly newsletter *Context*, now in its 31st year. Dr. Marty has authored 50 books including a three volume *Modern American Religion* and *The One and the Many: America's Search for the Common Good*. He is currently on the U.S. President's Committee on the Arts and Humanities, and Chairman of the Board of Regents at St. Olaf College. He is also past director of both the Fundamentalism Project of the American Academy of Arts and Sciences and the Public Religion Project at the University of Chicago. His numerous honors include the National Humanities Medal, the National Book Award, and the Medal of the American Academy of Arts and Sciences. He is also and elected fellow of the American Philosophical Society and the American Academy of Political and Social Sciences. Dr. Marty has received 64 honorary doctorates.

SANTOSH C. SAHA is now Associate Professor of History at Mount Union College in Ohio. He earned his Ph.D. in African History from Kent State University, Ohio. He previously taught Asian and African history in colleges and universities in India, Africa, and the U.S. Dr. Saha was Editor-in-Chief of the *Cuttington Research Journal* in Liberia. He is the author of several books including *Dictionary of Human Rights Organizations in Africa, Culture in Liberia,* and *Indo-U.S. Relations,* and many articles, some of which appeared in the *International Journal of African Historical Studies*; *The Journal of Negro History*; *Journal of Asian History*; *Pakistan Historical Journal*; *Indian Journal of Asian Affairs;* and *Canadian Journal of African Studies*. Currently he is on the editorial board of the *Indian Journal of Asian Affairs*.

RUDOLF T. ZARZAR is Professor of Political Science at Elon College, North Carolina. He received his B.A. in history and his M.A. and Ph.D. in political science from the University of North Carolina at Chapel Hill. He has taught at Elon College since 1968 and is also visiting professor at the University of North Carolina at Greensboro. He served as president of the Learning Disabilities of Alamance County, the North Carolina Chapter of the Arab-American Anti-Discrimination Committee, and the North Carolina Political Science Association. He is a frequent contributor to professional and civic organizations. His current research interests include Islamization, democratization, privatization, and pluralization in the Arab World and the Arab-Israeli conflict.